Sharon K. Unsing

D0912007

The Theology of Calvin

Wilhelm Niesel

Translated by
Harold Knight

BAKER BOOK HOUSE
Grand Rapids, Michigan

Reprinted 1980 by
Baker Book House Company
with permission of The Westminster Press
ISBN: 0-8010-6694-8

First Published in Great Britain in 1956
by Lutterworth Press

This book originally appeared as DIE THEOLOGIE
CALVINS, Chr. Kaiser Verlag, Munich, 1938. Some
revision of the original text has been made by the author for
this English edition.

PHOTOLITHOPRINTED BY CUSHING - MALLOY, INC.
ANN ARBOR, MICHIGAN, UNITED STATES OF AMERICA

CONTENTS

CONTENTS

CONTENTS

Abbreviations Used in the Notes

CR = *Corpus Reformatorum* (Calvin's Works, ed. Baum, Cunitz, and Reuss, vols. 1–59; Brunswick, 1863–1900).

OS = *I. Calvini Opera Selecta* (ed. Barth and Niesel, vols. 1–5; Munich, 1926–1952).

In. = *I. Calvini Institutio Christianae Religionis*, Geneva, 1559 (*CR* vol. 2; *OS* vols. 3–5).

Chapter 1

THE PRESENT STATE OF CRITICAL STUDIES

IN a report about the progress of Calvin studies since the memorial year 1909 we find these words in reference to the theological aspect of the Reformer's work: "We do not yet seem to have found the basis for any systematic exposition, and in view of Calvin's method and type of thought all such attempts would encounter special difficulties."[1] This has remained very true in recent years. Monographs have been increased by a series of very useful contributions; but we have not yet attained any conspectus of Calvin's theology as a whole.

Further, existing works, dealing with individual aspects of his doctrine, cannot simply be combined to form a composite picture. It would not help us to publish a collected edition of these Calvin studies; for the thread is lacking on which we could string together the various contributions and make of them a single whole. Calvin research suffers from the defect that the golden thread which runs through it has not yet been discovered. Certainly we are well informed about this or that individual feature or doctrine; but what is really in question when he writes his *Institutes of the Christian Religion*, what his governing intention is in constructing his theology, remains as yet unknown to us. So long as we have not clearly grasped the kernel of the whole nor understood the essential inspiration, no attempt at an exposition of the whole can succeed. Thus it is not superficial but quite fundamental difficulties which so far have hindered the writing of a work on the theology of Calvin.

[1] Gustav Krüger in *Die evangelische Theologie. Ihr jetziger Stand und ihre Aufgaben*; Part 3: *Die Kirchengeschichte*, II, I, Halle, 1929, p. 27.

9

THE THEOLOGY OF CALVIN

In recent years attempts have been made to master these difficulties. There are studies the purpose of which has been to discover the problem of the theology of Calvin and thus to complete the most important preparation for a systematic exposition of his work. Again, there are others which in passing have adopted an attitude towards this question.

I

In 1922 Hermann Bauke made certain classifications in the Calvin literature which had so far appeared.[1] According to him it falls into three groups, which again are capable of sub-division. The factors which determine such groups are the sources of conflict between the various authors. The first group of investigators bears a confessional character. Here Reformed and Lutheran confront each other in their interpretation of Calvin's doctrines. The second group is distinguished by the nationalistic tendencies of the writers. The French and all the Western nations understand the theology of Calvin differently from the Germans. Lastly, the third group is decided by the characteristics of a particular theological school. Here Albrecht Ritschl and his followers stand in one camp and Dilthey and Troeltsch with their pupils in the other. Bauke thinks that the very possibility of such varied divergences among Calvin's interpreters must in the last resort have its origin in the special character of his theology itself. Hence arises the question: "What is the peculiar characteristic of Calvinistic theology which makes possible such contradictory views?"[2]

Bauke considers that the key to the understanding of Calvin "cannot consist in any one intrinsic feature, any single point of dogma, any central or root doctrine from which everything else could be derived".[3] Such an opinion would at most only serve to bring about a new division among Calvin's exponents. If the study of Calvin has shown anything, it is this: that he is no systematic theologian who

[1] Hermann Bauke: *Die Probleme der Theologie Calvins*, 1922.
[2] *Op. cit.*, p. 7.   [3] pp. 11 ff.

speculatively deduces his theology from one or two root principles. "The theology of Calvin has in fact no basic principle."[1]

On the contrary, Bauke thinks he has found the clue to a true understanding of the teaching of Calvin in the *form* which his theology assumes: "Form not of course in the sense of its outward vesture, style, classification, and arrangement, etc., but in the deeper more comprehensive sense of the inner development and structure of the whole theological contents."[2] He distinguishes three essential traits in the structural formation of Calvin's doctrine. The first is its rationalism. By this he does not mean intrinsic but formal rationalism: Calvin gets to grips with the doctrines of theology by means of formal dialectics. The second mark of its structural development is the "*complexio oppositorum*", i.e. the capacity to integrate doctrines even though they are opposed from the point of view of logic or metaphysics. The third characteristic Bauke finds in Biblicism: not the literal kind which derives all materials from the Bible but "the formal kind springing from the principle that dogmatics must be essentially an exposition of Biblical themes".[3] On the basis of this peculiar mould of Calvinistic dogmatics Bauke endeavours to explain the divergences between Calvin's exponents. He sees the problem of Calvin's theology, not in the fact that it is the learned expression of a new type of religion, but in the fact that Calvin has given to the Lutheran content a new framework stemming from a different structural evolution. In this respect Calvin shows himself to be an eminent representative of the French mind, for which form is decisive.[4] In other words, the special feature of Calvin's doctrine is this: it is a reformed theology stamped by the mind of a Frenchman. Bauke understands Calvin from the standpoint of his French nationality, precisely in accordance with the dictum of the French critic Jacques Pannier: "Calvin's spirit is essentially the spirit of the French race itself."[5]

[1] *Op. cit.*, P. 31. [2] P. 12. [3] P. 20. [4] P.14.
[5] Jacques Pannier: *Recherches sur la formation intellectuelle de Calvin*, Paris,

THE THEOLOGY OF CALVIN

Some time ago another writing appeared which is immediately concerned with the problem of Calvin's theology.[1] This work of Hermann Weber is not very different in its conclusions from the one we have just discussed. Calvin in his theology gives expression to much the same ideas as Luther, but he experiences them and thinks them afresh in terms of his Latin mind.[2] Some differences result above all from the different method which Weber employs and recommends. In the arguments of Bauke he desiderates especially any psychological motivation and feels that the basic Calvinistic principles of thought disclosed are often used in a merely formal way, without recognition of the deep personal life of Calvin in which they are rooted.[3] When Weber seeks to understand the thought of Calvin from a psychological standpoint he has in mind a purely medical psychology which reveals the physiological bases of mental phenomena.[4] According to this anthropological psychology the thought and the total outlook of individuals are to be explained as reactions produced by varied personal structures.[5] Since these psycho-physical structures vary according to the individual, so that it is possible to distinguish several types of personalities, given data are variously interpreted by men according to their innate personal tendencies.[6]

From the standpoint of his concern with psychological structures Weber reaches the following conclusions:

1. In opposition to Bauke, he is of the opinion that the

Alcan, 1931, p. 55. Cf. also W. Niesel: "Calvin und Luther", *Reform. Kirchenzeitung*, 81, 1931, pp. 195 ff. Ernst Pfisterer in a study entitled "Die rassische Zugehörigkeit Calvins" (*Dtsch. Pfarrerblatt*, 39, 1935, pp. 375 ff.) has similarly tried to show—while realizing that he was thereby saying nothing of theological significance—that Calvin belongs to the Nordic races. We may await with interest the reaction of French Calvin scholars to this most recent, well-founded thesis. It is unimportant for our own study.

[1] Hermann Weber: *Die Theologie Calvins. Ihre innere Systematik im Lichte structurpsychologischer Forschungsmethode*, Berlin, Elsner, 1930 (*Monographien zur Grundlegung der philosophischen Anthropologie und Wirklichkeitsphilosophie*, published by E. Jaensch, Vol. 4).

[2] *Op. cit.*, p. 62.   [3] P. 16.   [4] P. 6.   [5] P. 5.   [6] P. 7.

whole edifice of Calvinistic theology rests upon a certain fundamental principle. This principle is certainly not "anything formal but is something lived out in the depths of the soul": the honour of God.[1] The existence of such a basic principle belongs necessarily to the formalistic mode of Calvin's thought[2] and to his schizophrenic disposition. Individuals with a fissure in their soul-life like that of Calvin would not be content to accept things as they are but would seek to reinterpret them according to the measure of their own psyche.[3] In the case of Calvin this is the idea of the honour of God.

2. But Calvin feels this final principle of understanding not as something subjective but as an objective reality standing outside himself to which all other beings are related. This type of thought, according to which all things lie outside the subject and are means to an ultimate end, rests upon a positivist world view such as is proper to the French mind. From it flow two principles basic to Calvin's system of thinking: (a) The teleo-causal law of thought which supposes that all continuities are subordinate in a causal series to a supreme end or value. Thus Calvin causally infers everything from the ethical idea of God, derives all things from the thought of the honour of God, and likewise traces them back to Him. Because causal thinking may often merge into judgments of value and vice versa, we get the development in Calvin of peculiar and apparently contradictory thoughts.[4] (b) The law of antithetic forms of thought: this means that the opposite of what a complex of thought suggests can become a reality. For example, in regard to the doctrine of justification: according to the Calvinistic system of thought (gloria Dei) justification is a work of God alone, but in reality there always exist the fact of sanctification and the exercises of piety. This apparent contradiction is not a genuine one for Calvin, because the primitive character of the soul-life, peculiar to the Latin people, brings it about that the connexion between idea and reality is on the one hand very close and on the other may cease altogether. Thus idea and

1 P. 21.   2 P. 24.   3 Pp. 18 and 25.   4 P. 38.

reality had only a formal dialectic connexion. But this formal solution of the problem is for the Latin Calvin a real one.[1]

This contribution of Weber to the understanding of Calvin's theology is itself a testimony to a largely primitive mentality.[2] Weber criticized Bauke for not having sufficiently shown in regard to the particular doctrines of Calvin how far the laws of thought which he discloses are really related to the thinking of Calvin. Yet it must be conceded to Bauke that he has at least attempted to do this. Nor has Weber done better. The second part of the latter's work, in which he sets out to show the application of his previous methodically prepared categories to the substance of Calvin's theology, is the weakest; for the exposition of certain of the main doctrines of Calvin is unfortunately troubled by very slender factual knowledge, so that it is not astonishing if he finds in Calvin everything as he must find it on the basis of his psychological presuppositions about schizophrenia in a Frenchman. Thus in the last analysis the study of Weber does not take us beyond that of Bauke. The main difference is that Weber, unlike Bauke, adheres to the idea of a supreme category for the understanding of Calvin's theology and seeks to deduce it from psychological considerations. This means: Weber approves the efforts of those scholars who have tried to understand the doctrine of Calvin on the basis of its content; but he has also points of contact with Bauke who rejected such attempts and endeavoured to understand the theology of Calvin from the standpoint of structure. For Weber everything hangs on typological psychology. The natural disposition of Calvin serves him as a basis of interpretation, and from it both the substantial and formal elements in the doctrine of Calvin are inferred.

But what is really gained for our understanding by such an analysis of types of thought?[3] One thing is certain—that the

[1] P. 53.
[2] Cf. the critique of A. Lang: "Calvin 'schizoid'?" *Reform. Kirchen-Zeitung*, 81, 1931, pp. 147 ff.
[3] Cf. Weber, *op. cit.*, p. 9.

Reformers themselves did not wish the differences between them to be thus reduced to insignificance. Luther did not reproach Zwingli with his Upper German mentality, but said that his way of thought was different. Calvin in judging Luther no doubt took into account the latter's natural disposition; but in the last resort his chief concern was that Luther held wrong views on the question of the Eucharist. If the Reformers concentrated their attention so wholly on the one thing, can we clever modern men come along and say that had they only had the insights afforded by anthropological psychology they would have realized that their whole strife was personally conditioned? To pose the question is to answer it. By such modern methods of enquiry we can at best modestly contribute to the biography of the Reformers; but these attempts are not appropriate as far as their theology is concerned, and hence not of scholarly value. This applies to the work of Weber, although he considers his methods to be alone strictly scientific.[1] What we mean by scientific quality in this connexion must be discussed later.

2

Thus it is not surprising that further efforts have been made to understand the theology of Calvin from the point of view of its content. Mülhaupt in his study has maintained, in opposition to Bauke, that it is not a question of making a virtue of necessity as regards the position of Calvin research and of viewing the apparent lack of system in Calvin as a natural outcome of his structural procedure and his humanist French type of mind.[2] Of course Mülhaupt's own attempt to trace everything in Calvin's theology back to the idea of God does not overcome the difficulties experienced in the previous course of research. He has to conclude with the observation that Calvin fails to attain the compactness of Luther's theological system and did not aim at the unity of

[1] Pp. 8 ff.

[2] Erwin Mülhaupt: *Die Predigt Calvins, ihre Geschichte, ihre Form und ihre religiösen Grundgedanken*, Berlin, de Gruyter, 1931, p. xiv.

Melanchthon's rationalistic nomism.[1] Hence the conclusion he reaches is the usual one: in Calvin we find obscurities and contradictions.

While Mülhaupt tries to find evidence for his thesis that the foundation of Calvin's doctrine of God is the idea of a gracious will,[2] Otto Ritschl in expounding Calvin's theological system holds that God for the Genevan Reformer is essentially the righteous God.[3] Love is only instrumental to His justice. The divine *"gloria"* consists in the fact that God manifests His justice in the salvation of the elect and the punishment of the reprobate, as in fact already in election and damnation as such. The thought of the *"gloria Dei"* interpenetrates the whole theology of Calvin and provides the real key to its understanding.[4] The doctrine of predestination so closely connected with this thought of God stands at the head of this theological system and all else is derivative from it.[5] Ritschl's approach to the problems of Calvin's theology contains nothing new, and has often been represented in the history of Calvin research. We shall not here be concerned with the fact that Ritschl's demonstration is often inaccurate[6] and that the doctrine of predestination itself is misrepresented by him, but we shall only be occupied with a comparison between his attempt at a solution and that of Mülhaupt.

The two monographs of Ritschl and Mülhaupt on the doctrine of Calvin are the only ones which have appeared since the work of Bauke.[7] In contrast to the latter, both seek

[1] *Op. cit.*, p. 169.   [2] *Op. cit.*, pp. 169 f.

[3] Otto Ritschl: *Dogmengeschichte des Protestantismus*, Vol. III, Göttingen, 1926, pp. 175 ff.

[4] *Op. cit.*, pp. 169 and 178.   [5] P. 167.

[6] Cf. simply p. 166, the wrong use of a quotation in a decisive passage.

[7] We set aside two unsuccessful theses: Hans Engelland, who in his work *Gott und Mensch bei Calvin*, Munich, 1934, aims at giving an introduction to the *Institutes*, summarizes the contents of this book from the wrong points of view and makes of Calvin a mediating theologian who tries to build a bridge between reason and revelation. Günter Gloede has written the most comprehensive work which has for long appeared about the theology of Calvin: *Theologia naturalis bei Calvin*, Stuttgart, 1935. He tries to show by abundant quotation that Calvin's doctrine of creation contains the key to his position. This fulness, however, cannot

the problem of Calvin's theology in its content and they come to conflicting conclusions.

Mülhaupt thinks that the God of Calvin is in the last analysis a God of grace, Ritschl that He is righteous will directed towards "*gloria*". Thus we are again faced by the antitheses of Calvin research, which Bauke hoped to explain and dissolve by the argument that the real problems of Calvin's theology arise from the peculiarities of its formal structure. His argument did not succeed, any more than did the recent attempt of Ritschl and Bauke to show that these problems have to do with the substance of that theology. Must we not then agree with Weber, who, taking as his point of departure structural psychology, *could* regard as valid the effort to seek a solution both in the substance and in the form and in his own opinion could take us all the nearer to the goal? If all other proposals fail, must we not accept the solution recommended by anthropological psychology?

3

We must not and we cannot do so, because the idea of theology being determined by its object, which we owe to Karl Barth, has produced a revolution in Calvin studies as elsewhere.

Peter Brunner[1] has the merit of having approached the study of Calvin with this idea in view. We certainly cannot agree with him in some respects. Among other things he has read into Calvin notions proper to modern theology. But that is not the essential thing about his contribution; his originality lies in his realization that the fundamental problem has to do neither with form nor with substance and sequence of thought, but with something more ultimate. Structure, substance, and sequence of thought can do no more than point

conceal a disastrous lack of scholarly depth, so evident as to make his arguments invalid. Details with regard to both books in the *Theol. Literaturbeilage der Ref. Kirchenztg.*, 1934, p. 16, and 1936, pp. 15 ff.

1 Peter Brunner: *Vom Glauben bei Calvin*, Tübingen, Mohr, 1925.

to this ultimate object of relationship, which cannot be directly apprehended or described.[1]

Alfred de Quervain in his excellent introduction to the theology of Calvin, which appeared at almost the same time, says much the same thing in regard to efforts to understand Calvin's doctrine from the point of view of the "*gloria Dei*": the honour of God "is not an approach, a principle, in a theological system. It is the transcendent goal and equally the presupposition of Calvin's whole life."[2]

Or, as Udo Smidt puts it: "Seen from the beyond it is a question (with regard to the honour of God) of the revelation implied in that unconditioned declaration: The Lord is my name and I will not give my honour to another (Isaiah 42:8). Seen from man's point of view it means that, in all the relations of life, with the zeal of upright obedience and the trustful confidence of faith, we apply all our powers to secure that God's honour shall remain intact upon earth and God's truth retain its value."[3]

Peter Barth has summarized the essence of these statements by saying: "The Biblical presupposition that man has to do with the living God is through and through the vital nerve of Calvin's instruction in the Christian religion."[4]

Whereas the last-named theologians do not consider the question how Calvin in his teaching can speak of an object which is not an object, Matthias Simon continues the thoughts of Brunner along these lines. He says: "God is necessarily for us a *coincidentia oppositorum* about which it is just impossible to speak directly. But this means: we cannot speak of God except dialectically in terms of thesis and anti-thesis."[5] "If we were to concentrate all our attention on the

[1] *Op. cit.*, p. 4.   [1926, p. 6.

[2] Alfred de Quervain: *Calvin, Sein Lehren und Kämpfen*, Berlin, Furche,

[3] Udo Smidt: "Calvins Bezeugung der Ehre Gottes", in: *Vom Dienst an Theologie und Kirche, Festgabe für Adolf Schlatter*, Berlin, Furche, 1927, p. 119.

[4] Peter Barth: "Calvin", *Zeitwende*, 7, I, 1931, p. 310.

[5] Matthias Simon: "Die Beziehungen zwischen Altem und Neuem Testament in der Schriftauslegung Calvins", *Ref. Kirchenztg.*, 82, 1932, p. 34.

statement that God is holy, then this holy God could become for us an idol, did we not remember at the same time that the same God is love. If on the other hand we thought of God only as love, then this gracious God could become for us a mere thing, if the message of His holiness did not remind us of the fact that He is the living God whom we can never apprehend or describe by means of one thought or one affirmation alone." [1]

If Simon thus endeavours to explain the contradictoriness of Calvin's theology by reference to its object, Alfred Göhler, adopting the same approach, says rightly with regard to the relation between its individual portions and the whole: "There is no central doctrine in the theology of Calvin; rather all his doctrines are central in the sense that their aim is to understand independently from their several viewpoints what is central and essential." [2]

The decisive contribution which all these theologians who are led to study Calvin in the light of contemporary emphases make to the understanding of the Reformer is this: The problems of his theology do not arise from questions of structure nor from those of content, but from the fact that it makes a serious attempt to be theology. This means: in Calvin's doctrine it is a question of the content of all contents —the living God. The effort to bear witness to Him makes itself felt both in structure and substance. It is impossible for either of these two factors to remain unaffected when the aim is to allow the voice of the living God to be heard through doctrine.

Certainly the question may be posed whether this solution of the problem really corresponds to Calvin's own intentions. Is it not rather that once again modern theology is being read into Calvin's doctrine? Well, the contributions of these theologians are already to some extent a proof of the

---

[1] *Op. cit.*, p. 35.
[2] Alfred Göhler: *Calvins Lehre von der Heiligung*, Munich, 1934, p. 81. Of course the author then falls into the trap of seeing in the special object of his study the decisive factor and of speaking of "the centrality of sanctification in the vision and interest of Calvin" (p. 105).

correctness of their thesis, and in the meantime we have received other studies which point in the same direction.[1]

But all these are dissertations which treat of individual doctrines, and which only partially, and then only in passing, attempt an answer to the question in what the essence of Calvinistic theology consists. A twofold task remains to be accomplished: the theology of Calvin must be examined at as many points as possible in order to discover his underlying intention. In this connexion the essence of his theology must be more clearly elucidated than has been the case hitherto.

I wrote thus in 1938 when I published this book about the theology of Calvin in the midst of the struggles of the church. In the meantime great strides have been made in this field of research. The conclusions of my own work have as a result been strengthened and completed. Let me mention above all the book (which appeared soon after my own) by the Calvin scholar who died recently—Wilhelm Kolfhaus: *Christusgemeinschaft bei Johannes Calvin*; Neukirchen, 1939, and his further work: *Die Seelsorge Johannes Calvins*; Neukirchen, 1941. Finally I should like to refer to the fine study by T. F. Torrance: *Calvin's Doctrine of Man*, London, 1949, and to the good survey by François Wendel: *Calvin, Sources et Evolution de sa pensée religieuse*, Paris, 1950. The revolution in the approach to the theology of Calvin is unmistakable.[2] We are sure that the publication which has been begun in Geneva of extant but hitherto unprinted manuscripts of the sermons of Calvin[3] will furnish further conclusive evidence for the correctness of the new view. (See page 251 for a brief survey of recent studies of Calvin's theology.)

What is offered in the following pages is no comprehensive

[1] Here we may mention the contributions of Peter Barth to Calvin research. They are listed along with other recent Calvin literature in the report of Peter Barth: "Fünfundzwanzig Jahre Calvinforschung 1909–1934", *Theol. Rundschau, Neue Folge VI*, 1934, p. 162.

[2] Cf. also W. A. Hauck: *Christusglaube und Gottesoffenbarung nach Calvin*, Gütersloh, 1939: *Vorsehung und Freiheit nach Calvin*, Gütersloh, 1947.

[3] J. Calvin: *Predigten über das 2 Buch Samuelis*, in *der Ursprache nach der Genfer Handschrift*, Hanns Rückert, Neukirchen, 1936 ff.

survey of the theology of Calvin in the sense that the chief points of his doctrine are enumerated and presented in every detail. Our aim is to illuminate the whole body of his teaching by a few fundamental examples. The problems of his theology must disclose to us the essential problem and bring it to the attention of our own theology and church.

Chapter 2

THE KNOWLEDGE OF GOD

I. THEOLOGY AND HOLY SCRIPTURE [1]

(*a*) If we wish to grasp the problem presented by the theology of Calvin, our best course will be in the main to keep well in view what he himself tells us about it. This will give to our study the most unexceptionable and solid point of departure. In his chief work, the *Institutes*, Calvin has provided the reader with an introduction. Here he imparts to us his basic purpose in giving an exposition of Christian doctrine.

"My intention in this work", he says, "has been then to guide and instruct theological candidates in the reading of the Word of God, so that they may without hindrance proceed upon the right lines. I have therefore thought fit to summarize the whole body of religious doctrine and to reduce it to such order that whoever rightly studies it will not find it difficult to decide what he must especially seek in Scripture, and to what end he must judge of its contents (*quem in scopum*). Accordingly if, after fixing these outlines, I give some exposition of Scripture it will not be necessary for me to engage in lengthy arguments about disputed points and to discuss general principles, and I can always try to be brief. Hence the pious reader will be spared trouble and annoyance if only he proceeds to read Scripture with a knowledge of

[1] J. A. Cramer: *De Heilige Schrift bij Calvijn*, Utrecht, 1926: *Calvijn en de Heilige Schrift*, Wageningen, 1932. D. J. de Groot: *Calvijns opvatting over de inspiratie der Heilige Schrift*, Zutphen, 1931. R. Bach: "Unsere Bibelnot und Calvins Schlüssel zur Schrift: Das innere Geisteszeugnis", *Reform. Kztg.*, 72, 1922, pp. 225 ff. M. Simon: "Die Beziehung zwischen Altem und Neuem Testament in der Schriftauslegung Calvins", *Reform. Kztg.*, 82, 1932, pp. 17 ff.

this book as a necessary part of his equipment."[1] In similar terms Calvin describes his intention in the introduction to the French translation of the *Institutes*. The work is to serve the purpose of finding the sum of what God wished to teach us in His Word. "To this end he proposes to treat the principal and most important things which are contained in Christian philosophy."[2] According to these fundamental considerations it seems to be the aim of Calvin in the *Institutes* to attain and expound a synthesis of the contents of Scripture.

Of course the *Institutes* itself begins with the words: "All our wisdom, in so far as it is to be held true and perfect, consists in two things: namely, a right knowledge of God and of ourselves."[3] But this first sentence about the knowledge of God and of ourselves is not meant to be the foundation for subsequent speculations of human reason about God and man, but rather, in enunciating this principle, Calvin is already carrying out the programme announced to the reader in the introduction. The latter is not found in the first Latin edition of the *Institutes*; but the French translation already contains in a preface the words just quoted. But it should above all be noted that the first *Institutes* does not contain in its opening the words "all our wisdom"; instead we find unmistakably: "All sacred doctrine consists in two things: the knowledge of God and of ourselves."[4] Thus Calvin in fact begins in the first sentence of the *Institutes* to expound the sum of what God teaches us in Holy Scripture.

But even if all this were not made so plain, the first words of the *Institutes* could not mean that Calvin in what follows was about to develop his own thoughts about God and man. Theologians and philosophers attempt that again and again; but Calvin knows very well that "all that we think and speak about God or ourselves is but vain folly and empty words".[5] The human mind is too weak to be able to fathom and comprehend the being of God.[6] If we wish to say anything apt about God and His relation to mankind then we must

---

[1] *OS* 3, 6, 18 ff.   [2] *OS* 3, 7, 28 ff.   [3] *In.* I, 1, 1.
[4] *OS* 1, 37.   [5] *In.* I, 13, 3.   [6] *In.* I, 6, 4.

be taught by God Himself. This is what happens in Holy Scripture, which alone discloses to us the nature of God and ourselves. "We must go to the Word, in which God is clearly and vividly mirrored for us in His works, and where the works of God are appraised not by our perverse judgments but by the criterion of eternal truth."[1] The fact is "that no one can understand the smallest part of true and saving doctrine unless he be a student of Holy Scripture".[2] Hence the aim of Calvin's theology seems to be not an unfolding of *"philosophia humana"* but an exposition of the *"philosophia christiana"* which God gives us in the Bible.

But we cannot understand without more ado the *"philosophia christiana"* which God offers us in Scripture. Even in reading Scripture we remain men "who are born in darkness" and "ever more and more are hardened in their blindness."[3] Hence Scripture remains for us in our present condition "like a dead and ineffectual thing".[4] Of course we hear its words and discover its teachings: but we make of them according to our fancy some philosophy or speculative system.[5]

Since our natural disposition is utterly contrary to everything spiritual, the inclinations of our heart must be changed if our study of the Bible is not to be so much lost time.[6] We must be given eyes and ears to register the truth of the Bible if we are really to recognize and grasp it.[7] When we turn to God, God effects this change in us through His Spirit.[8] The Holy Spirit alone is the true expositor of Scripture.[9] By His agency the word of Scripture is "powerfully imprinted upon our hearts"[10] so that we truly receive and understand it.

When Calvin proposes in his *Institutes* to interpret those fundamental principles of Christian philosophy which God has granted us in the Bible, then, in accordance with what has just been said, it must be remembered as we consider the fulfilment of his purpose that "no one can understand the

---

[1] *In.* I, 6, 3.   [2] *In.* I, 6, 2.   [3] *OS* 3, 63, 2.
[4] *CR* 54, 285.   [5] *CR* 8, 395.   [6] *CR* 9, 825.
[7] *CR* 52, 383.   [8] *CR* 9, 825.   [9] *CR* 6, 270.
[10] *In.* I, 9, 3.

secrets of God except those to whom it is given".[1] May we not then describe in the following terms the purpose which Calvin has in view in writing theology: for him it is a question of expounding the contents of Scripture, the "*philosophia christiana*" which he has apprehended and experienced in his own heart as the truth of God vouchsafed to him thus through the illumination of the Holy Ghost? Whereas the philosophers are able to teach only human wisdom and, further, the theologians, in so far as they rely upon reason, merely misuse the Bible in order to extract from it the materials for a doctrinal edifice of their own devising, may we suppose that Calvin reproduces in his theology words and teachings which by the action of the Holy Ghost in response to his faith he has understood as divine words and teachings?

(*b*) It is thus that Calvin in fact has frequently been understood. Whether, as dictated by our theological position, we say that Calvin wishes to expound the divine word of Scripture as he has apprehended it in faith, or that his purpose is to present the content of Scripture which he has inwardly assimilated, makes no great difference. Calvin in fact is concerned with something quite distinct. Certainly as "one who has received from God more light than others"[2] he wishes to discuss in his *Institutes* the principles of that Christian philosophy which the Bible offers us. He says this quite plainly in his preface, where he indicates also that he does not merely intend to draw up a list of such principles but that he has imposed a certain order upon this sum of religious truth.[3] But all this is not the essential. Of course he does all this and must do it; but the purpose which he has set himself is not to compose a synthesis of the divine teachings which in faith he has derived from Scripture in order thereby to instruct his brethren. No doubt to teach is part of his purpose. This is suggested by the very title of his book. But he does not mean that by an exposition of the principles of Scriptural doctrine—which in fact he gives—he can simply impart to his readers the matter which he has at heart.

[1] *In.* I, 7, 5.   [2] *OS* 3, 7, 26.   [3] *OS* 3, 6, 23.

Calvin, firstly, intends much less. What he says in the *Institutes* is not conceived as an end in itself, but as a sort of key by means of which readers can then find for themselves the right approach to Scripture.[1] The coherent presentation of Scriptural teaching has only the subordinate purpose of enabling each one to know "what he must primarily seek in Scripture and to what end he should relate its contents".[2]

But what kind of a "*scopus*" or "end" is it to which the reader of the Bible must relate the whole contents of the Scriptures? And—this question may now be asked—if all that Calvin adduces in the *Institutes* is only meant to draw the attention of the reader to the "*scopus*" of the Bible, what is then the problem of problems raised by Calvin's theology itself? To this Calvin gives a very plain answer in another preface. We mean the preface to the editions of the Genevan translation of the Bible.[3] This preface and that to the *Institutes* are complementary to each other. In the preface to the *Institutes* the reader is referred to the Bible and in the preface to the Genevan Bible he is referred to the *Institutes*.

In his preface to the Genevan translation of the Bible Calvin speaks chiefly about the supreme value and importance of Holy Scripture. Thus he there explains how the reader must prepare himself if he is to study the Bible with profit. This preparation has two aspects: "That we on our part shall be alert and ready, as is seemly, and that we realize the end to which we must strive."[4] After saying something on these lines, Calvin continues: "I now refrain from speaking in more detail about these two aspects (the value of Scripture and right preparation for the reading of it) because if this matter is to be rightly treated it requires not a simple introduction but a whole book."[5] On reading this, who does not think of the book which according to his own confession Calvin has written in order that each should know "what he

---

[1] *OS* 3, 8, 5; 6, 19.
[2] "quid potissimum quaerere in Scriptura et quem in scopum quicquid in ea continetur referre debeat", *OS* 3, 6, 24.
[3] *CR* 9, 823 ff.   [4] *CR* 9, 824.   [5] *CR* 9, 825.

must primarily seek in Scripture, and to what end he should relate its contents"?[1]

But what is the end of Bible study? Not that we should seek, in Scripture, food for idle speculations or material for frivolous questions. It is given to us not for the satisfaction of our foolish curiosity but for our edification. "If you ask in what this whole edification consists, which we are to receive thereby, in a word, it is a question of learning to place our trust in God and to walk in the fear of Him, and—since Jesus Christ is the end of the law and the prophets and the essence of the gospel—of aspiring to no other aim but to know Him, since we realize that we cannot deviate from that path in the slightest degree without going astray."[2] In other words: since the end, the fulfilling of the law, calling us to the fear of God is Jesus Christ and the theme of the gospel inviting us to trust is also Jesus Christ, the aim of all our attention to the Bible should be the recognition of Jesus Christ.

This statement of Calvin is not an isolated one. In a sermon he speaks in similar terms: "When we read Scripture our aim must be to be truly edified in faith and in the fear of the Lord, to become drawn to our Lord Jesus Christ and to recognize that God has imparted Himself to us in Him that we may possess Him as our inheritance . . ."[3] Elsewhere we find: "We must read Scripture with the intention of finding Christ therein. If we turn aside from this end, however much trouble we take, however much time we devote to our study, we shall never attain the knowledge of the truth. Again, can we be wise without the wisdom of God?"[4]

From these two quotations it also becomes quite plain why the goal of our Biblical study must be Jesus Christ: He is the Mediator in whom alone God communicates Himself to us. This again is what was implied in our previous statement that Jesus Christ is the end of the law and the essence of the gospel. This means further that law and gospel are not simply words but that they proclaim a word of God through which He reveals Himself to us men: Jesus Christ.

[1] OS 3, 6, 24. [2] CR 9, 825. [3] CR 53, 560.
[4] CR 47, 125; cf. CR 45, 817; 50, 45.

Finally we would refer to a passage of the *Institutes* itself in which Calvin expresses himself in a similar way in regard to the word of Scripture: "When by the power of the Spirit it effectually penetrates our hearts, when it conveys Christ to us, then it becomes a word of life converting the soul." [1] This too makes quite plain that Scripture ultimately is concerned with the living Christ. But something else is also implied. When it was stated previously that the aim of reading the Bible is to know Christ, we can now see that this knowledge is a knowledge which the Holy Ghost imparts to us. We have already been told that God the Holy Ghost is alone the true interpreter of the Bible for us. It is by His action that the Word of Scripture is powerfully conveyed to our hearts and that the words of the Bible become the one word radiating the presence of Christ and bestowing it upon us.

It now becomes clear that Calvin, in writing his theology, is concerned about something far deeper than an exposition of Scriptural truths apprehended by faith. The "end" of the Bible at which his work is aimed is, of course, as we have just heard, truth itself: Jesus Christ. But Calvin is not the controller of that truth. He cannot mediate it to his readers; he can only point to it. For the latter purpose he develops his "*philosophia christiana*" of the Bible and expounds in due order the main points of Biblical doctrine. By this theology he can serve the reader of Holy Scripture only as it were by marking out the path which leads to the one end on which the whole Bible is focused. Thus the various doctrines which he explains are so many signposts guiding the traveller again and again in the right direction and preventing him from going astray. [2] Calvin's design is thus purely and simply to expound doctrine, the affirmations of faith, "*philosophia christiana*". But this exposition of Christian doctrine is not the same thing as the "end" of his theological task. This ultimate purpose lies beyond the immediate one; it is the same as that of the Bible itself; our Lord Jesus Christ. Calvin in his theology is concerned fundamentally about this living Lord; not about certain doctrines which he has extracted from Scripture.

[1] *In.* I, 9, 3.   [2] *OS* 3, 7, 24.

To show that what we are here urging is not something read into Calvin, but the governing purpose which he himself entertains, we will make in conclusion the following observation. The first Latin edition of the *Institutes* is not headed by the preface from which we have quoted, but contains as an introduction the letter to Francis I. The opening of it runs thus: "My purpose has been simply this—to provide a preparation by means of which such as feel some zeal for religion should be brought to true piety. And I undertook this work principally for our own French people, many of whom, as I realized, hunger and thirst after Christ but of whom very few are instructed even moderately in the true knowledge of the Lord." [1]

In these introductory words to his *Institutes* Calvin has declared his intention unmistakably. He wishes to guide the reader to the attainment of true piety and this true piety consists in the knowledge of Christ. By the exposition of the contents of Scripture he wishes to proclaim to his countrymen this living Lord; nothing more.

(c) Thus our contention has been that Calvin's purpose was not to convey to his readers Scriptural truths recognized by faith; he knows that he can perform only a modest auxiliary service and cannot mediate to others the heart of the matter itself. In recognizing that as a true theologian he could only be a servant, and in being content that his theology should bear the character of an allusion and proclamation, he was doing more than offering his readers a compendium of divine teachings culled from the Bible. He performs his service as a teacher in the certitude that the centre of the Bible towards which his own theology is orientated—Jesus Christ Himself—constantly draws near to our soul in His living reality and power as we meditate on the words of Holy Scripture.

In the Bible we are confronted by God Himself.[2] He speaks to us to-day through the words of His witnesses and ever and anon reveals Himself to us.[3] Through all the words of the Bible the living Word of God itself resounds. There we

[1] *OS* 1, 21. [2] *CR* 8, 395. [3] *CR* 6, 269; 9, 824.

encounter Jesus Christ, the Word of words. Hence Holy Scripture is the sole criterion of the teachings of the church.[1]

In view of this interpretation of the heart and centre of Scripture there is little sense in describing this principle as the formal principle of Calvin's theology. Christ Himself, the Son of God made man, cannot become a formal principle. Nor is the expression "material principle" any more apt. Calvin does not consider his theology subordinate to any sort of body of materials. Christ the living Word of God spoken to us is not an element in a synthesis from which all the other elements are derived. Christ Jesus is the content which transcends all contents. He is the Lord whom Calvin awaits with burning desire: "How long O Lord?"[2] The Bible proclaims Him. Hence the theology of Calvin is linked to the word of Scripture and is bidden to do nothing more than point to the "end" of the Bible, Jesus Christ Himself.

2. SCRIPTURE AND SPIRIT

We have seen that the focal point of the Bible to which Calvin wishes to bear witness in his theology is not comprehensible by the unaided reason. It is by the grace of God that Scripture mediates to us the living Christ. The Holy Spirit must unfold to us the treasures of the words of Scripture if our study of it is to lead to this goal.

If the Holy Spirit must thus act upon us in order that we should recognize and gain Christ, why then is there any need of Holy Scripture at all? And if our attention must be turned to the latter, what role then does the Holy Spirit properly play? We must now more precisely determine the relation of Spirit and Scripture and also enquire into the exact reference of both to the "end" of the Bible, Jesus Christ.

On this point Peter Brunner puts forward some excellent arguments in his book.[3] There would be no need to add much to them if recently the opinion had not again been expressed

[1] Cf. *In.* IV, 8, 8.   [2] *CR* 21, 161; *In.* III, 9, 5.
[3] See above p. 17, note 1.

that Calvin taught the literal inspiration of Holy Scripture.[1] No doubt the thesis has been modified to the extent that he did not understand inspiration in any mechanical fashion. He did not think that the inspiration of the Bible could be demonstrated to all and sundry. He differed from later orthodoxy by the mode of his belief in the divine inspiration of the Scriptures; but he did truly believe in it all the same.

(*a*) First, we might point out that in the Scriptural exegesis of Calvin there is nothing to suggest a belief in literal inerrancy.[2] He expressly guards himself against exegesis which consists in the patching together of texts.[3] But we are not much advanced by making such observations. However important they may be in preventing us from reading orthodox views into Calvin's doctrine, they do not shed much light upon the problem itself. Does not Calvin then speak of a divinely inspired Scripture, and what does he mean by that? Of course Calvin speaks of it, but only very rarely—a fact which may be regretted by the champions of theories of inspiration, but which cannot be altered. In the chapters of the *Institutes* in which he puts forward his doctrine of Scripture he fatally omits to mention it at all. Elsewhere he expresses himself in detail on the point, so far as we are aware, only in three places. Once he discusses it with reference to the well-known text 2 Timothy 3:16, and in two other places, while not positively developing a theory of inspiration, he comes to speak of it in his debate with Romanists who wish to found the authority of the Bible on that of the church.[4] The circumstances which induced Calvin in these three passages to expatiate on the inspiration of Scripture will make a critical estimate of them very cautious.

(*b*) After making these observations of fact we will consider the matter in itself. Peter Brunner has already drawn attention to the fact that Calvin is fond of comparing the word of Scripture with a mirror. He makes two remarks on the point: "The mirror clearly reflects an image but this reflection is

1 De Groot in his above-mentioned book against Cramer.
2 Cf. E. Doumergue, *Jean Calvin*, IV, 76 ff.   3 *In.* I, 13, 3.
4 *In.* IV, 8, 5–9; *Contra Pighium, CR* 6, 270 ff.

not identical with the image itself."[1] In proof he quotes especially Calvin's exegesis of 2 Corinthians 5:7 where we read: "We see indeed, but as in a glass darkly—i.e. instead of having the thing itself we have to be content with the message about it."[2] Calvin expresses the same point when he describes the word of the Bible as an instrument of the Spirit.[3] This means that the Holy Spirit uses the word but it does not mean that it has so penetrated the word as to be identical with it. In this connexion we may remember that Calvin describes the elements of the Eucharist as instruments which the Holy Spirit uses in order to work in the souls of the elect.[4] God wills to make use of these elements as His instruments. That must strictly be borne in mind; but these means are not the thing itself. They must be carefully distinguished from God Himself. If this is true of the visible signs of the Eucharist, the same consideration applies to the word as the instrument of the Spirit. Instrument and thing are not to be divorced, but they are plainly to be distinguished.

Finally, we are led to the same interpretation of Calvin's attitude towards Scripture by a third series of passages. We have seen that he considers the word of the Bible as a dead and ineffectual thing for us if it is not divinely vivified. But this does not mean that the Holy Spirit has only to move within us for us to be able rightly to understand Scripture. No; the written word itself must be made alive. When Calvin speaks of the law he reminds us that Christ is the end of the law and indeed the soul which animates it. So soon as it is separated from Him it becomes a dead body of letters without soul. Christ the soul of the law alone can make it live.[5] "But what", he adds, "is true of the law is true of the Scriptures as a whole. If they are not focused upon Christ as their sole 'end', then they are completely warped and distorted."[6] Here again we recognize the two factors: the theme of the Bible cannot be divorced from its letters and

---

[1] Peter Brunner: *Vom Glauben bei Calvin*, p. 93.
[2] *Op. cit.*, p. 94; *CR* 50, 63; cf. *CR* 9, 823.
[3] *In.* I, 9, 3; IV, 11, 1.   [4] Cf. *OS* 1, 508.
[5] *CR* 40, 395; *CR* 49, 196.   [6] *CR* 50, 45.

words, from the extant book. And yet this theme is not identifiable with these words. In themselves they are dead words. The theme alone to which they bear witness makes them live; and this theme is Jesus Christ.

Jesus Christ is the soul of the law, the focal point of the whole of Holy Scripture. When we hear Calvin assert so much we realize how misleading it is to regard him as the exponent of a literal theory of inspiration. As though the living Lord could be identified with the written words of the Bible! In that case He would be simply an idea or some other thing, but not the Christ Himself. The Word of God the incarnate Logos must be distinguished from the words of Scripture.

(c) Why in any event does Calvin bring these two things into such close connexion? How comes it about that he describes Jesus Christ as the soul of the law and of the Bible as a whole?

He tells us this just at that point in the *Institutes* where he discusses the inspiration of the Bible to counter the authoritarian claims of the Roman church: "As truly as Christ tells us that no one has seen the Father save the Son and he to whomsoever the Son willeth to reveal Him, so certainly all those who have wished to come to the knowledge of God have always had to be guided by the same eternal wisdom. For how could they have understood or spoken of the secrets of God by their unaided reason unless they had been taught by Him to whom alone the mysteries of the Father are disclosed? Hence the holy men of long ago did not know God otherwise than by viewing Him in His Son as in a mirror. When I say that, I mean that God has never revealed Himself to men otherwise than through the Son; that is through the unique wisdom, light, and truth of the Son. From that wellspring Adam, Noah, Abraham, Isaac and Jacob and others have drawn all that they knew of divine things. And from it too all the prophets have derived whatever divine prophecies they have left behind them in their writings." [1] Calvin says just the same of the apostles, viz. that

[1] *In.* IV, 8, 5.

33

no more was granted to them than aforetime to the prophets, that they expounded the ancient Scriptures to show the fulfilment of them in Christ and that they could do this only through the power of the Lord, "the spirit of Christ speaking within them and in some sense dictating to them the words."[1] Thus Jesus Christ is the animating spirit of the Bible and both belong together because the hidden God has revealed Himself to us in Him alone, and it is just this revelation of God in Jesus Christ which the Bible attests.

No way leads from man to God. The only connexion between man and God exists in the one bridge which He Himself has built and which is the one Incarnate Lord. It is this position of affairs which Calvin desires to indicate in the passage just referred to, by the fact that, like Luther, he describes Jesus Christ as the mirror in which God's witnesses have beheld God Himself. In the countenance of Jesus Christ God allows us to see His own very image.[2] To be sure, continues the Reformer, "the Turks to-day affirm that they worship God the Creator of heaven and earth; but they worship only an idol. How so? They call Him the Creator of heaven and earth and they have no images of Him. So much is true, and the reason is that they have an idol instead of the living God because they refuse to accept our Lord Jesus Christ, who is the living image of God his Father."[3] Calvin research up to the most recent past is full of attempts to impute to Calvin's theology this kind of deity worshipped by the Turks. In this matter we have Calvin's own sharp disowning of Turks, Jews, and all their kin. The characteristic of Islam is seen in the fact that it understands Jesus Christ as one manifestation of the divine among others, and hence relativizes Him; the essence of Judaism consists in the fact that it denies Jesus Christ to be the Son of God. Both like to speak of God, but, since they dissociate the name of God from Jesus Christ, God can be no more to them than a phantom.[4] Calvin realizes that we are utterly dependent for our knowledge of God upon His self-revelation: upon the fact that He

[1] *In.* IV, 8, 8.   [2] *CR* 9, 816.
[3] *CR* 26, 427; cf. *In.* II, 6, 4.   [4] *CR* 47, 115.

Himself has come down into our world. We meet God personally only in Jesus Christ, who in His living personal reality is the image of God the Father.

The incarnate Christ is indeed no longer among us; but He has left us the word of His witnesses. As He Himself is the mirror of God, so the word of Scripture reflects for us the grace and truth of Christ. In this respect there is a certain parallelism: as God was in the man Jesus, so the incarnate Son is the animating soul of the Bible. We must not await God's living word from any source but solely from Holy Scripture. God has willed that there should be this fundamental witness to His revelation, that we might hold fast to it with assurance. He does not come down from heaven to speak to us every day. "But Scripture exists, by which God has seen fit to proclaim and uphold His truth throughout all ages."[1] In this purpose God's grace and favour towards us men declares itself. As once He condescended to dwell with us in our flesh, in order that we should encounter His living presence, so again in Holy Scripture He adapts Himself to our nature and speaks with us mortal men in our fashion that we may understand and endure His words. That the God of majesty speaks to us to-day in the word of Scripture and babbles with us, as it were, in this book, is a token of His condescension.[2] Because that is so, Calvin so frequently utters the word of command: "*Ad verbum est veniendum*".[3]

We have seen why Calvin does not confuse but distinguishes the one Word and the words of Scripture, Jesus Christ the soul of the Bible and the extant written message which bears witness to Him. Now we see too why he does not divorce them. For precisely thus he shows that he takes with real seriousness the unique, perfect, and exclusive revelation of God in Jesus Christ.

(*d*) All this should have made it plain that Calvin neither championed the idea of the demonstrable mechanical inspira-

[1] *OS* 3, 65, 11.

[2] *CR* 26, 387. Calvin here compares God with a nurse who talks to the child in the child's own language. Cf. also *CR* 35, 312.

[3] "You must come to the Word"; *In.* I, 7, 1.

35

tion of the Bible nor did he believe in its inspired literal inerrancy. Although he may incidentally speak of the divine inspiration of Holy Scripture, such remarks must in no case be interpreted to mean that Scripture as such is identical with the truth of God. No; the truth of God is Jesus Christ, the Mediator, our Lord, and not a spirit incarnated as it were in the Bible. Calvin's doctrine of the inspiration of the Bible is more vital than some suppose. When the second epistle to Timothy speaks of the divine origin of the Scriptures, Calvin thinks that it is a summons to us that we should look for God to speak to us through the Bible: "Thus Holy Scripture is for us a dead and ineffectual thing until we have come to realize that God speaks to us and manifests His will to us therein. That is what we should understand when Paul assures us that Holy Scripture is divinely inspired."[1] Unlike later critics, Calvin did not develop any theory as to how God inspired prophets and apostles. Rather he was aware of being claimed by the Bible and read the book "as if the living voice of God were to be heard therein".[2] This did not encourage speculation but challenged to obedience in the present hour. The teaching about literal inspiration leads to Bibliolatry and overlooks the fact that there is only one incarnation of the divine word, of which Holy Scripture is the witness.

Because the testimony of prophets and apostles is no speech conceived on their own initiative, but is rather what they were commanded to declare, they themselves and their words being merely the instruments of God who wills thus to use them for His purposes, it is inevitable that Calvin should speak of the Holy Ghost in formulating his doctrine of the Scriptures.

Christ by His Spirit won for Himself the hearts of prophets and apostles and used them and their words in His service. Hence by the activity of His eternal Spirit He must still to-day control their testimony and through their words speak His own living word to us—if the Bible is to have any meaning for us at all. Precisely because the ultimate theme of Scripture is God's own all-quickening word which became flesh in

[1] *CR* 54, 285.   [2] *In.* I, 7, 1.

36

Jesus Christ, that miracle must come to pass by which God makes the word of His witnesses as we find it in the Bible His own piercing word. Here is the miraculous operation of the Holy Ghost.

(e) But that is only one aspect of the matter. It is not enough that God has revealed Himself to us in Jesus Christ and wishes to speak to us to-day in the testimony to this revelation. Again, it is not enough that He wills to confront us in this instrument of Holy Scripture. However much we assert that Scripture alone is for us the ground of our recognition of God, it avails nothing. Still more are all attempts to prove the uniqueness of Holy Scripture in the last resort unavailing. Calvin realized very clearly the hopelessness of all such apologetic.[1] Just because the concern of Holy Scripture is not with doctrine but with the all-quickening Word of God, we must confess that we are unable to grasp its meaning by our unaided reason and ability. We can understand Scripture, says Calvin, only when God Himself makes His divine presence manifest to us therein.[2] And this is ever afresh a divine action and event. The Holy Spirit who used prophets and apostles as His instruments and still to-day uses and quickens their word to ever new purposes, to make the voice of the Lord audible to us, must also perform His work in our hearts and must Himself speak in us the response to the word by which we are addressed. In this connexion Calvin refers us to Isaiah 54:13 (*In.* I, 7, 5). In this way the wondrous action of the Holy Ghost is

---

[1] *In.* VIII, 1, 13. In this connexion Calvin has written a whole chapter in the *Institutes* concerning the credibility of Scripture from the point of view of reason. He discusses its impressive power, its age, the authenticity of its writings, the evidence of miracles and fulfilled prophecies, its marvellous preservation, its successful resistance to all criticism, and the confirmation of its authority by the blood of the martyrs. Calvin regards these arguments as helpful in our weakness and not without justification once the true ground of the authority of the Scriptures is recognized. Thus he does not intend them as conclusive proofs. Hence they are not of great value and later, when their secondary importance was no longer recognized, let in the tide of orthodoxy.

[2] *In.* I, 8, 13.

completed. This is not an illegitimate interpretation of Calvin in the light of modern theology, for he himself says: "For as the all-sufficient testimony of God is contained in His word, the latter does not find the response of human faith until it is sealed by the inner witness of the Holy Spirit".[1] "Word and Spirit—both must be present if the sovereignty of God is to be established."[2]

(f) It has been said that Calvin's statements concerning the relation of Word and Spirit are contradictory. On the one hand the Spirit must be added to the Word in order to lend authority to the latter. On the other hand the witness of the Spirit is identical with the meaning of the Word, and only gains its legitimation through its agreement with the latter. Bauke saw in this position a splendid proof of the existence of the *complexio oppositorum* in Calvin. The fact was that the Reformer, without appreciating the full scope of the problem, combined these opposites in his dialectical manner.[3] Peter Brunner on the contrary has shown that Calvin was committed inevitably to such positions by the intrinsic nature of the subject and by his own theology of revelation.[4] We shall now elucidate this point in connexion with our own discussion concerning the "end" of Scripture. We can well understand why Calvin says in debate with Sadolet: "It is no less unreasonable to claim to give utterance to the Spirit without the authority of the Word than it would be to shelter behind the Word without possessing the Spirit."[5] Were we to attempt to convince another by Scriptural proof, forgetting that only God Himself by His Spirit can persuade man of the truth of the Word, then all our arguments would be so many words; we should not be using the Word, and all would be in vain. If on the other hand—as the ecstatics of that time did—we were to appeal to an immediate spiritually inspired knowledge of God, then the question would arise whether in fact the Holy Ghost were operative and not rather our own spirit. God does not constantly reveal Himself from the heavens;

[1] *In.* I, 7, 4; *In.* I, 8, 13; *CR* 39, 42.   [2] *CR* 45, 197.
[3] Bauke, *op. cit.*, p. 55.   [4] Peter Brunner, *op. cit.*, p. 97, note 3.
[5] *OS* 1, 466.

He has spoken once in His Son and the presence of the Son confronts us to-day in the word of those who witness to Him.

Calvin is aware of all this and therefore he does not forget that the Holy Spirit, which is the Spirit of Christ, stands wholly in the service of God's self-revelation. The task of the Spirit is to make us sensitive to the one Word which lies concealed in the words of Scripture; it must therefore use the written words and quicken them for our understanding. In order to bring the incarnate Word near to us the Spirit needs the written word, and proves itself as the Holy Spirit, the third Person of the Trinity, by respecting the testimony which prophets and apostles bear to the historical revelation of God in Jesus Christ. He does not speak otherwise to-day than as He once spoke through those men of old, He testifies to Jesus Christ, and thus we must await the action of the Holy Spirit from no other source but that of the Biblical witness.[1] These considerations should make it clear that Calvin's opinions about the relation of Word and Spirit are governed by the insight that the one theme of Holy Scripture is the incarnate Word itself.

3. THE QUESTION OF NATURAL THEOLOGY[2]

(a) This formulation of the problem which we must now consider does not mean that, after all the foregoing

---

[1] A whole chapter of the *Institutes* works this out in opposition to the libertines (I, 9).

[2] Emil Brunner, *Natur und Gnade*, 1934. Karl Barth: "Nein! Antwort an Emil Brunner", *Theol. Exist. heute*, V, 14, 1934. (Eng. trans. of both these, *Natural Theology*, E. Brunner and K. Barth, London, 1946.) Peter Barth: "Die fünf Einleitungskapitel von Calvins Institutio", *Kirchenbl. f. d. reform. Schweiz*, 1925, pp. 41 ff. "Das Problem der natürlichen Theologie bei Calvin", *Theol. Exist. heute*, V, 18, 1935. Peter Brunner: "Allgemeine und Besondere in Calvins Institutio", *Ev. Theologie*, I, 1934, 189 ff. Jean Daniel Fischer: *Le Problème de la theologie naturelle étudié d'après Calvin*, Dissertation, Strasburg, 1936. Günter Gloede: *Theologia naturalis bei Calvin*, 1935. Max Lackmann: "Conditio vitae est cognitio Dei. Wesen und Sinn der menschlichen Erkenntnis nach Calvins Institutio von 1559 lib. I, 1", *Ev. Theologie*, 2, 1935, 198 ff. Wilhelm Lütgert: "Calvins Lehre vom Schöpfer", *Zeitschr. f. syst. Theol.*, 9, 1931, 421 f. Pierre Maury: "La théologie naturelle d'après Calvin", *Bull. de la Société de l'Hist. du protest. franç.*, 84, 1935, 267 ff.

arguments, it is still an undecided question whether for Calvin a knowledge of God is obtainable from nature and history. Must we once again remind our readers of the fact that in emphasizing the necessity of Holy Scripture for the knowledge of God we have been taking seriously the plan which Calvin has outlined in all the prefaces to his work of dogmatics? Must we once again recall that the first sentence of the *Institutes* itself speaks about the "sum of all our wisdom" which is to be developed in the pages which follow, and which is nothing else but the sum of sacred doctrines and of Holy Scripture itself? Whoever overlooks or evades these programmatic statements of Calvin and discovers in his writings a *theologia naturalis* can hardly be regarded seriously as a scholar.

The critic who desires to find in Calvin a natural theology encounters yet other difficulties, although they are not so obvious at the outset as those which Calvin has erected in the preface to his *Institutes*. The whole subject-matter of the final edition of the *Institutes* is divided into the three main articles of the Christian faith (Calvin counts his statements about the church as a special fourth division). Calvin introduces his teaching in connexion with the baptismal symbol of the church, which is recited at the moment when the candidate is shown by the ritual of the baptismal water how he must die and rise again if he is to attain communion with God. This recognition of the baptismal symbol in the very setting of the doctrine which is to be expounded excludes at once all natural theology. Anyone who doubts whether Calvin understood so strictly as an elaboration of the baptismal creed those articles of faith on which the edifice of his doctrine is based, and hence whether the implications which we have deduced are legitimate, may be reminded that Calvin certainly regarded the sacraments as occupying a paramount position in Church life.

No interpretation of the theology of Calvin can with impunity disregard the fact that the first Genevan Church Order begins with the sentence: "It is certain that no church can be considered to be well ordered and governed in which the Holy Eucharist is not often celebrated and attended." [1] Calvin assigns to the sacrament this central significance because we are promised that by its means we shall truly share in the Body and Blood of Jesus.[2] The church which holds the true confession of faith is the sphere in which Christ the Son of God is present; and are we then to suppose that the theology by which Calvin aims to help such a church in the better understanding of its life, can be systematically characterized as "inspired by the God of creation"?[3] To pose such a question is to answer it. Otherwise one would have to go so far as to say that Calvin taught something completely different from what he willed and carried through in the ordering of church life. Whoever defends the view that Calvin offers us a natural theology is disregarding what the Reformer said and did and is introducing into his theology typically modern sequences of thought. It would be better for such people to content themselves with their own ideas and leave Calvin alone.

Nevertheless Calvin must give occasion for such attempts to make of him a supreme witness to the justification of natural theology. This pretext arises from the fact that Calvin—especially as a result of his humanistic tendencies—was well aware of the question of natural theology and that he answered it throughout his writings but with particular detail in his *Institutes*. We must now give consideration to this answer.

(*b*) There can be no doubt that Calvin recognized a self-declaration of God to mankind in the natural order. In the *Institutes* this fact is made plain and supported by detailed argument. God reveals Himself in nature (and above all in the nature of man) in the course of natural processes and in the history of humanity. "Thus he has revealed Himself in the design of the universe, allowing Himself to be recognized every day, so that men cannot open their eyes without seeing the traces of His presence."[4] There is nothing so tiny but it

[1] *OS* I, 369.   [2] *OS* I, 370.
[3] Günter Gloede: *Theologia naturalis bei Calvin*, pp. 207, 140.
[4] *In.* I, 5, 1.

41

gleams with some sparks of the divine glory.[1] But man in particular is a masterpiece produced by the omnipotence, goodness, and wisdom of God.[2] He is endowed with capacities from which we may infer divinity.[3] What must be said of the nature of man applies equally to his destiny and to the destiny of mankind in general: "the wisdom of God shines forth in that He disposes all things for the best, confounds the crafty devices of the world, entraps the wise by their wisdom and in short rules all things for ultimate good."[4] Similarly God permits Himself to be recognized surely and clearly in the course of natural processes.[5]

To be precise, however, we must note that God Himself is not to be encountered in the world of nature and history. He exists above the order of nature[6] and is thus not immanent within it. The world shows traces of His reality from which we may infer His existence. He has impressed upon His works sure signs of His glory,[7] "so that in the created world as in a picture His power is reflected".[8]

When we are told that Calvin is familiar with the argument from the book of nature,[9] the question suggests itself whether the relation between this book and God is not similar to that between the Bible and its theme. Should we apply here also the principle that God and the witness to Him should not be confused but neither should they be divorced? Are nature and history then a sort of second Bible, a second source of revelation?

It seems as if such an interpretation of Calvin's thought were inevitable, since he not only speaks of God manifesting Himself in nature and history but even sets it down as a rule "that the most correct way and most convenient method of seeking God . . . is to discover Him in His works through which He draws near to us in friendliness and at times communicates Himself to us".[10] Indeed we can say that

---

[1] *In* I, 5, 1.   [2] *In.* I, 5, 3.   [3] *In.* I, 5, 6.   [4] *In.* I, 5, 8.
[5] *CR* 48, 328.   [6] *CR* 34, 432.   [7] *In.* I, 5, 1.
[8] *In.* I, 5, 10. Calvin also uses at times the image of the mirror, cf. *CR* 6, 15; 23, 9 f.
[9] Gloede, *op. cit.*, pp. 51 ff.: cf. *CR* 33, 428.   [10] *In.* I, 5, 9.

according to Calvin we are compelled by God's self-declaration in nature to look upwards to the Creator.[1] These statements are the more significant since they are not meant to imply that through the natural revelation of God we are to receive nothing further than material for the construction of our own world view. Such means are not meant to satisfy our natural curiosity as to what God is as such; but we are to learn what kind of a God He is and what is fitting to His nature.[2] Calvin ascribes to this natural knowledge of God such importance that he can say: "Such knowledge should not only encourage us and establish us in the true worship of God but also lead us to the hope of eternal life."[3] This self-disclosure of God in nature and history is not imperfect or of slight significance. Its goal is none other than pure and true religion, i.e. faith, and it is thus bound up with the earnest fear of God.[4] The point is that a true knowledge of the living God is mediated by the intimations of divinity in nature.

Thus the conclusion would seem to be: Calvin teaches that alongside the Scriptures and the self-revelation of God in His Son to which they bear witness there is a second source of revelation and a second possibility of entering into communion with God. Calvin does in fact speak of a twofold knowledge of God.[5] In nature God is manifested to us essentially as the Creator, but in the countenance of Christ He is the Redeemer.[6] Thus are not the exponents of natural theology who claim Calvin as a chief support and witness fully justified?

(c) To this we may make the following reply: The self-disclosure of God in the worlds of nature and history is objectively real. As creator He has left in the world traces of His glory and still manifests His sovereignty in the processes of nature and in the events of history. But the knowledge of God which we may acquire from His works and deeds is subjective and unreal. It would only be fully real for us if Adam had not fallen but had "remained in his primal perfection."[7]

[1] *In.* I, 5, 1 : "ut aperire oculos nequeant quin aspicere eum cogantur."
[2] *In.* I, 2, 2.   [3] *In.* I, 5, 10.   [4] *In.* I, 2, 2.
[5] *In.* I, 2, 1.   [6] *Ibid.*   [7] *Ibid.*

Thus "it is undoubted that we with our senses and powers of understanding will never reach true knowledge of God."[1] "For this we lack not only the will but also the capacity."[2]

Faith is not inevitable for us, because our condition is one of revolt against God, and in consequence we have lost the capacity to recognize the traces of God's sovereignty in His works. This state of affairs has often enough been emphasized. All that Calvin says about the natural knowledge of God is subject to the one condition: if Adam had not fallen. In that very passage of the *Institutes* where he speaks about the two-fold source of our knowledge of God he goes on immediately to add that the simple knowledge of God from nature would only be possible to us if Adam had not fallen.[3] If in spite of all this we hear natural theology constantly spoken of, the fact can only be accounted for on the supposition that unconsciously people infer from the objective self-disclosure of God in nature our actual recognition of God through nature.[4] By jugglery of this kind we can prove anything and we make of Calvin a Castellio. Up to the present, in spite of all attempts, it has not been possible to prove that Calvin deduces from the actuality of God's self-manifestation in nature the actuality of our natural knowledge of Him.

(*d*) So far we have of course neglected one point in Calvin's argument. The correctness of what we have urged must in the last resort be tested by this further consideration. Although man does not see the tokens of the divine glory in nature and history and reaches no sure knowledge of the Creator on this basis, Calvin all the same asserts that there is implanted in man a natural religious disposition. God "has sown in man's heart the seeds of religious awareness".[5] For Calvin this is beyond all doubt. He has written a whole chapter of his *Institutes* on the fact that the knowledge of God is innate in the human mind.[6] Because in this respect it is a question of something with which the Creator has endowed His creation, this seed of religion cannot be uprooted from

---

[1] *CR* 29, 425; *CR* 33, 429.   [2] *CR* 49, 326.
[3] *In.* I, 2, 1.   [4] So typically Gloede, *op. cit.*, pp. 50 ff.
[5] *In.* I, 5, 1; *CR* 47, 6.   [6] *In.* I, 3.

man, his feeling for the divine cannot be choked[1] in spite of all the world's efforts to root out his natural recognition of God.[2] Thus it avails man nothing to deny that God has disclosed Himself in nature. The knowledge of God which he refuses to infer from the intimations of Him in the world is alive in the depths of his heart and springs in fact from a natural impulse.[3] "Hence the godless themselves illustrate the fact that the knowledge of God is always living in the human heart."[4] This religious disposition is not just vaguely present in man, but shows itself to be effectual.[5] "Even the godless are compelled to confess that there is a natural feeling for God. When things go well with them they mock at the idea of God . . . but when despair torments them they are forced to seek God and to ejaculate prayers to Him" (*In.* I, 4, 4). We cannot escape from God. He surrounds us on every side and does not leave us alone even in the solitude of our inner life. He still draws near to us and awaits from us an answer.

Calvin does not say all this somewhat vaguely on the edge of his theological arguments; he teaches it quite consciously and decisively. In fact he preaches with downright earnestness to the freethinkers and atheists of his time. In the passages from the *Institutes* to which we have referred he engages in a full-length debate with them. He shows them the power and the glory of God. It is as if he wanted to bring them face to face with all the tokens of the divine glory in nature and history, and finally at the place here quoted to exclaim: very necessity forces from you the confession that you do know something of God.[6] Were we to overlook these considerations in an interpretation of Calvin's theology we

[1] *In.* I, 4, 4; *In.* I, 3, 3.   [2] *In.* I, 3, 3.   [3] *In.* I, 3, 1.
[4] *In.* I, 3, 2.   [5] *In.* I, 3, 3; cf. previous note.
[6] A real knowledge of God? It may be asked whether Calvin in his anxiety to corner his adversaries has not gone too far at this point. Understandable as is his argument on this occasion, it is less so in the wider context of this thought. In a later period, which lost sight of the real aims of Calvin, natural theology insinuated itself just here, according to the well-known scheme: God is known (1) from nature and history; (2) from the revelation attested in Scripture.

should be omitting something essential. But we should equally be distorting the doctrine of the Reformer if we were to go no further than the arguments we have just been quoting. For Calvin assigns to this religious disposition of man no importance whatsoever as a link with the proclamation of the Christian verities. He does not regard it as a foundation on which the edifice of Christian theology might be erected. What we have just been citing concerning the natural religious endowment of men is for Calvin, as it were, only the first clause of a theological sentence—a clause which taken by itself has no meaning and which in any event does not express Calvin's essential doctrine. This is plain from a purely external linguistic feature. There are hardly any sentences in Calvin the point of which is to emphasize the natural religious consciousness in the sense just mentioned. In nearly every case a certain qualification is added which may not be overlooked.

If we suppose that, while not clearly recognizing the Creator in creation after the fall, an obscure impulse in our inner life (needing only elucidation) still points to Him, we are again mistaken. Here the interpretation of Calvin in reference to our problem falls constantly into the second error; to wit, that we are apt to forget that, for Calvin, man can never adopt a neutral attitude towards God. The words "if Adam had not fallen" are not only the all-inclusive condition governing Calvin's arguments: it would be better to say they are the minus sign preceding the whole sum of what Calvin teaches about man and his relation to God. The fall means that man's whole relationship to God is reversed. Thus it introduces not a quantitative change but a qualitative one. We are not only blind and deaf with regard to the intimations of God in nature; we are crazy.[1] Our deadness and perversity darkens everything, so that any insight which we gain becomes nothing more than a monstrous deception.[2] Calvin illustrates this in detail. Instead of allowing our minds to be turned to the Creator by the signs of the divine glory in nature, our gaze remains fixed on the creature; we invest it

[1] CR 49, 326; cf. 9, 796 ff.   [2] CR 47, 6 ff.

with godlike worth and turn it into an idol.[1] Or by contemplating the universe we are merely impelled to follow the trend of our own speculations, to build our personal world view, thus evading the living God.[2] Even the working of God in history does not suffice to check us in this attitude. "Since the overruling of human activities shows so clearly the divine providence that it cannot be denied, men's only resource is to suppose that all revolves by the blind whims of fate: so dreadful is our natural inclination to vanity and error."[3]

Instead of praising the foreknowledge of God, we speak of blind destiny which determines the lot of man thus or thus.[4] We are called to the service of God and as a matter of fact we are constantly falling into idolatry either crudely or subtly. The religious tendency innate in us, despite the keenness with which it makes itself felt, alters not at all this fundamental fact. For it has not been unimpaired by the Fall. Just where Calvin stresses that the seed of religious awareness can never be eradicated from our hearts, but remains rooted therein, he adds: "yet it is so corrupted that it produces only the most evil fruits".[5] Hence Calvin's judgment on philosophies of religion is severe but pertinent: "I do not deny that here and there the philosophers give us various opinions about God very shrewdly and cleverly expressed; but they always smack of a sick fancy."[6] Even what looks like a genuine knowledge of God proceeds from a perverse attitude and has a false bearing. We cannot take "one single step" to attain a right knowledge of God.[7]

(e) The fact that men, instead of putting their trust in God, centre their confidence in themselves or in the creatures and neglect the Creator[8] has of course its consequences. "Thus in vain do so many lights shine in the universe; they cannot illuminate for us the honour of the Creator."[9] That is the humble opinion of Calvin. But the matter cannot end there. Since the failure of God's self-disclosure in nature must be imputed to our guilt, the notation of the fact that it

---

[1] *CR* 34, 297. [2] *In.* I, 5, 15; I, 5, 12. [3] *In.* I, 5, 11.
[4] *In.* I, 5, 11; *CR* 55, 145. [5] *In.* I, 4, 4. [6] *In.* II, 2, 18.
[7] *CR* 28, 489. [8] *In.* I, 4, 4. [9] *In.* I, 5, 14.

misses the mark is in no way sufficient. Just as we can never for one single moment adopt an attitude of neutrality towards God, so also He cannot be irresolute in His attitude towards us. "It was the order of creation that the structure of the world should minister to us as a school in which we might learn the fear of God, and in consequence be transplanted to eternal life and consummate felicity; but after the Fall, wherever we turn our eyes there meets us above and below the curse of God, which, because on account of our sin it affects and envelops the innocent creatures, must inevitably plunge our hearts into despair."[1] The tokens of divinity in nature and history which should show us the glory and the goodness of the Creator are now wrapped in obscurity because of God's curse, so that we are no longer led towards Him by these traces of His presence, but the more effectively separated from Him. The self-declaration of God which should serve for our salvation serves in fact in our actual condition to precipitate us to ruin.

This argument of Calvin only makes it plainer that he is fully serious in teaching that God wishes to disclose Himself in nature and history. If our rebellious attitude towards the signs of the Creator's glory were not to bring about our damnation as a consequence, then it would not be a question of a word of the living God uttered in the works of nature and the events of history. God is not mocked. His goodness cannot be despised with impunity. Thus we come to the following curious conclusion: All those who wish to make Calvin a champion of natural theology and to this end assert that he teaches the reality of a natural knowledge of God, even though it may not be properly developed in man,[2] in fact deny any true self-disclosure of God in nature at all; for in regard to the living God there is no more or less preparatory disposition which might lead up to a sensitive religious outlook.[3] On the contrary, Calvin affirms in the strictest sense that God does reveal Himself in nature and history, and he must in consequence dispute the reality of a natural knowledge of God.

[1] *In.* II, 6, 1.   [2] Gloede, *op. cit.*, p. 67.   [3] *Op. cit.*, p. 69.

(*f*) Why then does he consider it so important to develop fully the doctrine of a natural knowledge of God? In so doing his intention is to make clear, like the apostle Paul, that in face of God we cannot shelter behind the excuse that we have no knowledge of Him.[1] In saying that Calvin denies the possibility of natural theology we must be rightly understood. We did not mean that the religious disposition of man does not bear fruit. On the contrary, we have shown how strongly it makes itself felt. But the use man makes of it is to turn not towards God but towards His creatures and the phantoms of his own religious speculations. If these religious acts of man are truly appraised, it will be found that all natural knowledge of God has no other effect but to make man inexcusable before God.[2] On occasion Calvin distinguishes between a saving knowledge of God which we derive from Christ and a natural knowledge such as is proper to all men. But this does not mean that the universal knowledge of God forms an integral part of the saving special knowledge imparted by Grace. Here there is no question of degrees. Calvin says expressly that "natural theology which exists solely for the purpose of making us inexcusable is to be sharply distinguished from saving knowledge of God".[3] By his very wish to know God man fails to know Him. The religious quest, of which the object is that man should gain a knowledge of God, ends in separating him from his Creator and in making his guilt clear. The end actually reached by the self-disclosure of God in the world and by the immediate religious awareness innate in man, is this: that man stands forth burdened with guilt as an apostate who refuses to know God and despises all the friendly help which has been given him.

The fact that Calvin answers the question of natural theology in this way sheds light upon and shapes his doctrine of the knowledge of God which we gain from Holy Scripture.

[1] *In.* I,3,7; *In.* I. 5, 15.

[2] *In.* I, 10, 3; 5, 15. *CR* 23, 9 ff.; 28, 495; 40, 246; 47, 418 ff.; 48, 328; 55, 145, etc.

[3] *CR* 49, 24; 49, 326; 48, 327.

If through Scripture and its content, Jesus Christ, we gain access to God the Father, this does not mean that apart from the fact of our being addressed by the Biblical message we are left to our own devices. The God who reveals Himself to us in Jesus Christ is not to be confined to a special religious department of our minds or to a precisely delimited sphere within the world's life. He is rather the Lord of our whole life from its beginning to its end. At every moment we stand before Him in responsibility and not only when the Word of Scripture strikes us.

(g) Since the discussion of the question of natural theology in Calvin leads to this conclusion, viz. that we are not attuned to our responsibility before God and therefore, laden with guilt, fall into condemnation, its final outcome is the praise of God's self-revelation in Jesus Christ. That is the ultimate purpose at which he aims in this section of his theological treatise.

Seeing that it is impossible for us men ever to come to the true knowledge of God: God has revealed Himself to us in His word.[1] The incarnate Word attested in Scripture, the Son of God Himself, has entered into the breach between God and ourselves[2] and has taken upon Himself and diverted to Himself the curse of God which was meant to strike us. In Him and in His cross is to be seen the judgment of God falling upon the world; but that cross also signifies the end and the cancellation of the divine judgment against us, because Christ has really borne the curse for our sakes. Thus He opens up for us the path which leads us to God. "By the help of His cross we are raised from the deepest hell high above all heavens."[3] "Hence, although the preaching of the cross is not compatible with human reason, yet we must accept the same in all humility if we desire once more to enter into relationship with God our Creator (from whom we are estranged) in such a way that He again becomes our Father."[4]

We need Holy Scripture as our leader and teacher if we

[1] CR 29, 425.   [2] CR 47, 7.   [3] CR 23, 9 f.
[4] In. II, 6, 1; cf. II, 6, 4.

would attain the knowledge of God—and precisely and above all God as Creator.[1] "We confess", we read in the Confession of 1537, "that we will follow Holy Scripture alone as the rule of our faith and religion without mixing therewith anything derived from human understanding apart from the Word of God" (*OS* I, 418). In the same moment when we depart from the guidance of Scripture, all knowledge of God fades from our minds.[2] In Jesus Christ, the theme of Holy Scripture, we recognize also the glory of God as Creator shining in the world. "For Christ is the image in which God makes visible to us not only His heart but also His hands and His feet." "By the heart", says Calvin, "I understand that love with which He has enfolded us in Christ, by the hands and feet I understand the works which are manifest to our eyes. As soon as we deviate from Christ there is nothing big or little about which we do not inevitably fall into misconceptions."[3] What we describe as God apart from the Biblical revelation in Jesus Christ is nothing but an idol.[4] We find God nowhere else but in the Mediator. "For since Christ is the sun of righteousness we see nothing if we look outside His reality; it is He too who opens the eyes of our spirits."[5] All this is fully elucidated by the treatment of the problem of natural theology.

(*h*) Calvin goes yet a step further. He is conscious of the captious question: "Has God then never revealed Himself to one of the heathen?" He does not refuse to answer it. He was not indeed in the position of Zwingli, who opened wide the gates of heaven to the heathen; but he nevertheless realized that he was not justified in concluding that they are completely excluded. Calvin was sufficiently a theologian to understand that, whilst we are bound to the channels through which God wills to act towards us, God Himself is not so confined. He can act in other modes towards men if He so wills. Perhaps God reveals Himself uniquely and

---

[1] *In.* I, 6; cf. *CR* 23, 9 ff., etc.   [2] *In.* I, 14, 1.
[3] *CR* 23, 11 f., quoted after Peter Barth, *Das Problem der natürlichen Theologie bei Calvin*, p. 25.
[4] *CR* 51, 169; 52, 85.   [5] *CR* 48, 209.

extra-ordinarily to the heathen if it pleases Him without using the medium of Biblical testimony. But precisely in facing this difficult issue Calvin proves himself to be a theologian of revelation in the strictest sense. He does not admit in simple and generous terms that the boundary can be crossed and that God may by way of exception be apprehended through nature and history, or immediately through the religious consciousness, but gives the appropriate answer "that among the heathen there has been no revelation of God apart from Christ as also among the Jews".[1] If therefore the recognition of God is ever to be realized by the heathen, who have not access to the witness of the Bible, then it must be through the Word which became flesh in order to overcome our alienation from God and remove from us the divine curse. Although such heathen do not hear the message of Holy Scripture, yet they attain to the knowledge of God only through the essence of it—if it pleased God thus to treat them.

This statement, which stands in indissoluble opposition to modern historical thought, throws much light upon our previous argument about the end and aim of Holy Scripture. The heart and soul of the Bible, not contained therein but only attested by it, namely, Jesus Christ, is not simply one admittedly pre-eminent figure among other historical figures. His Person, whose historical existence was lived at one particular point in the course of world history, is of decisive significance for all ages and all men. Jesus Christ is decisive too for those men who lived on the earth before Him and never heard His name. "For His word 'I am the way' applies not to one particular time or to one particular people; rather it declares that He is the only one through whom all may come to God."[2]

(*i*) Finally, one last observation may make it clear how completely the theology of Calvin revolves around the Person of Jesus Christ. We have heard that a seed of religion is implanted in the heart of man and that consequently he possesses a feeling for the divine. If the religious consciousness is not directed towards God but finds satisfaction in

[1] *CR* 51, 169 ff.　　[2] *CR* 51, 170.

idolatry, then man stands before God without excuse. What is the ultimate ground of this fact? To this Calvin gives an answer which is very characteristic: "The world was created by the eternal Word of God and by His power the life of all creation is preserved. In particular, man was endowed with a certain special gift of knowledge; and though in consequence of the Fall he has lost the full light of wisdom, yet in spite of everything he is still able to perceive and know; so that what was his natural faculty, by the grace of the Son of God, is not completely extinct." [1] If man is still man, if after the Fall he has not been annihilated by the curse of God but stands guilt-laden in responsibility before his Lord, the reason for this is not that his alienation from God was not radical and complete and that he still retained a residual relationship with Him. Nor does the reason for it lie in the goodness of a so-called Creator God; but rather simply and solely in the grace of the Son in whom God turns His countenance towards us and through whom He bestows upon us all that we have and are. Even as we note the universal responsibility of men we cannot evade the *Deus incarnandus* and *incarnatus*.

[1] *CR* 47,7; cf.57, 481 ff.

Chapter 3

THE TRINITY

AFTER discussing how we can come to know God, we must now enquire about the content of such knowledge. For this purpose our previous discussion must be kept well in view. "God alone is an adequate witness to Himself and cannot be recognized except through His own testimony."[1] Hence we must understand Him in the guise in which He has revealed Himself to us."[2] This means that we may not seek God "elsewhere than in His holy word, nor think of Him except in the terms which His word illuminates for us, nor speak of Him except in so far as our words are taken from His word."[3]

I. CALVIN'S ATTITUDE TO THE DOCTRINE OF THE EARLY CHURCH

Calvin does not use his knowledge of Scripture to produce any original description of the being of God. As a hearer of the Word he knows that he belongs to the multitude of those who have interpreted Scripture before him, and in connexion with the witness of the early church establishes the principle: "Thus God proclaims Himself as the One and yet presents Himself to our view as distinguishable into three persons."[4]

But what has this theological affirmation to do with Holy Scripture, which alone Calvin recognizes as authoritative? Do we not plainly see here the philosophical apparatus of ideas distinctive of a particular age? In thus accepting the early church doctrine of the Trinity, is not Calvin in fact binding himself to human modes of thought in spite of all

[1] *In.* I, 13, 21; *In.* I, 11, 1.   [2] *In.* I, 13, 21.   [3] *Ibid.*
[4] *In.* I, 13, 2.

counterbalancing assertions? All such questions, including the modern one whether the use of such theological concepts does not injure the teaching of love, were before the mind of Calvin.[1] They were by no means alien to him. He put them to himself from the start of his theological work. The question is how far such theological conceptualism is justified.

In debate with one Caroli, Calvin represented the standpoint—even at the risk of being Arian—that even the most venerable concepts associated with the doctrine of the Trinity have no final authority.[2] He went yet a step further and expressed the same attitude in regard to ancient church creeds.[3]

Theological ideas, even when they are the fruit of religious attitudes, even church confessions, are not interchangeable with the thing itself. Their function is only to serve the truth and to bear witness to Christ.[4] Hence they must be used in the church in the spirit of freedom and not be allowed to exercise any tyranny.[5]

The reason for insisting on freedom in the use of theological ideas and the profession of church creeds is that all theological thinking must be rooted in Holy Scripture. But greatly as Calvin stresses that in the last resort we are bound to Scripture alone, yet precisely in connexion with this particular discussion he bears well in mind his arguments concerning the relation of Holy Scripture to the truth which it attests. He expressly refuses to fetter the theologian by requiring that his thought should formally correspond with the literal truth of the Bible.[6] Of course he admits: "We should find in Scripture a criterion for our thinking and speaking so that both the thoughts of our heart and the words of our mouth are in harmony with it." [7] The Bible is the standard by which dogmatics must be tested, but it is

---

[1] *In.* I, 13, 3; cf. *OS* 1, 72–74.

[2] *CR* 7, 318 f.; 10b, 120; cf. *In.* I, 13, 5.

[3] *CR* 7, 315 ff.; 10b, 121.

[4] "Nulla esse vera religionis symbola nisi quae ad Christum conformantur", *CR* 55, 99.

[5] *CR* 10b, 120.   [6] *In.* I, 13, 3.   [7] *Ibid.*

not a collection of material for the theologian. An orientation of theological thinking towards Scripture is not at all the same thing as a slavish confinement to Biblical expressions. If we forget this, we are making an idol of the Bible. Our aim should be to express the truth to which the Bible bears witness. If this truth requires it, special theological concepts must be formed in its service in order to express clearly the matter in hand.[1] This necessity always exists when the truth of Scripture is obscured by erroneous doctrine.[2] Precise theological ideas and definitions serve to expose false doctrine and to bring the truth to its full and proper expression.

For this reason Calvin took over from the early church fathers the doctrine of the Trinity with all the theological equipment which accompanied it, e.g. "as when we confess that we believe in one God, and that by the word 'God' is to be understood an undivided and simple being in whom we apprehend three persons or modes of being".[3] Thus we see that Calvin in full awareness makes use of the ideas contained in this theological principle; and his right to do so is indisputable. The question is only whether what Calvin expresses by the help of these Trinitarian ideas is compatible with the content of Holy Scripture. Is the God implied by Trinitarian doctrine the same as the Incarnate Lord attested by Scripture according to Calvin's own confession? Is not the self-revelation of God overlooked by Trinitarian doctrine and is not an abstract idea of God developed in place of it?

2. THE AIM OF THE DOCTRINE

We must briefly draw attention to the fact that in his writing directed against Servetus, *Defensio orthodoxae fidei de sacra trinitate*, Calvin contrary to the expectation aroused by the title does not so much propose to defend the orthodox doctrine of the Trinity as to refute the Christology of Servetus with its soteriological presuppositions and inferences.[4] This

---

[1] *In.* I, 13, 3.   [2] *In.* I, 13, 4.   [3] *In.* I, 13, 20.
[4] Ernst Wolf: *Deus omniformis, Bemerkungen zur Christologie des Michael Servet*, in *Theologische Aufsätze, Karl Barth zum 50 Geburstag*, 1936, p. 450.

view finds surprising confirmation in the fact that the position is the same in Calvin's commentaries and sermons.[1] If Servetus is there attacked and the understanding of the being of God is in question, the debate as a rule turns upon the question of the true Godhead of Jesus Christ.[2] Calvin sees the supreme heresy of Servetus in the fact that "he confounds the Son and the Holy Ghost with the creatures".[3] Calvin opposes the other anti-Trinitarians because they dissolve the divinity of the Son; for Gentilis and his compatriots are really concerned to assert that the Godhead of Christ is derivative.[4] Thus they make of Christ "a figurative God" "who is only apparently and nominally God and not God at all in reality".[5]

The purpose of Calvin's Trinitarianism is to secure the Biblical message "God is revealed in the flesh" against false interpretations. In revelation we are not faced by a second divine being somehow derivative from God, or a part of the one Godhead, so that God the Father would thus have an additional element. "Rather the truth is that the being of God is one. Hence the whole Godhead is revealed in the flesh."[6] Calvin repeatedly refers to the fact that for this reason the name Jahwe is rightly applied to Christ.[7] This Biblical proof of the strict Godhead of the Son occupies much space in the positive exposition of the doctrine of the Trinity in the *Institutes*.[8] He concludes with observing that this practical recognition is more secure and reliable than all idle speculation. "For here a Godfearing heart sees that God is wonderfully near and as it were grasps Him by the hands in the assurance that it is quickened, illuminated, sustained, justified, and sanctified by Him."[9] The message of Holy Scripture is radically different from other religious testimonies, and a truly joyful message, because it proclaims that

---

[1] This remark is also supported by the arrangement of Calvin's treatise on the Trinity; cf. below p. 249.

[2] Cf. for example *CR* 23, 16; 24, 145, etc.   [3] *In.* 13, 22.

[4] *CR* 9, 368.   [5] *In.* I, 13, 23.   [6] *CR* 40, 56.

[7] *CR*, 9, 325, 400, 708; 24, 263; 44, 163, etc.

[8] *In.* I, 13, 7.   [9] *In.* I, 13, 13.

God Himself has entered wholly into the sphere of our death-doomed life in order to approach us more nearly and to bestow Himself upon us. Whoever does not pay regard to this, no matter how often the words of Scripture are in his mouth nor how fervently he speaks of Christ, as did the anti-Trinitarians of the Reformation, he is not preaching the incarnate God but emptying the gospel of its specific content. "No one can accept Christ as God in his heart who does not see that the distinct divine persons are gathered into the unity of the divine being."[1]

3. THE TRINITY

But in this unity there is a distinction of persons. The Son who took upon Himself our flesh is to be distinguished from the One who sent Him. There is a "whence" of the Son— not of His divine essence but of His person. And equally the Son of God is to be differentiated from the Comforter, the Holy Ghost, promised to us as He who would open our hearts to the Saviour.[2] The incarnate Son of God has not only an origin of His person but also aims to reach the God in us. Thus it will not do to content ourselves with the observation that God Himself has wholly revealed Himself to us in Jesus Christ. Just when we take this insight most seriously we go on to confess: "I cannot think of One Person without being enfolded with the radiance of three: nor can I distinguish the three without immediately recollecting the One Being."[3] In order to give expression to the distinctions which find a place within the one divine Being, Calvin uses the concept of person which he has taken from the Trinitarian doctrine of the early church. He defines it in the following way: "I call a person a mode of being (*subsistentia*) in the being (*essentia*) of God, which when contrasted with the other modes is distinguished from them by such characteristics (*proprietas*) as cannot be communicated to any other mode."[4]

[1] *CR* 9, 331.   [2] Cf. *In.* I, 13, 17.
[3] Phrase of Gregory of Nazianzus. *In.* I, 13, 17.
[4] *In.* I, 13, 6.

THE TRINITY

This explanation of the traditional concept is extremely important. When it is said that there are three persons in one God, such a statement is precisely not meant in the sense which is normal "when we describe three human beings as three persons". "But in this case the word person serves to express the special qualities which exist in the being of God."[1] It must be remembered that the word person is intended to translate the Greek term *hypostasis*. But the exact Latin translation of the latter is *subsistentia*.[2] "Although the mode of being is inseparably bound up with the being, yet it has its peculiar characteristics by which it is distinguished from the being."[3] The quality of any one mode of being in the one divine essence is thus something other than a mere quality. To speak of God the Father, God the Son, and God the Holy Ghost, means something other than observing that "God is strong, righteous, and wise."[4] "These words, Father Son and Holy Ghost, assuredly indicate real distinctions, so that no one should suppose them to be mere additional designations by which God is described now in one way, now in another, according to His works."[5] If these existing distinctions in God are not taken seriously, and the persons are dissolved into ordinary qualities, then God Himself would not become accessible to us in the word of revelation but only one of His qualities or modes of action. He Himself would exist behind what is disclosed to us; that is to say, He would remain veiled.

How are the three modes to be described in their peculiarities? Each is distinguished in relation to the others by some particularity.[6] Thus what is in question here is the complex of relations within the Godhead. "We confess", says Calvin, "that the Son originates from the Father in that He is the Son; not of course an origination in the sense of time or being—which would be an absurd supposition—but in the sense of priority."[7] "In this sense it can be said that the Son alone proceedeth from the Father and the Spirit from the Father and the Son."[8] Hence there is in God a

[1] *CR* 47, 473. [2] *In.* I, 13, 2. [3] *In.* I, 13, 6.
[4] *In.* I, 13, 4. [5] *In.* I, 13, 17. [6] *In.* I, 13, 6.
[7] *CR* 9, 369. [8] *In.* I, 13, 18.

certain ordered manifoldness of being (*dispositio vel oeconomia*) which in no wise affects its unity.[1] When in Scripture God is referred to simply and without further qualification "the word applies as much to the Son and the Holy Ghost as to the Father. But as soon as the Father is compared with the Son, the Son's characteristic mode of being is distinguished from the Father's."[2] "Such distinctions imply that to the Father we ascribe the origin of all effects, the origination of all things; to the Son wisdom and counsel in the administration of creation; and to the Holy Ghost power and effectiveness in operation."[3]

But "in each several mode of being the whole nature of the Godhead must be understood to be included together with what is proper to each."[4] "These distinctions do not relate to the essence of divinity." It would be wanton to imagine a multifarious divine being.[5] "We have to do here with distinction, not separation."[6] For Calvin the unity of God is shown above all by the one manner of baptism summoning us to the one faith. "What else does Christ wish when He bids us baptize in the name of the Father, the Son, and the Holy Ghost, but that we should believe with unified faith in the Father, the Son, and the Holy Ghost? What is it but a public testimony to the belief that Father, Son, and Holy Ghost are one God?"[7] Here once more it becomes quite clear that Calvin does not indulge in speculation in formulating his doctrine of God. His intention is simply and solely to exalt the one God who declares Himself to us in word and sacrament. This one God manifests Himself as the true God as distinct from all vain phantoms which we are accustomed to call God, precisely by the fact that He is one God in three modes of Being.[8] The doctrine of the Trinity secures the unity of God by distinguishing Him from idols[9] and proclaiming Him as the Lord whom we encounter in the process of revelation.

[1] *In.* I, 13, 6. [2] *In.* I, 13, 6; *CR* 40, 56; 9, 370.
[3] *In.* I, 13, 18; *CR* 6, 13. [4] *In.* 13, 19.
[5] *In.* I, 13, 2; cf. I, 13, 19. [6] *In.* I, 13, 17.
[7] *In.* I, 13, 16. [8] *In.* I, 13, 2. [9] *Ibid.*

Chapter 4

CREATION AND PROVIDENCE[1]

I. CREATION

(a) If, as we have seen, Holy Scripture proclaims the incarnate God, and the aim of the theology of Calvin is none other than to glorify this God made man, we should not therefore conclude that theology has only to concern itself with the theme of our redemption. The argument of Calvin is Christo-centric, but this does not mean that redemption is given the central place in his scheme of thought. He is far from diminishing the scope of his questions in this way. The fundamental point is the knowledge of God and of our own being. We attain the knowledge of God solely through the testimony of Holy Scripture; in other words, only through the content of this testimony, Jesus Christ, do we gain access to God. But God in revealing Himself to us thus approaches us primarily as our Creator. "It is one thing to feel that God our Creator sustains us by His power, guides us by His providence, nourishes us by His goodness and lavishes upon us eternal blessings, and quite another thing to grasp the grace of the atonement set forth to us in Christ."[2] Calvin distinguishes between a general Scriptural teaching and the knowledge of our salvation.[3] This general religious doctrine brings before us God the Creator, and thus fulfils the task which the signs of God in nature should have fulfilled but could not because they were concealed from us by the curse of God.

[1] W. Lütgert: "Calvins Lehre vom Schöpfer" (*Zeitschr. f. syst. Theologie*, 9, 1931, pp. 421-40). J. Bohatec: *Calvins Vorsehungslehre* (*Calvinstudien*, Reform. Gemeinde, Elberfeld, 1909, pp. 339-441).

[2] *In.* I, 2, 1.   [3] *In.* I, 2, 1; I, 10, 3.

After our study of Calvin's Trinitarian doctrine we shall not misunderstand this as suggesting that Calvin wished first to discourse about the God of creation and then about the God of redemption, as though implying that our knowledge of the Creator should gradually be deepened until it emerged in an understanding of the Redeemer. The general religious teaching of Scripture is just as much determined by the central message of the Bible as is the preaching of grace in the narrower sense. The truth is, that we can recognize the creative work as well as the saving action of God in Christ alone.[1] This does not mean simply that through Christ we catch a glimpse also of the Creator God. It is rather that Calvin wishes to show how through Christ, the Word of God, all things are created.[2] The Logos is the means by which the Father has accomplished the work of creation.[3] Thus, in the general teaching of Scripture which is concerned with the theme of creation, God is not spoken of in general philosophical terms. Of course it does not treat of the redemptive action of God; but it does treat of the triune God in so far as He is the Creator of the world and of mankind. The creation story of the Bible does not speak only of "the essence of divinity but also displays before us the eternal wisdom of God and His Holy Spirit".[4] Because in Christ God Himself, God in His fullness, inheres, it must even be said that Christ Himself is the Creator. Thus, if it is stated in general terms that God is the Creator, God the Son is implied as well as God the Holy Ghost. But in regard to the person of the Son the statement that He is the Creator can only be understood in a general rather than specific sense. To speak more precisely, it must be said that He is the instrument of the creative process and that God the Father is the Creator of heaven and earth.[5] As Person, God the Father is the Origin of all things[6] and also the Creator of the world. But precisely when we affirm that God the Father is Creator we must remember that He has created all things through the eternal Word. Hence we do

[1] See above p. 51, note 3   [2] *CR* 47, 477.
[3] *Loc. cit.*; cf. *CR* 31, 328.   [4] *In.* I, 14, 2.
[5] *CR* 9, 369; 47, 477.   [6] See above p. 60, note 3.

not by any means evade this Word which, the Bible attests, became incarnate, when we wish to speak specifically, i.e. Biblically, about the work of creation.

(*b*) From Scripture we learn "that God by the power of His Word and Spirit created heaven and earth out of nothing."[1] The statement that He brought the world into being out of nothing proves Him to be the One who alone is eternal and self-existent.[2] In relation to Him everything else stands on another plane. In this respect we must note that God created not only the visible but also the invisible. In the *Institutes* Calvin devotes much space to showing that the good and bad angels are also creatures of God and subject to His dominion. The divine creation has a wider scope than our senses can be aware of.[3] It is more animated than we suspect. We are surrounded by powers, all of which in the last resort must serve God. Here Calvin is attacking in particular the suggestion that there are two principles in the world: God and the devil. Such a creed undermines the creative glory and sovereignty of God—in fact the very divinity of God— and must therefore be rejected.[4]

A second point is clearly implied in the affirmation that God created all things visible and invisible through His word. His operation is thus seen as effectual without the agency of any creature. He needs no means alien to Himself in order to realize His purpose. He summoned the world into being purely by His word of command "in order to exhibit the unfathomable might of His word".[5]

Creation is not controlled by the power of a blind fate, but by the might of the word of God. Hence it discloses at the same time the grace of God.[6] That is the third point which we must notice. It is made quite clear in the creation story of the Bible that the creation of man is the ultimate purpose of the whole creative process. God has called all things into being for the sake of man, and has ordered all things for our good and well-being.[7] This of course does not imply the greatness of man; we are intended rather to

[1] *In.* I, 14, 20.   [2] *In.* I, 14, 3; I, 14, 1.   [3] *In.* I, 14, 3–19.
[4] *In.* I, 14, 3.   [5] *CR* 31, 328.   [6] *In.* I, 14, 22.   [7] *Ibid.*

recognize in consequence the power and the goodness of the eternal self-existent God. "As often as we describe God as the Creator of heaven and earth we must remember that the government of all things which He has created is in His power and control, but that we are His children whom He has undertaken to preserve and bring up in His faith and protection, so that we may await all good from Him alone, and may entertain the sure hope that He will never suffer the things which are so needful to our salvation to fail us; so that we may aspire to receive as His gift whatever we desire, and may recognize all the benefits which we receive as coming from Him, and may confess them as such with hearty thanks; that thus, drawn by the great sweetness of His outpoured mercies, we may bestir ourselves to love Him and to worship Him with all our hearts." [1] To such an extent does Calvin see the end of the whole creation in the recognition and adoration of the omnipotent and gracious God that he can say: "if on earth such praise of God does not come to pass, if God does not preserve His church to this end, then the whole order of nature will be thrown into confusion and creation will be annihilated when there is no people to call upon God". [2] That then is the position: not because the world exists do we attain a certain knowledge of God, and then after a deepening of this knowledge an understanding of the church; but just the opposite—because there is a church there is also a world. The will of the Creator is from the start directed towards the people who shall serve Him. The church is that body of people who hearken to the message of Holy Scripture and therefore recognize God as the Creator. In its midst the power and the grace of His Word is exalted; for the Word, the theme of Holy Scripture, Jesus Christ, is Himself present in the church.

(c) The full depth of this insight is only realized when we consider what Calvin teaches about the creation of man. Man is the crown of the creative process, a microcosm, whose being unfolds such mysteries and marvels that it can only strike us with astonishment.[3] He embodies the com-

---

[1] *In.* I, 14, 22.　　　[2] *CR* 32, 192.　　　[3] *CR* 33, 481.

plexities of the whole of the rest of the creation because he is that creature who participates both in the visible and the invisible orders. Man is composed of body and soul.[1] The soul is the nobler part of man. It comprises reason and will,[2] and thus distinguishes man from all unreasoning creatures. Latent within it is the germ of the religious awareness and it forms in consequence the state of responsibility in which man faces his Lord.[3] "If the soul were not something essential to man (*essentiale quiddam*) distinct from the body, Holy Scripture would not teach that we dwell in houses of clay and through the gate of death travel elsewhere, that we put off what is perishable, so that each one of us may receive on the last Day his recompense and reward according as he has acted in the flesh. For assuredly these and similar passages which recur here and there not only make a clear distinction between the soul and the body, but also show, by designating man as a soul, that it is the noblest part of a human being."[4]

From these words it becomes clear that the special feature which discriminates the soul from the body is above all its immortality,[5] the effect of which is that man after the death of his body is not freed from responsibility before God. In regard to the immortality of the soul and the mortality of the body it must be said that the body is the prison house of the soul, in which it lies enchained.[6] In spite of this antithesis of the body and the soul, a basic affinity between them arises from the fact that the soul, like the body, is created.[7] Although it possesses so many advantages over the body and belongs to the sphere of the invisible world, yet it has been

[1] *In.* I, 15, 2.

[2] *In.* I, 15, 7. With regard to the linguistic usage of Scripture Calvin observes as follows: "quum voces animae et spiritus varie sumantur in scriptura, simul tamen coniunctae duas animae praecipue facultates denotant. Spiritus enim pro intelligentia capitur, anima autem pro sede affectuum". *CR* 45, 37; cf. 52, 179.

[3] *In.* I, 15, 2.

[4] *Ibid.* Calvin refers to 2 Corinthians 5:6, 8; 2 Corinthians 7:1; Matthew 10:28.

[5] *In.* I, 15, 2.   [6] *CR* 5, 196.

[7] *In.* I, 15, 2; *CR* 25, 222; 26, 150.

created by God exactly as have the angels.[1] The Biblical account of man's creation is not to be understood in the sense that God has implanted in man as his soul a part of His own eternal being.[2] "Creation is not such a transmission (*transfusio*) but a beginning of being out of nothing."[3] Even the best thing in us men, our soul, has been created out of nothing.[4] The immortality of the soul is not the same thing as eternity. There is no such thing as an eternal soul substance. Each time a man is born, God creates his soul also out of nothing.[5] The immortality of the soul is and remains God's gift of grace, for God wills to hold men after the death of the body in the expectation of His Day of Judgment. "If God withdraws His grace, then the soul becomes a passing breath just as the body is dust."[6] "It has no quality of permanence in itself."[7] At times Calvin expresses this state of affairs very vigorously: "If God did not wish to preserve the distinctive life He has given man, then the death of a man would be exactly the same as that of a horse or dog; for we are in no sense nobler or worthier, but we owe all to the fact that it has pleased God to give us this special pre-eminence that we are immortal."[8] "Because it entirely depends on the grace of God to preserve the life of the soul beyond the death of the body, and thus to cause man to stand before Him in full responsibility until the Day of Judgment, the man who is estranged from God knows nothing of this immortality. Only believers can rejoice in it, to whom it is attested by the Word and the Spirit of God."[9] What had to be said in regard to the creation of the world, applies here with still greater force: God is recognized and honoured as Creator within His church alone. Hence the church alone understands the true being of man. Right knowledge of God and of oneself are connected in the most intimate way.[10] Man is not eternal, like God, nor is he perishable in the same way as the beasts of the field. His

[1] *In.* I, 15, 5.   [2] *Ibid.*   [3] *Ibid.*   [4] *CR* 44, 401.
[5] *CR* 33, 162.   [6] *CR* 32, 81; cf. 33, 491, 674; 34, 455; 53, 92
[7] *Op. cit.*   [8] *CR* 53, 621.   [9] *CR* 50, 61.
[10] *In.* I, 1, 1; *In.* I, 15, 1.

essential being consists in the fact that during his pilgrimage on this earth, and also after the death of his body until the Day of Judgment, he is permitted to live in the presence of God.

So far in this exposition of the creaturehood of man we have not said explicitly that man was made in the image of God[1]; and yet this must not for one moment be forgotten. God has given man not only body and soul, but has also lavished both upon him and the creation splendid gifts.[2] He did not leave man to shift for himself but established him in such a relationship to His own being that man "became a mirror, as it were, of that great splendour whose full brightness shines in the Godhead".[3] "Man found himself placed in such a right spiritual attitude (*rectitudo*) that the glory of God shone forth in the various parts of his soul and even in his body." [4] Because the heart of created man was turned to his Lord, a reflection of the divine glory was visible in him, and he stood forth as the image of God on earth.[5] The right orientation of man, his likeness to God, was seen in the fact that "he was gifted with enlightened understanding and his will was fixed in obedience to God".[6] "He was characterized by faith, love of God and neighbour, desire and application to live in righteousness and holiness."[7] Thus man's similitude to God implies something more than his psycho-physical constitution[8], it signifies his right attitude towards his Creator and thus his right attitude towards all other creatures. Calvin admits without more ado that this fact impresses itself on the very body of man. He has no objection "if anyone wishes to count as part of the image of God the fact that, whereas all other creatures are bent earthwards, to man alone it is given to walk uprightly; man alone is called to look upwards to the sky and stars."[9] The body of man is endowed with such pre-eminence "that in it alone one can detect the image of God".[10] But we must not say that the

[1] *In.* I, 15, 3.   [2] *In.* I, 15, 8.   [3] *CR* 33, 660; cf. *In.* I, 15, 3.
[4] *CR* 10a, 166.   [5] *In.* I, 15, 3; 15, 8.   [6] *CR* 10 a, 166.
[7] *In.* II, 2, 12.   [8] *Ibid.*   [9] *In.* I, 15, 3.
[10] *CR* 32, 620; *In.* I, 15, 3.

body in itself is this image. Similarly with regard to the soul of man; although Calvin here admits that it is not absurd if man "is described as the image of God on account of his soul".[1] But the invisible aspect of man's being as such is not the divine image. We should rather say that the latter "has its true seat in the soul".[2]

The divine similitude consists not in the fact that man is endowed with reason and will, but in the fact that these faculties in original man were directed wholly towards knowledge of and obedience to God. Thus Calvin can echo the expressions of the church fathers and say that body and soul are natural gifts which man has received, whereas the similitude to God on the contrary is a supernatural gift.[3] It is superadded to the psycho-physical constitution of man and is imparted from outside. This is illuminated by the fact that it is restored to us through Christ.[4] But it should not be asserted that the similitude to God is an addition to the creaturely status of man, that the former might even be absent. There is no neutral psycho-physical constitution of man. The fact that man was originally created in the image of God means rather that his whole psycho-physical existence was thereby moulded; what consequences the loss of the image entails we shall have to consider later. In using traditional theological concepts in this connexion Calvin wishes to express clearly that man owed the right orientation of his being wholly to the goodness of his Creator. Body and soul in themselves live uniquely and solely by the preserving grace of God. Man does not possess them firmly in his own right. This applies the more forcibly to the divine similitude which the first man bore. This special distinction which exalts him above all creatures[5] is thus not to be understood in the sense that man in creation was given something divine as his permanent possession. It is not that to his body and soul was added a spark of the divine essence.[6] The divine

[1] *In.* I, 15, 3.   [2] *Ibid.*   [3] *In.* II, 2, 12.
[4] *Ibid.* "Haec omnia quum nobis restituat Christus adventitia censentur et praeter naturam".
[5] *In.* I, 15, 3.   [6] *CR* 10a, 166.

similitude depends rather on man's relation to his Lord. Man was created by God to serve Him in freedom. He was endowed with freedom to choose the good.[1] When he threw away his opportunity his relation to the Creator and consequently the divine image in him was destroyed.

But on what does Calvin base these assertions? How does he know that the divine similitude of man consisted in the original right orientation of his being towards his Creator? The answer which he gives to this question is decisive for his whole teaching concerning the creatureliness of man. Once again at this point the essence of Calvin's theology is revealed. Calvin says that the restoration of the image of God in man shows plainly in what it originally consisted.[2] Thus he does not content himself with discussing the ideas of the creation story which are relevant in this regard. Rather he refers to Colossians 3 and Ephesians 4.[3] He directs our thoughts to the second Adam, to Christ who is the perfect image of God.[4] In Christ, the incarnate Word of God, we see in what this divine image in man consists. The true being of man is disclosed to us in Him alone. We cannot recognize it by exploring our own nature. Nor can we find grounds for it by considering the creaturely status of man apart from the God revealed in Christ, and with this end in view appealing perhaps to the Biblical story of creation. The first chapter of Holy Scripture proclaims no other God than that preached by Saint Paul in the two epistles just mentioned. The Bible is concerned not with teaching ideas about God but with proclaiming the Teacher and Saviour sent to us. In Him we perceive whence we have fallen; through Him who is Himself the image of God we are restored[5] and brought again into a true relation with our Creator. We are redeemed by being made like unto Christ, so that we may bear the image of God in "true godliness, righteousness, purity, and knowledge"[6]—that image which we had lost. Whatever is taught about humanity in disregard of this sovereign claim

[1] *In* I, 15, 8.   [2] *CR* 23, 26; *In* I, 15, 4; II, 2, 12.
[3] *CR* 23, 26; *In.* I, 15, 4.   [4] *In.* I, 15, 4; L. 255, 4.
[5] *In.* I 15, 4; *CR* 51, 209.   [6] *In.* I, 15, 4.

of Christ is nothing but a conspicuous error; for we are inevitably led astray in so far as we do not experience Christ as Lord.[1] There is no theological anthropology which can exist apart from Christology. We cannot truly confess the first article of faith if at the same time and by implication we do not confess the second.

2. PROVIDENCE

(a) "Herein lies the unfathomable greatness of God: not only did He once create heaven and earth but He also guides the whole process according to His will. Thus he who confesses God as Creator while supposing that He remains tranquilly in heaven without caring for the world, outrageously deprives God of all effective power."[2] Calvin thinks that we can only truly confess God as the Creator of all being if at the same time we appreciate His power as effectually at work in the present.[3] After its creation the world does not run on its own steam nor is it surrendered to the sway of some alien power. Thus there is neither chance nor fate in life.[4] God as Creator is and remains the omnipotent Lord. He is truly the Disposer supreme.[5] His present creative activity manifests itself in three ways. God alone sustains the created order in being[6]; apart from His action it would dissolve into nothingness. Daily He bestows on all things their effective reality as it pleases Him[7]; apart from Him they could neither live nor move nor have their being. And finally in His incomprehensible wisdom He guides all things to their appointed end.[8] This manifold and ever present relationship of the Creator to His creation is divine providence. Calvin derives this idea from Genesis 22:8 (*Deus providebit*) and explains that the word *providentia* denotes not so much the foreknowledge of God as His care for His creatures.[9] Providence lies not in the mere knowledge but in the effectual action of God.[10] Hence the archaic translation of

[1] *CR* 51, 209.   [2] *CR* 32, 359.   [3] *In.* I, 16, 1.
[4] *In* I, 16, 2, 3.   [5] *In.* I, 16, 3.   [6] *OS* 3, 188, 3.
[7] *In.* I, 16, 2.   [8] *In.* I, 16, 4.   [9] *Ibid.*   [10] *Ibid.*

the *Institutes* is right in rendering the word as "*provident care*".

(*b*) When we consider how Calvin explicates in detail this providential care we recognize that he focuses it upon the redemptive work of God in Jesus Christ.[1] The argument that Calvin's theology is primarily concerned with the thought of creation is here seen to be completely untenable. Just in this connexion it becomes clear that Calvin's theology does not proceed by successive thoughts, as though the recognition of a Saviour God were inferred from the recognition of a Creator God. It is rather that throughout his work Calvin praises the power and the goodness of the triune God who has drawn near to us in Jesus Christ. But let us listen to Calvin himself.

The fact that God is so fully the sovereign Lord of the created world that He preserves and rules it according to the counsels of His will is something which we could never discover for ourselves. This inability is not remediable by our piety. We have no possibility of obtaining for ourselves the comforting news that God cares for us like a true father. He himself must open up a way to us and declare to us what kind of a God He is. "Until God became my teacher"— thus Calvin interprets a text of the Psalms—"and I learnt from His Word what otherwise my understanding could not fathom, I failed to discover by my own reflections how the world is governed."[2] God speaks this word to us in Holy Scripture. There alone do we gain an insight into the providence of God.[3] By Christ Himself are we taught that God sustains and governs all things.[4]

As far as we are concerned this means: "We do not apprehend in a human manner nor in the light of natural feelings," "but by faith alone, the invisible providence of God."[5] The operations of God are understandable to us only by the message of God Himself. We are utterly dependent upon Him and can do nothing else "but obediently

---

[1] Cf. just the chapter headings of I, 17.   [2] *CR* 31, 682.
[3] *In.* I, 16, 2, 4; 17, 1; *CR* 8, 349.   [4] *In.* I, 16, 2.
[5] *CR* 31, 132; *CR* 8, 349; *In.* I, 16, 9.

accept what God teaches us through His Word and Spirit".[1] But faith directed to the Word and comforted by the providence of God does not consist simply in an inquisitive searching of the Scriptures. We attain understanding only when we perceive that God by His Word is calling us to Himself and adopts us as children out of the depths of His mercy.[2] Faith which recognizes the ceaseless controlling and sustaining might of the Creator arises from our thus being enfolded by the grace of God. This faith rests upon the gracious election of God.[3] This must be borne in mind if we would understand Calvin's assertion that only believers have eyes to trace the workings of divine providence.[4] By this statement Calvin does not intend to reject the idea of natural theology only to set up in its place and to glorify the religious certitudes of the pious Christian. He is concerned solely to exalt the mercy and the majesty of the God who addresses us through His Word and makes us His own.

When the Word of God addresses us and we receive it in faith, we are not merely informed about the providence of God but we experience the very power by which God maintains and governs the world. God created the world out of nothing by His Word, and by the same means He prevents it from dissolving into nothingness again.[5] Indeed we must go so far as to confess that the Word shares in the government of the world. The eternal Word together with the Father guides all created things.[6] Naturally such a statement can only be made about the Word inasmuch as it is divine and not inasmuch as it is a distinctive Person in the one Godhead.

(c) If we ask what object the sustaining and guiding action of the Word pursues, we find that Calvin first opposes the opinion that there is only a general providence (*providentia universalis*) in the sense that God is the power which animates the whole universe.[7] It is rather that God by His particular providence sustains, fosters, and cares for each individual thing and being which He has created, down to the tiniest

[1] *CR* 31, 682. [2] *CR* 31, 464. [3] *CR* 31, 330.
[4] *CR* 31, 89. [5] *CR* 47, 479; 27, 699.
[6] *In.* I, 13, 12; *CR* 51, 160. [7] *In.* I, 16, 4; I, 16, 1.

sparrow.[1] We do not realize the whole splendour of God until we see that He tends every creature and guides it to its goal.[2] He truly orders the life of every creature and type of existence. There is nothing in the world which is not directly under the control of God and subject to His will.

Calvin distinguishes various degrees in this special divine providence. As man is the most eminent of God's creatures and as it is for his sake that all is created both in heaven and earth, the providential care of God is exercised above all towards him. "Marvellous are the judgments of God who punishes the godless, schools believers to patience and mortifies their fleshly desires, purges through suffering the vices of the world, startles many people out of their indolence, destroys the pride of the impious, laughs to scorn the cunning of the prudent and brings to nought evil counsels. And on the other hand His incomparable mercy is evident when He helps the wretched, protects and assures the life of the innocent, and brings help when all appears to be lost."[3] "The life and death of men, the common lot of empires and peoples as much as the personal lot of each individual and whatever else is usually ascribed to fate, utterly depends upon the sole guiding providence of heaven."[4]

If Calvin thus discriminates between the special providence which God grants to each creature, even the tiniest living thing, and that in virtue of which He guides every man and nation, he introduces with regard to human beings a further distinction of the greatest importance: "Although God manifests Himself to the whole human race as Father and Judge, yet, because the church is the sanctuary in which He dwells, He reveals His presence there still more plainly; there He exercises His fatherhood, and deems the church worthy, as it were, to draw more closely to His side." "The church is the real sphere in which God carries out His providential purposes and the special theatre in which His providence operates."[5] God sustains and guides the whole world, each individual thing and being, but His providential

[1] *In.* I, 16, 1, 4.   [2] *In.* I, 16, 4.   [3] *CR* 8, 348.
[4] *CR* 8, 349.   [5] *Loc. cit.*; cf. *CR* 29, 241; 31, 19; *In.* I, 17, 1, 6.

73

goodness is directed above all to the human race and within it to the church.

In regard to this gradation in the exercise of divine providence it is not a question of a simple scale reflecting the degree of dignity of the various creatures. The position is rather this: God sustains the whole world and proves Himself the Lord of each individual creature, of men, and peoples, because He wills to be the Lord of His church. He guides the movements of nature and history because He wills to guide and maintain His church in this world. "God has unlimited power to secure the existence of His church, and, since He controls all creation, cannot be prevented by any resistance from fulfilling His purposes."[1] If we fail to realize this ultimate end of the divine providence, we have understood little about it. "For the providence of God is rightly honoured when believers do not despair in the hour of their greatest need, but rather out of the depths lift up their hearts to God in hope, because He allows His own to hunger in order to fill them when He wills and plunges them into the shadow of death in order to restore to them the light of life."[2] "We are superstitiously fearful if we become afraid whenever men threaten us or alarm us, as if they in themselves possessed any power to do harm, or could fortuitously injure us, or as if we did not believe that in God there is enough help against their attacks."[3] God cares for the world and for mankind in general only for the sake of that fatherly protection which He bestows upon His church.[4]

The church is indeed the real object of the divine providence. In this thesis we clearly recognize the focusing of Calvinistic teaching about creation and providence on the revelation of God in Jesus Christ; for the church is the body of Christ. But the full scope of the thesis will not be appreciated if we fail to see that Calvin goes one step further in his argument; the church is the object but not the final goal of God's providence. The church is not a society whose basis lies in itself, but the sanctuary of the Lord where Christ is the

[1] CR 32, 184.   [2] CR 31, 333.   [3] In. I, 16, 3.
[4] CR 8, 349.

chief corner stone. Hence the providence of God is not concentrated upon it in order that we should devote ourselves to it as such. Rather in focusing His providence especially upon the church He wishes to encourage us to call upon Himself, the living God, and to set our hope upon Him.[1] We are neither to be occupied with ourselves nor with the dangers which surround us, but to aspire to God in prayer and trust.[2] This is no impossible demand; for God confronts us in Christ. We must cling with all our hearts to Him, for He cares for us.[3] Such is the ultimate end of divine providence. In the last resort it is only a question of one thing—that we should recognize and exalt the grace and the power of our God.[4]

(d) The fact that God cares for us does not relieve us of our own responsibility. Providence does not imply that in this world we can simply let ourselves go. Here again there is no immediate relation between man and his Creator. Calvin decisively rejected the teaching of the Quintinists who because they felt the effectual operation of the divine spirit taught that man must surrender himself to the stream of life without reflection.[5] No; God has endowed man with reason and will-power so that he may use them and make decisions.[6] God has given us resources for the mastery of life.[7] If we do not use them, if we allow our own capacities to slumber within us, we have no right to take comfort in the thought of the divine providence. In the exercise of the latter, God takes into account the fact that we men are gifted with reason and will-power. All that we are able to devise and set in motion is integrated into His plan.

By stressing the responsibility of man, Calvin does not mean to lessen the power of the Creator. It remains true that God makes possible the decisions and actions of men and subdues them to His purposes. The providence of God must

---

[1] *In.* I, 17, 9.   [2] *CR* 8, 350.   [3] *CR* 10b, 201.

[4] *CR* 31, 271 f.

[5] Cf. W. Niesel, "Calvin und die Libertiner", *Zeitschr. f. Kirchengesch.*, Vol. 48, new series, 11, pp. 58 f.

[6] *In.* I, 17, 4, 6; *CR* 36, 222.   [7] *In.* I, 17, 4.

not be watered down to a merely permissive attitude[1]: "as though God sat enthroned on a high watch-tower and simply beheld how events by chance worked out."[2] Men really depend on the will and plan of God; such, Calvin thinks, is the clear teaching of Holy Scripture.[3] The point is that "in affirming that the will of God is the cause of all things we make the divine providence the controlling force behind all the purposes and activities of men, and further imply that its effect is apparent not only in the elect, who are guided by the Holy Spirit, but also that it constrains the reprobate to obedience."[4]

Here two serious questions arise for our human understanding.

Firstly: if all happens according to the will of God, are there not two wills in God, one which He has revealed to us in His Word and another hidden will opposed to the will which is revealed?[5] Calvin points out that according to the teaching of Holy Scripture God accomplishes His righteous will even through the evil designs and actions of men. We must realize that in discussing this question of divine providence we are in the last resort confronted by the cross of Christ: "If Christ had not been crucified by the will of God, how could we have been redeemed?"[6] The will of God is not dualistic, nor is it subject to change. It only appears to us in this light "because on account of the weakness of our understanding we cannot comprehend how God in a dialectical way can both will and not will that a thing should happen."[7] Here our understanding reaches its limit. But because of this inability we should in no case postulate absurdity in God. Rather we should confess our weakness and bow before the mystery of the divine dispositions[8] whereby the one righteous will of God is always triumphant.

Secondly: is not God then the author of evil, if everything that happens owes its origin ultimately to Him?[9] Calvin

[1] *In.* I, 18, 1. [2] *Ibid.* [3] *Ibid.* [4] *In.* I, 18, 2.
[5] *In. I*, 18, 3. [6] *Ibid.* [7] *Ibid.* [8] *Ibid.*
[9] *In.* I, 18, 4; 17, 5.

headed a whole chapter of the *Institutes* with the words:
"That God uses the service of the godless and directs their
hearts in such wise as to exercise His righteous judgments
but that He Himself remains pure and unsullied by any
sin."[1] In this sentence everything is already said. There is
no independent reign of evil in opposition to God. All is
subject to the Creator. He has the reins of all things in His
hands and directs all to the fulfilment of His purposes. He
uses even evildoers as the instruments of His providence in
order to accomplish the judgments which in secret He has
determined.[2] Even Satan must stand ready in His service.[3]
But this does not mean that God has the ultimate responsibility for evil and that evil deeds are thus excused. "In this
respect we should not think of any violent coercion, as
though God led men into evil against their will"; but "in a
marvellous and incomprehensible way He overrules all the
impulses of men so that their free-will remains intact."[4] If
men act wrongly, they break the commandment of God by
their own free-will and yet through their conduct God fulfils
what in His hidden counsels He has determined.[5] Again in
this aspect of the doctrine of providence we are confronted by
the mystery of the cross of Christ. It is precisely there that we
see "how in the same event the guilt of men is declared and
the righteousness of God shines forth."[6] When God yielded
up His Son, and Judas betrayed his Lord, in that one
happening God showed Himself to be the Just and man the
unjust. Calvin is aware that human curiosity cannot be
satisfied with this kind of illustration or with the discussion
which he devotes to the subject. The question of God and
evil cannot be solved. It exceeds the capacity of our understanding. In regard to it we can only listen to the message of
Holy Scripture and the appeal of the cross of Christ.[7] But to

---

[1] *In.* I, 18; *OS* 3, 219, 4.   [2] *In.* I, 17, 5.   [3] *In.* I, 18, 1.
[4] *CR* 36, 222.   [5] *In.* I, 18, 4.   [6] *In.* I, 18, 4, 1.
[7] *In.* I, 18, 4. A comparison which Calvin was fond of is intended less
to explain the matter than to cut short curious questions: "Et unde,
quaeso, foetor in cadavere, quod calore solis tum putrefactum, tum
reseratum fuerit? Radiis solis excitari omnes vident; nemo tamen illos

that extent we must not evade the question. "For our wisdom must be nothing but an acceptance with humble and docile hearts of all (without exception) that is put before us in Holy Scripture"[1]; and here it must be admitted as a fact "that no concord can exist between man and God if the former does through God's just instigation what is against the law".[2]

The question: What are we to do? has not to be answered from the standpoint of our own reflections. It is answered for us by the divine command which is given in Holy Scripture.[3] Our already accomplished actions must be tested solely by the criterion of this law, and with regard to decisions which we are about to make we must refer wholly to the word of Scripture which is both admonishing and comforting. Here we are not secure against the danger of separation from God. Inward and outward enemies press upon us and seek to gain the mastery over us. In the midst of this oppression in which we must daily make our decisions it behoves us to recollect that God has not given us only His Word as a light on our path. He has also placed in our hearts the desire to pray and has commanded us, His own for whom He cares, to call upon Him in our distress. He does not as it were leave us to do the best we can with His Word, but Himself wishes to place us in the way in which His Word directs us.[4] We must pray that strengthened by His Word we may overcome all our difficulties. The Biblical teaching about the providence of God leads neither into brooding care nor into carelessness, but drives us rather to the Word and to prayer. Here once again it becomes clear how the doctrine of providence belongs essentially to the sphere of church life. The Word and prayer live only in the midst of the church.

When we use these means and thus await all things from God, we make real progress and our pilgrimage in this world is comforted and strengthened. Then when we enjoy fortunate success we render hearty thanks; in misfortune, we

---

foetere ideo dicit. Ita quum in homine malo subsideat mali materia et culpa, quid est quod inquinamentum aliquod contrahere putetur Deus, si ad suum arbitrium utatur eius ministerio?" (*In.* I, 17, 5).

[1] *In.* I, 18, 4.   [2] *Ibid.*   [3] *In.* I, 17, 5, 3.   [4] *CR* 12, 454.

are patient, and with regard to the future we look forward with wondrous fearlessness.[1] As members of the Church we are relieved from our weight of cares.[2] Hence it is understandable that Calvin comes to the conclusion that "the greatest thing in our extremities is that we know nothing of God's providential designs and again that the highest blessedness is based on the recognition of divine providence".[3]

[1] *In.* I, 17, 7.   [2] *In.* I, 17, 11.   [3] *Ibid.*

Chapter 5

SIN [1]

I. ORIGINAL SIN

MAN who is thus sustained and guided by God in the way which we have described shows no longer any trace of the original goodness in which he was created. When philosophers and even church teachers think very highly of man and ascribe to him the utmost moral dignity [2] they are deceiving themselves about the ground of his being. What man is becomes clear only when he is confronted by the truth itself. We attain a true knowledge of ourselves only when we view ourselves in the truthful mirror of Holy Scripture. [3] The reference to this authority which stands over against every man shows plainly what Calvin is here concerned about. He does not wish to oppose a pessimistic to an optimistic view of man. "If it were only a question of the pre-eminent natural endowment of man, then we might"—he admits without more ado—"pay regard to the extraordinary gifts which he has received from God; but in so far as he is confronted by God he must crumple up into utter nothingness." [4] The real question is what man is in the presence of God, whether he can stand before God; and such a question can only be answered by God Himself. "The Holy Spirit assures us in Holy Scripture that our understanding is so smitten with blindness, our heart in its motions so evil and corrupt, in fact our whole nature so depraved, that

[1] W. A. Hauck, *Sünde und Erbsünde nach Calvin*, Heidelberg, 1938; T. F. Torrance, *Calvin's Doctrine of Man*, London, 1949.

[2] Cf. *In.* II, 2, 2 ff; *OS* 3, 242, 26 f.   [3] *In.* II, 2, 11.

[4] *CR* 36, 535.

80

we can do nothing else but sin until He Himself creates in us a new will." [1]

The divine image in man is destroyed and effaced.[2] Calvin makes this ruthless assertion, although in a more exact description of the state of affairs he is bound to admit "that it has not been completely eliminated".[3] Man has not become a beast. He has no reason to boast of the fact; for properly speaking he belongs to a still lower grade.[4] But he has remained man, a being gifted in contradistinction to the beasts with reason and will-power. Yet the divine similitude in man in the strict sense and his original uprightness no longer exist.[5] Alienation from God has taken the place of his original orientation towards his Creator.[6] Calvin teaches with the whole church that this change in the state of man is rooted in the fact of the fall of Adam. The first man created by God fell away from his Creator and thus decided the fate of the whole human race.[7]

This revolt from God is the primal sin (*peccatum originale*) of man. It is noteworthy that in a mild debate with Augustine Calvin does not consider the pride of man to be the real ground of all evil.[8] According to his insight the root of the trouble lies much deeper. The defection of man is grounded in something purely negative, in the fact that he no longer cleaves to the word of God, in his radical unbelief and disobedience.[9] And this unbelief engenders and is indeed itself separation from God, it spells the loss of the divine likeness and is the root sin of man. These negative expressions must be noted and from them we must infer that sin is not an element native to the being of man, of which he might even boast. Nor does it consist simply in a moral defect. It can only be described as a surrender of man's right relation to his Creator. The effects of this change in the

---

[1] *CR* 14, 35. [2] *CR* 23, 26; 51, 208; 28, 205; 51, 253.

[3] *In.* I, 15, 4.

[4] *CR* 51, 253. "Brief, nous ne sommes pas dignes d'estre mis au reng des bestes brutes, si nous demeurons en la condition telle que nous avons de nature."

[5] *In.* I, 15, 4. [6] *In.* II, 1, 4. [7] *In.* II, 1, *OS* 3, 228 f.
[8] *In.* II, 1, 4. [9] *Ibid.*

attitude of man extend to his entire being. Just as his nature was originally moulded by his turning Godwards, so now it is affected to its inmost depths by his estrangement from the source of life. "We know that the injury wrought by the primal sin is not confined to one part of man's being but completely embraces body and soul."[1] Also in regard to the soul it is not simply a matter of the baser sensual impulses.[2] "As long as we do not understand that sin has injured every part of the soul we have not yet realized the full extent of its power. Hence if we refuse to admit that the understanding of man is completely depraved and his heart evil, we have little insight into the significance of original sin."[3] "The whole man from head to foot is thus, as it were, drenched in a flood of wickedness so that no part has remained without sin and so everything which springs from him is counted as sin."[4] In "the whole of his nature no element of integrity remains".[5] Calvin takes up the Biblical expression and affirms that the entire man in this fallen condition is "flesh".[6] "To put it bluntly", "men have nothing in themselves but sin". "This does not mean that the substance of our bodies and souls is evil, for we are God's creatures." But "every part of us is saturated in evil".[7] Man is an abyss of every sort of corruption and depravity,[8] and indeed it is precisely our souls which are a sink of iniquity.[9] If we noted just now that the primal sin must be described as essentially negative, as a revolt from God, it becomes apparent from the above that this nothingness can be transformed into something positive from which evil springs continually. "Although those who have described the primal sin as a lack of the original righteousness which we were intended to have understand the general position well enough, yet they do not bring out clearly enough the power and effects of sin. For our nature is not merely poor and devoid of all good, but it is, further, so

---

[1] CR 32, 230.   [2] In. II, 1, 9 : II, 3, 1.
[3] CR 31, 514, 513; cf. CR 26, 121.   [4] In. 11, 1, 9.
[5] CR 47, 57: "in tota natura nulla rectitudinis gutta superest".
[6] In. II, 3, 1; CR 49, 128; 40, 246; 50, 252 ff.
[7] CR 33, 728.   [8] CR 46, 598.   [9] CR 13, 70.

fertile and pregnant with all wickedness that it cannot be idle."[1] Thus unbelieving and disobedient man, devoid of original integrity, is as a whole, and in himself, "nothing but a well of vain and wicked desires" (concupiscentia).[2]

This original sin in its terrible negativity and power still exists in man, even though it may not be immediately apparent, as is the case with little children.[3] Although it may not be manifest in particular sinful actions, that is no proof that sin itself does not live in a man.[4] Already from our mother's womb we have sin within us; "for we belong to a damned and corrupt race".[5] "Let men therefore cease to boast; even kings and princes who say: 'I have sprung from such or such a family.' It is certain that in our body and soul there is in the eyes of God nothing but repulsive filth. In that lies their whole nobility and worth!"[6]

2. ADAM'S SIN OUR SIN

We must now consider the question how it is possible that the sin of the first man should be our sin—the sin of the whole human race. How can it be that this sin should live on in every child that is born, before the first movements of the conscious mind have been awakened in it? The usual answer given is that we have inherited sin from our first ancestor. Calvin realizes that this answer is not quite correct,[7] although he himself, following tradition, describes original sin as "the hereditary perversity and corruption of our nature".[8] In fact, there is no real solution to the problem.[9] Calvin endeavours to clarify the matter in the following way: "The guilt of one man could not concern us at all if our heavenly Judge had not delivered us over to eternal ruin."[10] "Because of the guilt of one man God has placed us in a condition of universal indictment."[11] Thus what is presupposed is an act of divine judgment. God views all men

[1] In. II, 1, 8.   [2] Ibid.   [3] CR 46, 843; In. II, 1, 8.
[4] CR 25, 207.   [5] CR 33, 654.   [6] CR 46, 358.
[7] In. II, 1, 7.   [8] In. II, 1, 8.   [9] CR 33, 661; 28, 192.
[10] CR 9, 289.   [11] CR 9, 290.

as sinners and treats them as such. Thus Calvin rejects all naturalistic attempts at explanation. Original sin does not devolve upon us through any physical process such as biological heredity. It is no inherited malady. "For posterity did not entail corruption in any physical manner through its descent from Adam; but the fact is rather dependent on the ordinance of God, who, just as He endowed the entire human race with the most splendid gifts in the person of one man, also deprived it of the same through him."[1] "And why is that? Because we were all represented in his person according to the Will of God. There is no occasion in this matter to work with rational considerations, in order to find out whether this is so or not; we should rather recognize that it was the Will of God to bestow upon our ancestor what it was the divine intention that we should receive, and when those gifts were taken from him we were all involved in the same ruin and confusion. Let us therefore pay heed to this divine judgment and hold fast to it and not trust our own understanding and fantasy."[2] Adam was not just an individual[3] but the embodiment of the whole human race. It was the will of God that we should be represented in him. His behaviour was our behaviour, his deed was our deed. "Hence it is not so much that each one of us has inherited vice and corruption from his parents but rather that we have all been at the same time corrupted in the one Adam."[4]

Ultimately this state of affairs is only understandable to us through Jesus Christ. All naturalistic attempts to explain original sin, the biological one which regards it as a matter of inherited depravity and the moralistic one which supposes that it has arisen through the evil imitation of the revolt of the first man, tend to neglect the revelation of God in Jesus Christ and the light which falls upon the mystery of human nature from that source. Calvin in this connexion points to Paul as the truest witness to the strange universality and actuality of original sin. The fact that Adam is so to speak the fountain of human nature is "made clear by the apostle

[1] *CR* 23, 62; 47, 57; 33, 660 f., *In.* II, 1, 7.
[2] *CR* 33, 661.   [3] *CR* 31, 514.   [4] *CR* 47, 57.

in the comparison between Adam and Christ".[1] "If it is undisputed that the righteousness of Christ is appropriated by us through our fellowship with Him, as is also eternal life, then it follows that both were lost in Adam and restored to us in Christ; hence sin and death entered in through the fall of Adam and have been destroyed by the work of Christ."[2] By the very nature of the gift which we receive in Christ we come to realize what is lacking to us. "Because all these things (faith, love of God and neighbour and the striving for holiness and righteousness) have been restored to us in Christ, they must be considered as something added to our nature rather as something belonging to it. Hence we conclude that they were utterly effaced in us."[3] Because Christ is the sole cause of our righteousness, our radical unrighteousness and incapacity for good is established.[4] In the light of Christ we realize that we are incorporated in Adam and find ourselves in a situation of wrong relationship with God, and thus are moulded and impelled by the fact of original sin. A right awareness of sin implies a glorification of the merits of Christ. "All of us without exception", so comments Calvin on Ephesians 2:3, "are indictable until we are justified by Christ...so that no righteousness, no salvation and in fact no good in general are to be found outside Christ."[5]

This fundamental insight illuminates the whole seriousness of our situation. Even the customary teaching on inherited sin deceives us about it by suggesting that we have to bear the burden of a dark and fateful inheritance. Only in the light of Christ do we see that we all stand before the light of God's countenance in utter corruption and perversity. "We are lost, there is no means of help; and whether we are great or small, fathers or children, we are all without exception in a state of damnation if God does not remove from us the curse which weighs upon us, and that by His generosity and grace, without His being obliged to do so."[6] Apart from Christ the judgment and the curse of God strike us. But

[1] *In.* II, 1, 6.   [2] *Ibid.*   [3] *In.* II, 2, 12.
[4] *CR* 49, 95.   [5] *CR* 51, 162.   [6] *CR* 26, 262.

what calls forth the vengeance of God is real sin.[1] Therefore no man is without sin; not even little children. For if they "are not free from the anger and curse of God it is surely not without reason if He visits them with punishment".[2] He knows well "why He punishes even the children who are still in the womb of their mother, and we must adore His judgments in all humility". "We are too weak and stupid to understand the judgments of God which are so high." [3] But one thing we must learn from the fact of Christ : the judgments of God which strike us are just; "for we are all guilty".[4] We are all involved with Adam in the solidarity of sin. We all stand with the first man in a state of estrangement from God.

All this brings out the fact that it is not innocently and without having deserved it that we have to bear the guilt of Adam's transgression.[5] Such a suggestion which flows from the usual doctrine of sin as inherited shows clearly the questionableness of the latter interpretation. The punishment which comes upon us proves that we have all in truth committed in Adam his transgression.[6] Even young children are involved not in the sin of others but in their own. The actual condition in which they are is reckoned in the eyes of God as sin in the true sense.[7] Although they have as yet committed no particular sins, they stand in the presence of the Lord as no more just than their parents. For there could not be a possibility of indictment without guilt.[8]

Every fatalistic feature must be removed from the doctrine of sin. "If we sin, it does not happen from compulsion, as though we were constrained to do so by an alien power; but all sin results from our own will and inclination." [9] This does not mean to say that we have indeterminate freedom of choice as between good and evil.[10] If we were able to effect anything against God we would not be able to attain full salvation through the grace of Christ. Redemption would then become in part self-salvation.[11] But it does mean that

---

[1] *CR* 49, 95.   [2] *CR* 26, 262.   [3] *CR* 28, 192.
[4] *CR* 28, 191.   [5] *In.* II, 1, 8.; *CR* 23, 62.   [6] *In.* II, 1, 8.
[7] *Ibid.*   [8] *Ibid.*   [9] *CR* 28, 560.   [10] *CR* 6, 303.
[11] *CR* 6, 483.

our perverse decisions take place with our full consent.[1] "We sin freely because sin would not be sin if it did not happen in freedom of will; but we are so given over to sin that we can voluntarily do nothing else but sin because the evil that reigns in us constantly impels us to do so."[2] Defection from God spells slavery for us, but it is of our choosing and is what we ever and again seek. In this connexion Calvin distinguishes between necessity and coercion (*necessitas* and *coactio*).[3] Our condition is one of estrangement from God; we decide for evil and follow it willingly. But we can no longer in our own strength free ourselves from the necessity of so deciding. We cannot depart from the path which we have chosen. That is the meaning of the necessity to sin to which we have freely subjected ourselves. Thus it is not a compulsion which comes to us and grips us from outside. The latter would be incompatible with our responsibility and would make guilt impossible. Here Calvin recollects that "from the character of the help which the Lord grants to us we can alone fully realize our defect and our need".[4] We are well aware of our own servitude and will glorify Christ alone as the One who frees us from it.[5] Christ does not release us from some external compulsion but renovates our will and our heart and re-orientates them towards righteousness.[6] The seat of the ill lies at the point where He begins His work of renewal. He lives within us. This must not be obscured. By faith in Christ we receive adoption as children of God and so true freedom.[7]

From this point of view Calvin tries to find an explanation of how man's fall from his Creator could come about at all. Of course Adam was created in a right relationship to God. "But he had no divine power, he stood on the ladder of creation and had the measure of a man, so that he was liable to change; and he evinced this only too truly."[8] "Thus there was something of weakness already in him." "He was subject to temptation."[9] That is to say that the man created

[1] *CR* 6, 303.   [2] *CR* 49, 128 ff.   [3] *In.* II, 3 5.
[4] *In.* II, 3, 6; *CR* 47, 202; 6, 279.   [5] *CR* 47, 203.
[6] *In.* II, 3, 6.   [7] *CR* 50, 221.   [8] *CR* 46, 598.   [9] *Ibid.*

good by God was still a man. Adam was not Jesus Christ. This observation does not cast doubt upon the rectitude of the original man: "We must distinguish between the natural weakness which has always been proper to man and the vicious weaknesses which have come upon us because of original sin."[1] The fall of Adam came about not because man was defectively created but because as man he had within himself no divine capacity for perseverance.

3. SINS OF ACTION

In order to complete the picture of Calvin's doctrine of sin we have something still to say with regard to the question of particular sinful actions. The fundamental attitude in which humanity is engaged determines the entire thinking, willing, and acting of man. "The spirit of perversity is never at rest within us but brings forth ever new fruits, viz. the works of the flesh . . . just as a roaring furnace gives off flames and sparks or as a spring without ceasing spouts forth water."[2] We are blinded, we fall into error and can make no right decisions.[3] Our will is so crooked that it can only engender what is vicious and impure.[4] Of course the various particular sins which we commit are of different kinds and degrees. There is a direct sinning against God and failure in our duty to our fellow men. In the last resort, however, all our evil deeds strike at the being of God Himself.[5]

But all this does not mean that Calvin depicts the moral state of mankind only in the blackest colours. He does not place Camillus and Catiline on the same level but admits that in the life of man there are virtues and vices.[6] In fact, we meet in history ethical accomplishments which tower far above the normal standards. Calvin does not try to deny that real heroism is to be found amongst men[7]; and what is true of the moral sphere applies equally to the activities of human intellectual enquiry and insight.[8] Calvin would have been the last to fail to esteem the results attained by the

[1] *CR* 46, 598. [2] *In.* II, 1, 8. [3] *CR* 55, 108. [4] *CR* 6, 362.
[5] *CR* 29, 338. [6] *In.* II, 3, 4. [7] *Ibid.* [8] *In.* II, 2, 18.

discipline of philosophy. But in saying this much we have not said the final thing about the worth of human achievements. For it must first of all be observed that God, in virtue of His providential designs, equips some people with special gifts because He has special purposes for them to fulfil.[1] Hence what we are inclined to accredit to men should in fact redound to the praise of God alone. And secondly it is to be noted that even in such cases men remain involved in the general condition of human depravity.[2] "What is the point", says Calvin, "of extolling man's capacity for good when in fact even those who give every appearance of virtue are being constantly tempted to do evil?"[3] In this respect it is not a question of the external accomplishments of man but of what he is in the realities of his inner life.[4] The human will is and remains perverted.[5] "The more outstanding a man is, the more he is unceasingly goaded by his ambition—an evil which sullies all his virtues, so that they lose all merit in the eyes of God. Thus we must esteem as valueless whatever appears praiseworthy in the impious."[6] In particular they lack "the zeal to glorify the honour of God".[7] This defect vitiates all that they attempt to do. This is their essential fault. Ambition and self-seeking, which both inspire and ruin every good work of man, are only the obverse side of the fundamental defect which clings to him. And so, in spite of all differences, men in the last resort all stand on the same level. The fact is that sin is something other than moral failure.

In spite of all the excellence which they are able to show, men are cramped within themselves instead of being expanded outwards to God in the desire to do His will. Calvin demonstrates the truth of this by reference to Christ. That is typical of his whole theological method. There has lived on this earth only one man on whom the spirit of the fear of God rested.[8] In the light of His life it becomes clear to us that we do not stand in a right relation with God, but that each one of us seeks his own; and hence all our thoughts,

[1] *In.* II, 3, 4.   [2] *Ibid.*   [3] *Ibid.*   [4] *Ibid.*
[5] *Ibid.*   [6] *Ibid.*   [7] *Ibid.*   [8] *Ibid.*

words, and works, however well they may appear, cannot stand the test of divine judgment. Only in Christ are we freed from the tyranny of sin and placed in the service of God.[1]

It is Christ who first discloses to us the truth about our human situation. "If His grace is the sole means by which we can be freed from our blindness and from all the evil which it engenders",[2] then all our capacities come under condemnation. "For, if we need a new heart and a new spirit, it follows that our soul in every part is not only injured but to such an extent depraved that its perversity can only be called death and destruction, at least in comparison with its original integrity."[3] Without Christ we stand under the judgment of God and thus are subject to the death of body and soul—the punishment for our sin. "I do admit", says Calvin, "that there remains to us a residue of life even when we are as yet far from Christ. For our unbelief does not efface our understanding, our will, and the various capacities of our soul. But of what value is all that in comparison with the kingdom of God? Or in comparison with the life of blessedness, seeing that everything which we think and will is dissolute and decadent? Hence it must be held that the only and true life of our soul consists in communion with God, and that apart from Christ we are completely dead, because sin reigns in us with its inevitable consequence of death."[4] It is precisely that part of our soul which "most of all seems to have been spared injury", our understanding, which most needs renewal. How easily that determines the ruin of our whole nature.[5] And note well: our plight is so evil that no mere healing will help our understanding even. However much its acuteness may be praised, it needs radical renovation.[6] The renewal which must embrace our whole existence must not be understood as simply an improvement of the faculties which we already possess; what is in question is rather a new creation. We recognize this fact in Jesus Christ. Through Him we receive a share in the second creation "where everything is effaced

[1] *In.* II, 3, 4. [2] *In.* II, 3, 1. [3] *CR* 40, 245.
[4] *CR* 51, 161. [5] *CR* 51, 208. [6] *In.* II, 1, 9.

which is part and parcel of our ordinary nature".[1] Jesus Christ means for us the turning from death unto life, and hence all those illusions which we entertain about our being and its capacities pass away from the moment when His name is named and His work is praised.

[1] *In.* II, 3, 6.

Chapter 6

THE LAW OF GOD

MAN who has become separated from God cannot now find his way back to his Lord. When in spite of this we fondly imagine that we can once more enter into a relationship with God, we encounter an idol instead of the living God. God is withdrawn from all approaches on the part of man. Yet He has not left man to himself, but has shown His sovereign Lordship by taking the initiative to restore the broken relation. God has given man His law and has declared His will therein.

What Calvin teaches about this initiative of God is so characteristic for his theology that it can by no means be neglected. If with the usual prejudices about the legalism of Calvin we come to his writings and really read them, it is just here that we shall find what a lot we have to unlearn.

I. THE LAW AS THE LAW OF THE COVENANT

Calvin's understanding of divine law is based on the recognition that the law of God is covenantal law. If in the New Testament Paul at times speaks of the law in itself, that is only because he wishes to expose the error of those who imagine that man can acquire righteousness by fulfilling the works of the law. But in point of fact the law does not stand thus as an isolated phenomenon. It is not simply a collection of commands about how to live well, but is included in the covenant of grace which God founded.[1] Abraham and his heirs, who belonged to God no more than other men, were

[1] *In.* II, 7, 2.

viewed and accepted by this triune God as His children. This act of adoption was not grounded in the worthiness of that family but solely in the mercy of God.[1] Hence the covenant of God is immutable, however men behave towards Him. The institution which God founded on behalf of men in spite of their unworthiness and infidelity cannot be destroyed by their conduct.[2] But from the angle of God, too, the covenant which He concluded is inviolable. The triune God is not at war with Himself but remains ever and unchangeably the same. "Hence He wills that from the covenant which He has made with His church His unchangeable loyalty should shine forth."[3] The law of God is embedded in this grace and loyalty which He shows towards His people, the church; God in entering into a covenant with His people makes an absolute claim upon them. This divine demand is the meaning of the law.

This point of view is of fundamental importance. "Of course God desires that each one of us should be consecrated to Him, that we should renounce self-will, that we should be subject to Him and surrendered to His guidance; but before He requires that of us He bestows Himself upon us."[4] Such is the background against which the divine law is set in relief. Here lies the origin of the radical difference between this law and all others. Whereas in other cases there is a sharp opposition between a law and those to whom it is applicable, and this implies compulsion and servitude for those whom the law affects, in this case the triune God imparts Himself to those whom He summons to walk in His way. "This must soften our hearts, even though they were harder than stone. Who are we then that our Lord should condescend so low in order to make a covenant with us, and to promise us that He will be our Father and Saviour, so that He comes before us as one who has concluded with us a contract that is a gift?" "This should so delight us as to cause us to yield ourselves to God without hesitation, since He persuades and invites us to do so by His example."[5] The grace of God is so

---

[1] *CR* 28, 549.   [2] *Ibid.*; *CR* 40, 396.   [3] *CR* 38, 645, 688.
[4] *CR* 28, 513.   [5] *CR* 28, 513.

great that He not only offers His help to His own but imparts
to them His very self. Thus His word can be heard by them
and find obedience.

All this is true also of the Mosaic law itself. The latter
belongs integrally to the covenant which God concluded with
His servant Abraham.[1] "For Moses was not made a lawgiver
in order to set aside the promise given to the seed of
Abraham; rather we see that he constantly reminds the
Jews of the covenant of grace concluded with their fathers
whose heirs they were, just as if his special mission were to
renew that covenant."[2] Through Moses' giving of the law
God recalled His people to their task, and by the hand of
Moses[3] He sealed His covenant. Moses is not the founder of
a so-called religion of law but the prophet of the covenant
God, witnessing to God's mercy and loyalty.

The same is to be said of that theologian among the
reformers who is usually regarded as the exponent of law. Of
course Calvin affirms with the Psalmist the blessedness of the
man whose delight is in the law of the Lord and who
meditates on His law day and night (Psalm 1:2); but the
legalistic Calvin has taught us to see most clearly the Biblical
conception of the law. He has praised the glory of the law
because he recognized it to be the covenantal law of the
gracious and faithful God, and imparted by Him to His
church.

2. THE LAW AND THE CULTUS

This insight leads Calvin to regard the law from a cultic
point of view. He sees moral and cultic laws as essentially
bound up together. "By the term law", he says in definition,
"I understand not only the ten commandments, which
prescribe how one should live in piety and justice, but the
whole cultus of religion which God communicated through
Moses."[4] Ceremonies prevent a moral misunderstanding of
the law. "God added them all in order to support the
commandments and to sustain and promote the faith."[5]

[1] CR 38, 688.   [2] In. II, 7, 1.   [3] CR 38, 688.
[4] In. II, 7, 1.   [5] CR 48, 305.

THE LAW OF GOD

Whilst the laws, as such, expose our unrighteousness, the sacrifices and signs which God instituted in conjunction with them mark out in the swamps of our life a path on which we can walk before God uprightly and in holiness according to His will.[1] These sacrifices and ceremonies remind us of the fact that the law is given by the gracious and faithful covenant of God in order to redound to His praise. They are meant to make still clearer what the commandments also proclaim: God guarantees by the gift of the law the fulfilment of the commandments; there is a life in accordance with the will of God because He has bestowed Himself upon His people.

3. CHRIST AND THE LAW

God has given Himself to us in Jesus Christ. The covenant of God with His people is grounded in the Incarnation. God has adopted us as children and declared His will to us because His only begotten Son has fulfilled that will in this world. "The main content of the law and the foundation of the divine covenant consists in the fact that the Jews have Jesus Christ as their Leader and Protector—the heart of their sacred history; without Him there can be no religion and they themselves would be the most wretched of men."[2] "Whatever the law teaches, prescribes, and promises is always orientated towards Jesus Christ its centre." "Thus no one can have a correct understanding of the law unless he constantly relates it to Him."[3] Before developing his interpretation of the law in the *Institutes* Calvin therefore writes a chapter on the theme: "That man after becoming corrupted in himself must seek his redemption in Christ",[4] and then continues: "Thus the law is not given in order to lay its fetters on the people but in order to maintain the hope of salvation in Christ until His advent."[5] Whoever does not pay heed to the soul of the law, whoever disregards the fulfiller of the law, must in any event perish by the law. He does not see it as an invitation from the Father of grace,

[1] *CR* 49, 59.   [2] *CR* 48, 289.   [3] *CR* 49, 196.
[4] *In.* II, 6.   [5] *In.* II, 7.

95

and strives in vain to fulfil its requirements in will and deed. "Without Christ the law is valueless and offers no sure ground of hope." [1]

This is true of the law in every part. The ritual and sacrifices are of no avail apart from Christ.[2] The whole cultus prescribed by the law would be a completely ridiculous affair if its value were intrinsic to itself and if it did not contain shadows and types symbolizing the truth.[3] "Jesus Christ is the grace and truth which the cultus and its ceremonies foreshadowed." "The power and efficacy of the ritual depended on Him."[4] Just because God has imparted Himself to us in Jesus Christ, the various rites of the Old Testament cult which body forth the covenant of God with His people did not cheat the Israelites.

Much the same is to be said of the moral law. It is primarily given to us [5] "in order that by disclosing the divine righteousness which alone is valid in the sight of God it should remind, convict, and picture to each one of us his own unrighteousness and finally condemn us because of it." [6] "This does not happen to the end that we should sink in despair and without consolation be plunged into ruin." [7] The pedagogic intention of the law is rather that we should lift up our hearts to the sphere where the righteousness of God is fulfilled. The point is "that we should be led to resign foolish delusions about our own strength and to realize that we can stand upright only in the strength of God, so that, naked and exposed, we flee to His mercy to lean wholly upon it, to hide ourselves utterly within it, appreciate that it alone is our true virtue and merit and is ever open to us in Christ as long as we desire it with all our hearts".[8] This must not be taken to imply that by the office of the law men are only admonished to depart from their false ways and to

[1] *CR* 47, 124   [2] *CR* 50, 603.
[3] *In.* II, 7, 1.   [4] *In.* III, 2, 32.
[5] As regards Calvin's idea of a threefold use of the law as contrasted with a twofold office of the law cf. A. Göhler, *Calvins Lehre von der Heiligung*, pp. 117 f.
[6] *In.* II, 7, 6.   [7] *In.* II, 7, 8.   [8] *Ibid.*

enter the right path. No, they obstinately cling to belief in their own powers; but in spite of that the law fulfils its function and reaches its goal. It arouses in men such terror of the judgment of God "that even against their own will they are attracted to the Mediator".[1]

But this is not the sole function of the moral law. It has a normative as well as a pedagogic significance. "Moses has well taught that the law which for sinners can only spell death is meant to have a better and more admirable purpose for the saints."[2] The law reminds us of the covenant which God has ratified with us and thus belongs to the essential life of the church. "It has its place among believers in whose hearts the spirit of God is already working to guide and inspire."[3] In this respect the law has its special function to fulfil. It is a "lamp to our feet so that we do not depart from the right way",[4] and shows us the goal towards which our life must be directed.[5] As long as we live in this world we must ever be reminded that God is our Saviour and Lord, and we need the summons and the claim mediated to us by the Word of God. The law performs this office of instruction and admonition.[6] When we accept this service and recognize in the law the gracious invitation of God to take upon us the yoke of the covenant which He has established with us, then we can walk in comfort under the law. For we then see it in closest connexion with Jesus Christ.[7] In Him the law has completed its function of judging and punishing, and this has effected the final fulfilment of the law and of the will of God which it represents. For our sakes, and in the sight of God, Jesus Christ walked in the way prescribed by the law; and now we must allow the law to invite us simply to follow in His footsteps. If we are thus taught and exhorted by the law, then the promises which are subjoined to the law gain significance for us: "For as God gives us all things of His free grace, so also among other things He confers on us this benefit: that He does not reject our imperfect obedience, but overlooking its defects he accepts it as perfect and on the

---

[1] *In.* II, 8, 1. [2] *In.* II, 7, 13. [3] *In.* II, 7, 12.
[4] *OS* I, 394. [5] *In.* II, 7, 13. [6] *In.* II, 7, 12. [7] *Ibid.*

score of it allows us to enjoy all the good which He has promised in His law."[1]

4. FREEDOM FROM THE LAW

Because God in Christ has made us His children, the service which is required of us under the law is no servitude. Rather through the law we are called to walk in the freedom of the sons of God. This freedom becomes effective in three directions.

As long as we are under the dominion of sin we are slaves. The law holds before our eyes the righteousness of God and exposes our sin, showing that it means for us corruption and death. But we must not remain imprisoned by the law. We must think of Him who for our sakes has taken upon Himself the punishment of the law.[2] We must accept the faith that the law has been fulfilled by Jesus Christ. Hence when we wonder how we can stand before God we must rise beyond the bounds of the law and forget all its righteousness.[3] "But when consciences are disquieted as to how they can find God gracious, what they are to answer and what can be the ground of their confidence, when they are summoned before the judgment seat of God, then they should not begin to calculate the requirements of the law but must plead as their righteousness the one Christ who surpasses all the perfection of the law."[4] In this sense Calvin admits the saying that the law is cancelled for believers; "not indeed in the sense that it no longer commands them to do what is right but that from henceforth it no longer possesses the authority which it did formerly, that it can no longer cause their conscience to torment them with terrors, and has no more power to condemn them finally".[5] Because Christ has fulfilled the demands of the law we are free from their coercive power and from the curse which every trespass entails.[6]

This aspect of Christian freedom implies the second, viz. "that consciences do not render obedience because compelled

[1] *In.* II, 7, 4. [2] *In.* II, 7, 15. [3] *In.* III, 19, 2.
[4] *Ibid.* [5] *In.* II, 7, 14. [6] *In.* II, 7, 15.

by the constraint of the law but are freely obedient to the will of God after being released from the yoke of the law".[1] Because Christ has taken our place we are able not only to live but also to act under the law. We know that God does not judge us according to our performance but is pleased to accept our service for the sake of Christ. The much discussed activism of Calvin is rooted in the fact that we belong to Christ and thus can go our way free from care and confess our membership in Christ; but it does not arise from any zealous desire to prove one's Christian life by good works. "Those who remain fettered by the yoke of the law are like slaves to whom certain daily tasks are assigned by their master. For they are worried about how little they have done and do not dare to come before their master unless their allotted daily tasks are completed. But children who are treated more gently and considerately by fathers are not afraid to show work which is only begun or half completed, or which has certain defects, because they trust that their obedience and willingness of heart will give pleasure even though they have not performed as much as they wished. We must be such children and have confidence that our obedience will be well pleasing to the Father in His mercy, however slight, frail, and imperfect it is. . . . Such trust is very necessary to us; for without it all our efforts will be in vain."[2]

"The third aspect of Christian liberty is that, in the sight of God, we are not under any obligation about outward observances which in themselves are matters of indifference, so that we are in a position to use them or not as we please."[3] In Christ God has made all things ours. Thus "we are to use the gifts of God without scruples of conscience or inward disquiet for the purpose for which they have been given us. By such confidence we have peace with Him and recognize His goodness towards us". There are no exact prescriptions about the ceremonies of the right form of divine worship and the outward order of the church, and hence the various rites which are of course requisite for the edification of the church

[1] *In.* III, 19, 4.   [2] *In.* III, 19, 5.   [3] *In.* III, 19, 7.

99

are not necessary to salvation.[1] In the observance of such externals, however important, there must be no superstition.[2] In any case they may not be substituted for the Word of God, for Jesus Christ in whose service they are intended to function. There are no intrinsically holy things, customs, seasons, or days; but naturally we may use whatever serves the edification of the church.[3] In this connexion it is to be noted that we are free from the ceremonial cult of the old covenant.[4] The sacrifices and ceremonies which the law prescribes were valid only until the advent of Christ and have been annulled by that event.[5] Were we to use them, we should be obscuring the clarity with which Christ has enlightened us by the use of types and shadows.[6]

What is true of the ceremonies of the Old Testament cult applies even more to the ordinances of the Mosaic law, which were meant to regulate the political life of the Jewish people. Even though such ordinances are connected with the divine law of love, they are to be distinguished from it.[7] In that form they were given only to the people of Israel.[8] Other nations are not involved in the political ordinance of the Old Testament law.[9] But their emancipation means also subjection to the command of love, to the essential content of the divine law.[10]

From all this it should have become clear that Calvin does not teach in the strict sense an abolition of the law. In this regard he is at one with the New Testament witness. Because he interprets the law exclusively in the light of Christ there can be no question of its annulment. Jesus Christ is the heart of the law. For this reason, while we are free from the curse and compulsion of the law, from its ceremonies and political ordinances, we remain bound to its inner content. Christ came precisely in order to fulfil the law and in view of our transgressions to provide relief. "Hence the doctrines of the law remain untouched by Christ,

---

[1] *In.* IV, 10, 30.   [2] *In.* IV, 10, 32.   [3] *Ibid.*
[4] *In.* II, 7, 16.   [5] *Ibid. CR* 26, 209; 245; 48, 190; 55, 89, 364.
[6] *In.* II, 7, 16; *CR* 48, 219.   [7] *In.* IV, 20, 15.
[8] *In.* IV, 20, 16.   [9] *In.* IV, 20, 15; *CR* 28, 63.   [10] *In.* IV, 20, 15.

for these doctrines by their warnings and admonitions and instruction are meant to prepare and dispose us to every good work."[1] When the New Testament speaks of the law as storing up wrath and slaying man, "the law is not thereby despised or anything detracted from its glory".[2] If the law fulfils the function of the stern judge against us, the fault is our own. "It is clear that through our own wickedness we are prevented from knowing that blessedness which is openly offered in the law."[3] Hence in any event "the law remains valid if regarded in itself; but by the guilt of man it has come about that the covenant of the law has been superseded".[4] Again this does not imply that Calvin praises the glory and significance of the moral law while thinking lightly of the institutions of the Old Testament covenant, which has been replaced by the new. Certainly the ceremonies of the old covenant have been cancelled, but not "with regard to their meaning, only with regard to their use".[5] As the moral law remained unimpaired in its validity despite the disobedience of man, so the sacrifices and other arrangements of the covenant are not disparaged as a result of the infidelity of men. "But the fact that they were cancelled by the coming of Christ detracts nothing at all from their sanctity, in fact they have been exalted and enhanced thereby."[6] "In bringing an end to the use of the ritual Christ sealed its efficacy in His blood."[7] This Old Testament cultus proclaimed to the people of Israel the reality of the Christ.[8] That is its meaning and this meaning is still reflected in the Old Testament account of it. The same applies to the political aspect of the Mosaic law. Its abolition does not mean its rejection. The foundation of those rules which were given to the people of Israel for the purpose of regulating its political life is abiding.[9]

[1] *In.* II, 7, 14. [2] *In.* II, 7, 7. [3] *Ibid.*
[4] *CR* 39, 42. [5] *In.* II, 7, 16; *CR* 50, 354. [6] *In.* II, 7, 16.
[7] *Ibid.* [8] *Ibid.* [9] *In.* IV, 20, 15.

THE THEOLOGY OF CALVIN

This concludes our exposition of the main features of Calvin's teaching on the law; but to it we must add a word about the question of the law of nature. In this connexion we are faced once more by the problem which we considered in our discussion of the question of natural theology. Calvin gives the same answer in both cases.

"Those things which we have to learn from the two tables of the law reflect to some extent and enable us to understand that inner law which is written and as it were impressed upon the hearts of all." [1] Such is Calvin's teaching in commenting on the apostle Paul. Man has not merely a dark surmise of the will of God but by the law of nature is sufficiently instructed how to live rightly. [2] "This instruction is carried out by the voice of conscience. As a seed of religious awareness is implanted in the heart of man so that he may recognize and honour his Lord, so conscience is given him that he may sufficiently distinguish between right and wrong. [3] The activity and insights of conscience are the language in which the law of nature is couched." [4]

The law of nature has only one purpose: namely, to make man inexcusable before God. [5] Since it becomes manifest in the dictates of conscience, the latter too has no other object but that of depriving man of the pretext of ignorance and making clear his responsibility before the judgment of God. [6] All this, however, does not imply that in this way man can attain a real knowledge of the divine will. "As man is enclosed by the darkness of error, the natural law gives him scarce an inkling of the kind of service which is pleasing to God." [7] The ability to distinguish between good and evil has ceased to be healthy and intact in the mind of fallen man. [8] While not completely effaced it has become so paralysed and corrupted "that only miserable broken fragments of it still appear". [9] It is for this reason that we have not the capacity

[1] *In.* II, 8, 1.   [2] *In.* II, 2, 22.   [3] *Ibid.*   [4] *Ibid.*
[5] *Ibid.*   [6] *In.* II, 2, 22; 8, 1; III, 19, 15.
[7] *In.* II, 8, 1.   [8] *In.* II, 2, 24; *CR* 35, 74.   [9] *In.* II, 2, 12.

within ourselves to know the chief features of the first table of the law.[1] But even with regard to the second table we cannot rightly reach the truth. In any event the natural man is unable to realize that his covetous desires point to the rottenness of his condition. "The light of nature is long extinguished before we gain any idea of this unfathomable gulf."[2] "It is more than enough that man's insight should reach so far as to deprive him of every excuse, and so, convicted by the testimony of his own conscience, to make him begin to tremble before the judgment seat of God."[3] Natural man is thus not relieved of his responsibility before God. He is rightly summoned before the bar of the divine judgment and condemned. This is the meaning of Calvin's arguments about the natural law imprinted on the soul of man. Conscience, in which the law of nature makes itself heard, does not on the other hand give sufficient indications to enable us to walk uprightly before God. It does not provide the starting point for a universal ethic which could develop into a Christian one.

In order to reveal His will to us and really to set us on the right way, God has given to us the written law.[4] This does not speak otherwise than the natural law; but it addresses us so decisively that we must hear it when it pleases God to open our hearts to its authority by the power of His Holy Spirit.[5] As sinners we constantly need to hear the divine demand and to be illumined by the light of the Holy Spirit. The emphasis on the natural law does not injure the law of God which is drawn up in Holy Scripture: on the contrary, it suggests to us the necessity of the divine law of the covenant which has its basis in Jesus Christ.

[1] *In.* II, 2, 24.   [2] *Ibid.*   [3] *Ibid.*   [4] *In.* II, 8, 1.
[5] *In.* II, 2, 25.

Chapter 7

THE OLD AND NEW TESTAMENTS[1]

I. STATEMENT OF THE PROBLEM

OBJECTIONS have again and again been raised to the doctrine of the law which we have just sketched out. Lutherans especially, but also Reformed Christians, have urged that Calvin's legalistic tendencies led him to blur the boundaries between the Old and the New Testaments.[2] "It is significant", says Wernle in his commentary on the *Institutes*, "that it was the Reformed Christians precisely who had a specially keen interest in this Christianization of the Old Testament. The Reformed Christians were the practical party in the Reformation movement; the New Testament was not sufficient for their ecclesiastical-political institutions; they were compelled to go back to its Old Testament background and hence needed a unified authoritative Bible. The evangelical national state church and the Christian state as ideally pictured by the Reformed Christians both rest upon the basis of Old Testament theocracy."[3] The modern theologian has so little understanding of Calvin's conception of the old covenant that at this point he is much more inclined to agree with the fanatics: "In his moral zeal, Calvin utterly denies the difference between the Old and the New Testaments, closes his eyes to all the new values which

[1] M. Simon: "Die Beziehung zwischen Altem und Neuem Testament in der Schriftauslegung Calvins", *Ref. Kirchenztg.*, 82, 1932, pp. 17 ff. H. H. Wolf, *Die Einheit des Bundes. Das Verhältnis von Altem und Neuen Testament bei Calvin*, Bethel, 1942.

[2] R. Seeberg: *Dogmengeschichte*, 4, 565 ff. A. Lang: *Johannes Calvin*, 1909, p. 75.

[3] P. Wernle: *Der evangelische Glaube*, III, *Calvin*, p. 268.

Jesus brought into the world, and degrades Him to the position of an interpreter of the ancient lawgiver Moses. How much more clearly the Baptists saw the truth in this respect." "The New Testament must be fitted in with the authority of the Old Testament; Christ is interpreted according to Moses." [1] Our reason for giving such extended quotations is that they have become widely regarded as of decisive importance. This is how people commonly think about Calvin's teaching on the law and his view of the Old and New Testaments.

A theologian such as Calvin does not understand the relationship of the two Testaments in such wise that he reads the Old into the New and vice versa. Certainly he uses the one to elucidate the other. But that is not the important thing. The decisive point is the recognition that the Old Testament promises what the New Testament offers to us in Christ.[2] The salvation of the saints of the Old Testament is founded, just as much as our own, in Jesus Christ.[3] Therefore in both cases what is in question is the one "body of Christ—the church"; the new covenant is no other than the old covenant instituted by God and broken by the people of Israel.[4] Christ is the foundation of the divine covenant to which both the Old Testament and the New bear witness.[5]

2. THE OLD TESTAMENT

If we consider the Old Testament by itself and enquire about its meaning we have to note the following: in Calvin's opinion the Old Testament does not reflect a primitive form of religion lower in degree than that of the New. It is not the expression of the religious laws and customs of the Jews, but from the first line to the last it preaches to us about Christ. "The law"—and in so saying Calvin does not mean merely the commandments but the whole corpus of so-called Mosaic religion—"was not laid down four hundred years after the

[1] P. Wernle, *op. cit.*, p. 13 and p. 30.   [2] *CR* 40, 395.
[3] *CR* 28, 288.   [4] *CR* 40 ff., 395 f.
[5] *CR* 48, 289; cf. *CR* 48, 569.

death of Abraham in order to lead the chosen people away from Christ, but rather in order to hold them upright until His coming, to stir up in them a religious zeal, and to strengthen them in hope lest they should languish and lapse through the long delay of His advent." [1] It is meant to maintain in the pious the expectation of the Christ that was to come. [2] The sacrifices and ceremonies served this end. "God did not ordain them in order to give His servants enough to do in earthly things, but rather to raise their minds to things above." [3] The same purpose was served by the strictness of the commands which caused them to look forward to Him who should perfectly fulfil them. [4] The kings and priests also of the Old Testament are, so to speak, mirrors in which the people can see reflected the one King and High Priest. [5] And the prophets were sent to prevent the people from becoming fettered to the cultus and commands as such; they were to guide the thoughts of the people to the one goal of all the doctrines and arrangements of the law: Jesus Christ. [6]

But the Old Testament does not merely in some vague sense adumbrate Christ; it proclaims Him in the strictest sense as the Mediator between God and man. He is the mirror in which the hidden God becomes visible to His people [7]; He is above all the Redeemer through whom alone the people could gain access to God. "When Jesus Christ was still not revealed in the flesh, He was already the Mediator, and all the patriarchs of old could approach God only when they were guided to Him by the Saviour and when the Saviour enabled them to find grace in the presence of God; and they could base their prayers only on the ground that they were pleasing to God because a Saviour was promised to them." [8] The efficacy of the one Sacrifice which He perfected is eternal, extending itself to all times. [9] The work of Christ is so decisively operative that even the destiny of those who were under the old covenant depends on it.

---

[1] *In.* II, 7, 1.   [2] *In.* II, 9, 1.   [3] *In.* II, 7, 1.
[4] *In.* II, 7, 2.   [5] *Ibid.*   [6] *In.* II, 7, 1.   [7] *In.* IV, 8, 4.
[8] *CR* 41, 555; cf. *CR* 41, 558; 44, 162; 50, 217, 224.
[9] *CR* 55, 118.

THE OLD AND NEW TESTAMENTS

Without Christ and His sacrifice all the promises of the Old Testament would be of no avail,[1] and the commands would bring death to their hearers. "Christ is the sustaining ground of the promises because in Him alone God the Father is gracious to us."[2] Christ belongs as much to the commands as to the promises.[3] The whole covenant of God with His sinful people is not only recognized as valid in Jesus Christ but is also centred in Him. In this sense the Old Testament as a whole proclaims the Christ.

3. THE NEW TESTAMENT AS DISTINCT FROM THE OLD TESTAMENT

The New Testament bears witness to this same Mediator Jesus Christ. But in contrast to the Old Testament its life-breath springs from the incarnation of the Son of God. "Those mysteries which the men of the Old Testament beheld in the form of shadows have been plainly revealed to us."[4] For this reason the Gospel may not be regarded as interchangeable with the promises of the old covenant. "The gospel in the proper sense is the solemn announcement of the revealed Christ in whom also the promises are fulfilled."[5] Because the New Testament declares to us the Christ who has come in the flesh, and the Old Testament Him who was to come in the flesh, Calvin is fond of elucidating the difference by saying that the New Testament is like a colourful picture whereas the Old presents the appearance of a shadowy outline.[6] In the *Institutes* Calvin has enumerated the differences, which on close examination he feels compelled to note between the two Testaments,[7] and we can therefore spare ourselves the trouble of mentioning them, especially as they are reducible to one—that between the clarity of the gospel and the obscurity of the word which was preached before the gospel.[8] But both Testaments testify to the same Word, both proclaim Jesus Christ, the one in one manner, the other

---

[1] *CR* 38, 407.　　[2] *CR* 50, 22.　　[3] *In.* II, 7, 2.
[4] *In.* II, 9, 1.　　[5] *CR* 49, 9.　　[6] *CR* 55, 121.
[7] *In.* II, 11; *OS* 3, 423 ff.　　[8] *In.* II, 9, 10.

in another manner.[1] Hence the differences which Calvin notes between the Old and New Testaments must not be misunderstood. If the New Testament proclaims Christ more clearly, it is not to imply that we now have Christ simply in our possession whereas the pious men of the Old Testament could only look forward to His coming. No; we too stand yet in hope.[2] We, like the people of Israel, are referred to the Word and to the Holy Ghost who makes this Word a living reality to us. "In so far as we accept Christ we do not possess Him otherwise than cloaked in His promises. Hence it is that while He dwells in our hearts we may walk far from Him because we walk by faith and not by sight."[3]

On the other hand it must be said with regard to the Old Testament that its function was not confined to that of foreshadowing Christ as the Mediator. Christ was truly presented and imparted to hearers through its words.[4] For the saints of the old covenant, as for us, these words were confirmed by sacramental signs which sealed the promises.[5] In this way the patriarchs ate the same spiritual food and drank the same spiritual drink as we Christians; and this was Christ.[6] Further, the Old Testament did not have this significance for the people of Israel only; it is given to us also for the same purpose. We say this not merely with reference to single parts but also with reference to the Old Testament as a whole. In discussing the problem of the law we saw that the Old Testament accounts of sacrifices and cultus have not lost their significance. "Although the ceremonies are no longer in use, their essential truth is still valid for us through the person of Him on whom their fulfilment depends."[7] The Old Testament is neither a superseded book as far as we are concerned, nor is it merely of auxiliary use enabling us to understand the New Testament better. We possess the Old Testament solely because it awakens in us faith in Jesus Christ. In that purpose the Old Testament is at one with the New.[8]

[1] CR 40, 396.   [2] CR 55, 121.   [3] In. II, 9, 3.
[4] In. I, 9, 3; CR 39, 64.   [5] In. II, 10, 6.   [6] In. II, 10, 5.
[7] CR 9, 747.   [8] CR 48, 569.

THE OLD AND NEW TESTAMENTS

4. THE JUXTAPOSITION OF THE TWO TESTAMENTS

The juxtaposition and succession of the two Testaments emphasizes the fact that they do not aim at giving us religious and moral instruction, or holding ideals before our minds, but at testifying to the Word which at a given moment in the history of the world became flesh. For this reason there is a before and after. Since at that moment not just any event, nor even a merely momentous event, took place in the history of humanity, but rather God's only begotten Son entered the world, the time before just as much as the time after was shaped by the operation of the event itself. But this must be rightly understood. Had Jesus Christ been only a man, a religious personality of the greatest dimensions, then His coming might well have been surmised in advance. But this is not what is meant when we say that the action of Jesus Christ shaped the time which preceded Him. What is meant is rather this: because the Incarnate Word is God, His efficacy is not restricted to our own Christian era. Hence He could already by the word of His witnesses and the sacramental cultus draw near to the saints of the old covenant and bestow Himself upon them. For this reason the Old Testament does not merely reflect a people's religious consciousness nor its words simply point as signposts to the one Word; rather they communicate the reality of that Word to the hearers when the Holy Ghost renders the latter responsive. If any one interprets the Old Testament otherwise, he is forgetting in his blindness that Christ "was true God who from the beginning and without intermission has spread the wings of His grace".[1]

[1] *CR* 9, 305.

Chapter 8

THE MEDIATOR [1]

THE insight which we have just expressed brings before us the mystery of the person of Jesus Christ.

Calvin considers that the Old Testament and the New Testament form in the strictest sense one single testimony to Christ. As we have tried to show, all the truths which Calvin expounds in his theology have thus but one end—to make intelligible to us the revelation of God in Jesus Christ. In the course of the history of theology many different ideas have been entertained about the person of Jesus Christ, and so it is not surprising that people have variously understood and appraised, also, what Calvin teaches about Jesus Christ. Thus, for example, in one of the most recent works on Calvin, Christ is understood as one of the peculiar tones of the gospel, a manifestation of the gracious attitude of God who says "Yes" to the sinner.[2] If after all that Calvin has so far taught us about Jesus Christ we feel a certain mistrust of such an interpretation as this, it is incumbent upon us at this point to go specially into the question as to who that One is around whom the entire thought of Calvin revolves.

The 12th chapter of the second book of the *Institutes*, where Calvin begins to develop his Christology, begins with the sentence: "That dogma has always been considered of the

---

[1] Max Dominicé; *L'humanité de Jésus d'après Calvin*, Paris, 1933. *Idem*, "Die Christusverkündigung bei Calvin" ("Jesus Christus im Zeugnis der Hl. Schrift und der Kirche", Supplement 2 to *Ev. Theologie*, Munich, 1936, pp. 223–53). E. Emmen: *De Christologie van Calvijn*, Amsterdam, 1935.

[2] E. Mülhaupt: *Die Predigt Calvins*, p. 120.

highest importance which states that he who was to be our Mediator is true God and true man." [1] Thus Calvin agrees with the confession of the ancient church: Jesus Christ is "true God and true man". What does this mean?

I. TRUE GOD

"To be sure, all would have been hopelessly lost if the divine Majesty had not condescended to come down to us, seeing that we are not in a position to reach upwards to it." [2] We have already in passing touched on this point: if Jesus Christ is to mean anything decisive to us, we must encounter in Him the majesty of God and find in Him the One "who is truly our God".[3] If we ask the reason for this, the sentence from the *Institutes* just quoted does not give any adequate answer. Why cannot we in our own powers reach the heights of the majesty of God? Why must the Infinite condescend to our own sphere if there is to be any encounter between it and ourselves? Calvin gives the following reasons:

"Firstly", he says in his Commentary on 1 Peter 1, 20 ff., "we have to bear in mind the greatness of the divine glory and the wretchedness of our own minds." [4] Peter Brunner thinks that Calvin in saying this is referring to the distance and the cleavage between God and man. If that be so, we should have to understand the first reason which Calvin urges in proof of the divinity of Jesus Christ in the following way: by reason of man's creaturely status there is a gulf between God and man which cannot be bridged from man's side. Hence God must Himself come down to us if we are ever to attain fellowship with Him.

We do not wish to dispute that the thought of the distance between Creator and creature plays its part when Calvin speaks of the majesty of God as contrasted with our own wretchedness. But it is questionable whether this thought alone is intended. For we must observe that in the *Institutes* Calvin expresses himself in quite similar terms as follows:

[1] *OS* 3, 437, 3.   [2] *In.* II, 12, 1.   [3] *CR* 53, 327.
[4] *CR* 55, 226; quoted after P. Brunner, *Vom Glauben bei Calvin*, p. 74.

"The majesty of God is far too high for mortal men, who crawl as it were like little worms upon the earth, ever to be able to attain unto it." [1] Here Calvin is speaking not of the distance between Creator and creature but of the fissure in creation caused by the Fall, and of the creature in consequence being burdened by the punishment of death. When Calvin says that God Himself must meet us in Christ because we ourselves cannot bridge the gulf which exists between Creator and creation, he is no doubt thinking of the radical distinction between God and His creatures. At the beginning of the Christological section of the *Institutes* it is said specifically: "Even though man had remained without any taint of sin, yet he is too limited ever to be able to come to God without a Mediator." [2] But Calvin cannot separate from this insight the other—namely, that this gulf is for us to-day a gulf between the Creator and a fallen creation. "How could man help himself when by the shameful fall he was degraded to death and hell, sullied with so many stains, fetid with his corruption, and wholly in the power of the curse?" [3] Hence God must Himself take the initiative and come to us; because the distance between Creator and creature, which in itself is unbridgeable by man, has become as a result of the Fall an impassable gulf.

In a third line of argument Calvin shows further how everything depends on the true divinity of Christ. In the Commentary just quoted on 1 Peter after speaking of the greatness of the divine majesty and our own wretchedness, he adds: "Sin which reigns in us makes us hateful to God and Him to us. As soon as God is in question, fear inevitably grips us. When we now approach Him, His justice is like a fire which utterly consumes us." [4] Now this implies: sin not only creates a cleavage between God and ourselves but actually widens it ever more and more. [5] Instead of engaging at all in the prospectless attempt to find God, we rather flee before Him. Any encounter between Him and ourselves can only come about if He confronts us in our path. How

[1] *In.* II, 6, 4.   [2] *In.* II, 12, 1.   [3] *Ibid.*
[4] See p. 111, note 4.   [5] Cf. P. Brunner, *op. cit.*, p. 77.

necessary is such a condescension of God becomes especially clear to us when we consider what it means to close the gap which is continually being widened by ourselves. Christ must be true God, "for his office was to overcome death. Who could have done so but life itself? His function was to conquer sin. What could do so except righteousness itself? It was incumbent upon Him to destroy the world rulers and the powers of darkness. What could do so except the power which ruled over them? In whom now is eternal life, righteousness, and the ultimate dominion over heaven and hell except in God alone? The infinitely merciful God became our Saviour in the person of His only begotten Son for the reason that He willed to rescue us from our plight." [1]

2. TRUE MAN

But Calvin lays no less stress on the other aspect of the matter: Jesus Christ is "true man".

Not without reason does Paul assert so emphatically, when he wishes to present Christ as the Mediator, that He is true man. "Because the Holy Spirit who speaks through Paul is so well aware of our weakness, He has used a suitable means of healing in order to meet its needs and has placed the Son in our midst as one of ourselves." [2] In the man Jesus Christ, Calvin means to say, "God, to bring Himself within the reach of human understanding, humbles Himself and makes Himself small." [3] Only because of the fact that God condescends to dwell upon this earth and to take humanity unto Himself have we easy access to Him. [4] This self-mortification of the divine means a concealment of His revelation. "We cannot behold God in the splendour of His majesty." [5] "The effulgence of the being of God is so excessive that it dazzles our eyes until it shines upon us in the face of Jesus Christ." [6] "Christ veils the majesty of God which otherwise would be

---

[1] *In.* II, 12, 2.   [2] *In.* II, 12, 1.
[3] *CR* 55, 227; quoted after Brunner, *op. cit.*, p. 75.
[4] Cf. *In.* IV, 17, 8.   [5] *CR* 53, 34; see Brunner, *op. cit.*, p. 69.
[6] *CR* 55, 12; see Brunner, *op. cit.*, p. 68.

terrible to us, so that it is manifest to us only as grace and fatherly kindness."[1] Calvin suggests that Christ must become true man since God can only draw near to us in that disguise without annihilating us. Hence the veiling of the revelation is to be understood as a sign of the goodness of God. Only in the second place does it happen in order to humble the pride of men and compel them to absolute surrender: "Men in their pride are ashamed of the lowliness of Christ; they aspire upwards to the unfathomable Godhead. And yet no faith attains to the heights of heaven except that which subjects itself to the Christ who discloses His divinity under the lowliest forms; and never will faith be firm until it seeks support in the weakness of Christ."[2] Of course the arrogance of man must be humbled to the dust by the Child in the manger; but it must be noted that this humiliation of man before the Incarnate must take place only in order to make clear to him the sole foundation of faith. Thus we may conclude that it is the divine love which triumphs in the condescension of God taking upon Him our flesh.

The second reason which Calvin urges for the necessity of the true humanity of Christ is the following: the fact that we encounter God in human flesh is an important pledge of our destiny to be related to Him. "We trust that we are the children of God because the eternal Son of God accepted a body like our body, became flesh of our flesh and bone of our bone", "so as to affirm His solidarity with us".[3] The true manhood of Jesus Christ is the presupposition for our communion with Him and so for our salvation. Because the Son of God has become one with us, in communion with Him there can be an exchange between what properly belongs to us and what properly belongs to Him.[4] By the brotherhood which the Son of God establishes between Himself and us in becoming man, the eternal inheritance which is His own is guaranteed to us also as our possession.[5]

The encounter between God and ourselves and our fellow-

---

[1] *CR* 55, 56; see Brunner, *op. cit.*, p. 69.
[2] *CR* 47, 322; see Brunner, *op. cit.*, p. 71.
[3] *In.* II, 12, 2.   [4] *In.* IV, 17, 2.   [5] *In.* II, 12, 2.

ship with Him implies that our hostility towards Him shall cease. At this point only we see the meaning of the true humanity of Jesus Christ in all its depth. Our Lord "has assumed the person of Adam and taken his name in order that in his place He might render obedience to the Father and offer our flesh as a ransom to the just judgment of God, and in the same flesh bear for us the punishment which we deserved".[1] By taking upon Him our flesh the Son of God substitutes Himself for us. He bears the punishment for our violation of the majesty of God and shows Himself obedient to the will of God as though it were we ourselves who performed all that. The true humanity of the Son is indispensable to His work of salvation. But in this connexion we see how difficult and dangerous it is to consider the true humanity of Jesus Christ in isolation from His divinity. For the work of Christ consists essentially in the fact that He bears the punishment of death which was to fall upon us. That implies according to Calvin: "Because God alone cannot suffer death and man alone cannot overcome it, therefore Christ unites the human with the divine nature, so that for the atonement of our sins He may subject the weakness of the one to the power of death and in the strength of the other may endure the struggle with death and obtain victory for us."[2]

3. UNITY BUT NOT FUSION OF THE TWO NATURES

It will not do at all to introduce a dualism into the person of Christ—true God and true man[3]; rather His two natures are closely bound up together. Calvin sharply opposed the heresy of Nestorius. The idea of a dualist Christ is not permissible.[4] Jesus Christ is not on the one hand God and on the other, and in isolation from the first fact, man also; rather, whatever distinctions are to be made, "the truth is that both natures are so closely bound up together that Jesus Christ is one Person only".[5] "If Jesus Christ had not

[1] *In.* II, 12, 3.   [2] *Ibid.*   [3] *In.* II, 14, 4.
[4] *Ibid.*; *CR* 46, 109.   [5] *CR* 46, 110.

assumed a human body, or had kept His Godhead in separation from it, where would be to-day our chances of salvation? But since He was both God and man in one, and the two natures are united, look—we can come boldly to Him and reckon Him as our brother, without doubting that He will own us as members of His body." [1]

We have already seen how intransigently Calvin, in view of this fact, holds fast to the one Christ and describes the divine being in Himself, honoured by Turks and Jews, as an idol. But he notices too a neglect of the fact of the Incarnation within the church itself. He finds in the scholastic theology of the Roman Church a speculation about God which is dissociated from revelation, and criticizes it as follows: "All thought about God which does not proceed from the fact of Christ is a fathomless abyss which utterly engulfs our faculties. A clear example of this is furnished not only by Turks and Jews who under the name of God worship their fantasies but also by the Papists. The principle of their theological schools, that God in Himself is the object of faith, is generally known. Hence they philosophize at length and with much subtlety about the hidden majesty of God while overlooking the fact of Christ. But with what result? They get entangled in curious and delusive ideas, so that their error has no limits." [2] These unequivocal statements make it clear that Calvin pursues a theology of revelation, that he thinks God is only to be found by us in Jesus of Nazareth, true God and man, and that there can be no question of separating the Godhead of Jesus Christ from His manhood.

But that is only one side of the question. The other must at least equally firmly be kept in view: there must be no fusion of the Godhead and manhood. "The confession that the Word became flesh is thus not to be understood as if it were transformed into flesh or fused with the flesh, but in the sense that it chose for itself from the body of the Virgin a temple in which to dwell; and thus He who was the Son of God

[1] *CR* 46, 110.

[2] *CR* 55, 226; see Brunner, *op. cit.*, p. 74. Cf. *In.* II, 6, 4; III, 2, 1; *CR* 26, 427; 47, 321 ff.

became a Son of Man not by a confusion of modes of existence but by the unity of His person. That is to say that according to our belief His divinity became conjoined and united with His humanity in such wise that each of the two natures constantly kept its distinct qualities, and yet one Christ arose from the union of both." [1] Right and necessary as it is that theology should be a strictly revelational theology and should unambiguously declare that God is to be found only in Jesus Christ, yet it must never come to the point of so emphasizing the unity of the Person as to destroy the distinctness of the two natures. [2] "The error of Eutyches must be rejected just as much as that of Nestorius. If it is not noted that the one Person of Christ consists of two natures, so that the characteristics of each remain intact, [3] then we are taught the existence of a hybrid thing which is neither God nor man." [4] Such a fusion of divinity and humanity in Jesus Christ would have serious consequences, as follows:

Firstly: the humanity of Christ would no longer be a true humanity if it participated in the characteristics of His divinity. The human nature conceived as the bridge built by God to reach us would be destroyed, the gracious condescension of God to our sphere of life would be called in question. But, above all, that community between Christ and men would be imperilled in virtue of which there can be an interchange between Him and ourselves and we can receive all that He has done for us. [5] From this it becomes obvious that Calvin does not object to the transference of the divine in Christ to the human on the ground that it would be incompatible with the laws of our thought. Calvin is no rationalist. His objections to the Christology of a Eutyches, as also to that of the Lutherans, have another basis. He sees that our salvation is jeopardized if Jesus Christ had not truly been such a man as we are. So far as we are concerned, everything depends on the true manhood of Jesus Christ.

[1] *In.* II, 14, 1.   [2] *In.* II, 14, 4.   [3] *In.* IV, 17, 30.
[4] *Ibid.*   [5] *In.* IV, 17, 29.

Secondly: by a fusion of the divinity and humanity in Christ His true Godhead would similarly be threatened.[1] It would then be a question whether God Himself were to be found in Christ or only divine powers. In that way again our salvation would be imperilled.

4. GOD REVEALED IN THE FLESH

Calvin has attempted to make quite clear that in Jesus Christ and in Him alone we encounter the revelation and the incarnation of God, but—it must be stressed—the revelation of *God*. He says that when we are thinking of God's revelation in Jesus Christ we must not be understood to mean "that the Godhead left the heavens in order to confine itself to the chamber of Christ's body, but that although it filled all things yet it dwelt corporeally precisely in the humanity of Christ, i.e. dwelt therein both naturally and ineffably".[2] The Godhead of Christ fills all things and while not being restricted to the manhood of Christ yet dwells within it.

The paradoxical principle: God wholly within Jesus of Nazareth and yet wholly outside Him, was termed later the *Extra Calvinisticum*. The above-quoted passage is to be found as early as the first edition of the *Institutes* of 1536, in the course of a discussion concerning the Lutheran doctrine of the Last Supper. Thus Calvin embraced this thesis from the very beginning. A second and more considered expression of it comes at the end of the debate with the Anabaptist Menno Simons which was added only in the edition of 1559: "Wondrous is the Son of God who descended from the heavens and yet did not leave them. In a wonderful manner He was willing to be born in the body of the Virgin, to dwell upon earth, to die on the cross, so that He might fill all things as He has done from the beginning."[3] With such statements Calvin radically rejects the idea of any mingling of humanity and divinity in Christ. The Godhead is not merged in the manhood of Christ. For our salvation it

[1] *In.* II, 14, 7.   [2] *In.* IV, 17, 30.
[3] *In.* II, 13, 4; cf. *CR* 47, 62.

remains what it is eternally. Hence as divinity it is also wholly without the manhood of the Son of God. It retains always its fundamental transcendence over human nature.

It might be objected that it is false to regard the *Extra Calvinisticum* as the most essential feature of Calvinistic Christology, as is customary. For the *Extra* of the Godhead is not expounded by Calvin in any positive doctrine but simply referred to in a very few passages arising in the course of debate with opponents. This objection is important. It is not the case that the *Extra* constitutes the centre of Calvinistic Christology. Calvin does not teach that God is to be found in Jesus Christ but is also to be encountered fully apart from Him. No; according to Calvin, God has disclosed Himself only in Jesus Christ and we must therefore hold fast solely to this One and not attempt to seek God outside the Mediator. But as a critical distinction the *Extra* has its value. In Jesus Christ we are faced not merely by enhanced nature, but the fact is that there God Himself stands revealed to us. Calvin expresses this unmistakably in the two passages quoted above, and he has repeatedly said the same thing elsewhere in speaking of the Person of Jesus Christ. "The Word chose the body of the Virgin as a temple in which to dwell." [1] Christ is—and the distinctive expression should be noted—"God revealed in the flesh." [2] It is this which must not be overlooked when we are speaking of Jesus Christ. There must be no fusion of the divinity and humanity, no destruction of the two distinct natures, because all depends on the truth that God disclosed Himself uniquely in Jesus of Nazareth, that eternity really entered time, and life this world of death. If we do not note this, if we make out of the "God revealed" the accessibility of God to man, if out of the unity of the two natures depending on the Person of the Logos we make their fusion, then our teaching endangers our salvation.

[1] *In.* II, 14, 1.   [2] *CR* 46, 110; 53, 327, etc.

Chapter 9

THE GRACE OF CHRIST WITHIN US[1]

THE goal of the theology of Calvin is Jesus Christ, because in regard to Him we must confess "God revealed in the flesh." It has become clear to us already in considering the doctrine of the Person of Jesus Christ that the revelation of God in the Mediator took place for our sakes and our salvation. It happened not in order to mediate to us the knowledge of a higher world but in order to save us from our lost condition. "In order that we might know to what end Christ was sent by the Father and what He has brought to us",[2] Calvin in the *Institutes* added to his teaching about the Person of Christ a special section on the Work of Christ in chapters 15–17 at the close of the second book. As we do not propose to give an account of all the doctrines of Calvin but rather to investigate the tendency of his teaching as a whole, it will be preferable to omit any consideration of this section. For what he has to say about the Work of Christ has inevitably been implied in his chapter on the Person of Christ.

I. COMMUNION WITH CHRIST

(*a*) At this point the question arises: "How can we become sharers in the grace of Christ?"[3] How can that which Jesus once was and effected be of decisive significance for us men of to-day? How can the interval of time between Him and ourselves be bridged? How can the work of another shape

---

[1] W. Kolfhaus, *Christusgemeinschaft bei Joh. Calvin*, Neukirchen, 1939.
[2] *In.* II, 15.　　　[3] *In.* book III.

our own destiny? "It must now be seen"—Calvin therefore begins his third book of the *Institutes*—"how the treasures which the Father has given to His only begotten Son are passed on to us, since He did not receive the same for His own benefit but that he might therewith enrich us who are poor and needy. And first we must understand this: as long as Christ is far from us and we dwell apart from Him, all that He has suffered and accomplished for the human race is useless and unavailing to us." [1] This gives us the first and fundamental answer to the question as to how we are to appropriate salvation.

Calvin asks how we can receive the merits which Christ has gained for us. But it is significant that in answering this question he does not in the first place speak of these merits but focuses our attention upon Christ. He has just been treating of His person and His office in several chapters, and now when the point arises about our appropriation of salvation and so the sequence of thought should be directed to ourselves at last, he just does not speak about us and our enrichment by these merits. Rather the theme is still Jesus Christ Himself. This has its good reason. The situation is not that Jesus Christ has obtained for us various benefits which are now simply there for us to seize. To be sure, what Christ has done has been done for our salvation. The merits He acquired were acquired not for His own use but for us. But in this respect it is to be noted that the Father has given these treasures to Him as the only begotten Son. He, the Son, possesses them. [2] Hence it is that just at this point of his theological reflection Calvin at once refers us to Christ.

On one occasion he described the position as follows: "When it is a question of the gifts of God which He offers to us of His free grace, it is my custom always to begin with Christ and rightly so; for we are necessarily devoid of all the gifts of grace, the abundance of which is hidden in the being of God until He becomes ours." [3] If we are thinking of the grace which God wills to bestow upon us it must be noted

[1] *In.* III, 1, 1.   [2] *Ibid.*   [3] *CR* 9, 88.

that we do not receive gifts of grace but the one gift, Jesus Christ. "For those gifts could never reach us if Jesus Christ had not already made us His own."[1] In other words, God's gift to us is not a something, not a power, not an improvement of our own nature. Nor does God give us part of His own being. Rather He imparts to us Himself, which means: He gives us Jesus Christ as our own. If we have Him then we have all things.[2] We are hostile and odious to God, "but if we are united to our Lord Jesus Christ as members of His body, then we cannot doubt that God numbers us among His children".[3] Communion with the Mediator produces a revolutionary change in our lives. "In the Person of Jesus Christ perfect salvation is found."[4]

(b) But the question of our appropriation of salvation is only in part answered by such considerations. The further question immediately arises: How then does Christ become our own? How does the Christ who is outside us become the Christ who is within us? The usual answer is: that comes about by faith. Calvin agreed with this answer.[5] He wrote a long chapter about faith in the *Institutes* and described Christ as the object of this faith.[6] But by faith in Jesus Christ very different things have been understood. The statement that we gain communion with Christ through faith needs elucidation: "It is true that we receive such communion through faith; since, however, it is clear that not all without distinction attain to that communion with Christ which is offered us in the gospel, we are inevitably led to go further and to enquire into the mysterious working of the Spirit through which it happens that we come to enjoy the presence of Christ and all His benefits."[7] If it is asked how the revelation of God in Jesus Christ becomes a living reality for us to-day, how we enter into relationship with the Mediator, it is not enough to point to faith as our "yes" to Christ. We cannot by our own insight recognize and accept the God

---

[1] *In.* IV, 17, 11; III, 2, 24; *CR* 6, 189. [2] *OS* I, 41, 88.
[3] *CR* 46, 436; 46, 358. [4] *In.* III, 1, 4. [5] *In.* III, 1, 1.
[6] *In.* III, 2, 1; 2, 32. [7] *In.* III, 1, 1.

revealed in flesh. We are not able in our own strength to establish a relationship with Him.

Hence at this point it is not sufficient simply to talk about faith, but it is necessary to go more deeply into the matter. If we are to attain contact with the reality of the God-man then this reality itself must seize upon us. We know what is meant by that. Calvin's doctrine of Holy Scripture in itself suggests what he must talk of at this point in his theology: "The Holy Spirit is the bond whereby Christ powerfully binds us to Himself." [1] When Jesus Christ stretches out His hand towards us and grips us, when He baptizes us with the Holy Spirit, we become participators in His life. [2] Our fellowship with Christ rests wholly upon an act of the exalted Lord Himself. Through His Holy Spirit He inspires in us the "yes" which we address to Him. He brings us to Himself and maintains us in communion with Him. This process is simply and without qualification a divine miracle.

(c) Provided all this is borne in mind it is legitimate to speak of faith in regard to the reaction of man. Faith is that surrender of ourselves to Christ which is the work of the Holy Ghost. It is "the fruit of a supernatural gift that those who otherwise would have remained petrified in unbelief should accept Christ in faith." [3] Thus it can be said without reservation that faith binds us to Christ, incorporates us in the body of Christ, [4] if only it is remembered that faith effects this spiritually, [5] that is, in the power of the Holy Ghost who inspires the attitude of faith.

If we spoke of faith otherwise and failed to understand it as man's response to Christ engendered by the Holy Spirit, then God Himself would not be bridging the gulf between Christ and ourselves and there would be no communion at all between the Mediator and us. If faith were only a human attitude, only the fruit of human insight and feeling, even though directed to the person and life of Jesus Christ, then what Christ has done for us would not help us at all. "Christ remains as it were without effect until our hearts are touched

---

[1] *In.* III, 1, 1.   [2] *In.* III, 1, 4.   [3] *Ibid.*
[4] *In.* III, 2, 30.   [5] *In.* II, 13, 2.

by the Holy Spirit; for we behold Christ as sluggish spectators outside ourselves and indeed far from ourselves. But we know that He saves only those whose Head He is and for whom He is the firstborn of many brethren; in short, those who have put on the Lord Jesus. Only this intimate union brings it about that He has not in vain accomplished the work of our salvation. This is suggested by the symbol of that holy marriage by which we become flesh of His flesh and bone of His bone and are utterly at one with Him. But it is only through the work of the Spirit that He unites Himself with us. By the work and power of the same Spirit we become the members of His body so that He feeds us with His life and again we possess Him as our own." [1] Hence we must conclude that "there can be no worse fate for us than to dwell outside of Christ and outside of faith in Him". [2]

Faith in itself has no value, no meaning for salvation. [3] It is nothing more than an empty vessel. [4] It acquires a saving significance only in relation to its content: Jesus Christ. In the life of faith we have all that is necessary to us, we have in faith communion with the Saviour Jesus Christ. But in no case must we entertain the error that faith is the matter of salvation itself. [5] Calvin sharply rejected the doctrine of Osiander that our union with Christ effects a merging of our being with His own. [6] It must be firmly maintained that the Holy Ghost is the bond which unites us with Christ. [7] The Holy Ghost proceeds from Christ and kindles faith in our hearts, thus bridging over the gulf between Him and ourselves. If we neglect this truth we fall into the error of supposing that there can be an immediate connexion between Christ and us. On the contrary, our fellowship with Christ depends utterly on the sovereign dispositions and authority of God. It is God who brings us into contact with the Mediator. But we remain what we are: men. And Jesus Christ remains what He is: the divinely Human Mediator. Were we in our Christian fellowship not to realize that this

[1] *In.* III, 1, 3. [2] *CR* 48, 543. [3] *In.* III, 11, 7; 2, 30.
[4] *In.* III, 11, 7. [5] *Ibid.* [6] *In.* III, 11, 5, 10.
[7] *In.* III, 11, 5.

distance between Christ and ourselves exists, then our whole salvation would be endangered. It would not be assured that our fellowship is really with the Mediator.

(*d*) It is in this sense that Calvin teaches the communion of the Head with the members, the indwelling of Christ in our hearts, the hidden union and the sacred marriage between Him and ourselves,[1] as the basis of our appropriation of the salvation which He has won for us. Again and again we find in the writings of Calvin the image of incorporation in the body of Christ.[2] He lays all possible stress upon that as the essence of salvation. By affirming that the process takes place through the activity of the Holy Spirit, he intends not to diminish but to secure our communion with Christ. The importance which Calvin attaches to this emphasis is to be seen from the following statement: "Christ is not simply united to us by an indissoluble bond of union but from day to day is increasingly knitted with us into one Body until He becomes utterly at one with us."[3]

This word "until" brings us face to face with an eschatological limit. Calvin does not think that we can gradually develop in this aeon towards a state of perfection. "If in this world you are united with our Lord Jesus Christ"—he writes in a letter—"and are a member of His body (since He took upon Him our flesh in order to establish full brotherhood with ourselves), and if you are living in obedience to His gospel which teaches us to seek all our bliss in Him, then you will reach the life promised to the faithful in so far as you wait for Him to resurrect us all to His glory at the last."[4] Communion with Jesus Christ is made a reality by the work of the Holy Spirit in this earthly life already and nevertheless it is subject to the "not yet" implied by the Day of Judgment. This eschatological reservation makes it clear that for Calvin the essential point is our relationship

---

[1] *In.* III, 11, 10: "coniunctio igitur illa capitis et membrorum, habitatio Christi in cordibus nostris, mystica denique unio; III,,1, 3: sacrum illud coniugium"; cf. *CR* 28, 94; 51, 186, etc.

[2] *In.* III, 11, 10; III, 2, 24.   [3] *In.* III, 2, 24.

[4] *CR* 12, 715.

with the living Lord Jesus Christ. That union of the faithful with Christ which Calvin teaches has nothing whatever to do with the absorption of the pious mystic into the sphere of the divine being. Precisely in this connexion Calvin proclaims the crucified and bodily risen Lord and Mediator who will come again at the last day to redeem His own. But this Lord is our Lord in present experience and we are His own children.

2. REGENERATION AND SANCTIFICATION [1]

We have seen that Christ is the one good which we receive; but we must now consider the gifts which in fellowship with Him are poured out upon us. Right from the start Calvin's answer to this was: we obtain through Christ the forgiveness of our sins and our sanctification,[2] or: justification and regeneration.[3]

(a) Regeneration

Christ becomes our living Lord and Saviour; we are incorporated into His body. The consequence of this is "that we live through His spirit and are also controlled by it".[4] When God seeks to have fellowship with us in Jesus Christ it is an event which must needs have repercussions upon our sinful way of life. Christ unites Himself to us that we might be faithful to Him; hence we must without question obey Him when He commands us.[5] The life which pleased us

---

[1] A. Lang: *Zwei Calvin-Vorträge: Rechtfertigung und Heiligung nach Calvin*, 1911 (*Beitr. z. Förder. christl. Theologie*, ed. Schlatter, Vol. 15, no. 6). Alfred Göhler: *Calvins Lehre von der Heiligung*, 1934. Hermann Strathmann: *Die Entstehung der Lehre Calvins von der Busse (Calvinstudien*, ed. Reform. Gemeinde, Elberfeld, 1909; pp. 187–245): *Calvins Lehre von der Busse in ihrer späteren Gestalt (Theol. Stud. u. Kritik*, 82, 1909; 402–47). Willy Lüttge: *Die Rechtfertigungslehre Calvins und ihre Bedeutung für seine Frömmigkeit*, 1909. Ch. Lelièvre: "La doctrine de la justification par la foi dans la doctrine de Calvin" (*Rev. de Théol. et de Phil.*, 1909, 699–701, 767–76). Wilhelm Niesel: "Calvin wider Osianders Rechtfertigungslehre" (*Zeitschr. f. Kirchengesch.*, 46, 1927, 410–30).
[2] *OS* I, 69.   [3] *In.* III, 11, 1.   [4] *CR* 55, 403.
[5] *CR* 28, 415.

when we were estranged from God must be renounced. We are claimed in an absolute sense by the Lord to whom by nature we are hostile. This sovereignty which Christ claims over the whole of our lives is one of the two gifts which flow from communion with Him. Calvin calls it rebirth or penitence or else renewal, sanctification, conversion.

In order to understand exactly what this gift implies for us we must realize that in fact it consists of two benefits: "Two things come to us through our communion with Christ. For as truly as we participate in His death, our old man is crucified by His power and the body of sin dies, so that the corruption of our first nature ceases to operate. In proportion as we participate in His resurrection we are awakened by it to newness of life corresponding to the righteousness of God. Hence I sum up the act of penitence by the one word rebirth, the object of which is that the image of God, which was defaced and almost blotted out by the transgression of Adam, should be renewed in us."[1] This change brought about in our life whereby the old man is slain and we are made a new creation is rooted in the fact of Jesus Christ.[2] He is the Crucified and Risen One and as such He brings us into communion with Himself. We must live as those who belong to the Crucified and Risen Lord. Because He accepted death as the wages of sin and offered up His life, the old nature common to all of us can no longer subsist but must perish. So we must be slain by the piercing sword of the Spirit and brought to nought.[3] But because Christ did not remain in the power of death, because He rose again, we also are awakened into a new creation. If He is "the most complete image of God", then "we shall be restored into His likeness so that we may bear the divine image in true godliness, righteousness, purity, and knowledge".[4]

In these considerations one point must be carefully noted. The role of Christ is not simply to set in motion a process of salvation within us when we encounter Him. No, He alone

---

[1] *In.* III, 3, 9.   [2] *In.* III, 3, 5.   [3] *In.* III, 3, 9.
[4] *In.* II, 15, 4.

127

has died the one decisive death and He alone has overcome death with the effect that in Him the divine image in man is restored. Our part is to share in His death and resurrection. In speaking of what Christ bestows upon us we may never speak merely of the gifts in themselves or of our own lives in so far as they are remoulded by those gifts, but we must ever keep well in view the *ex Christi participatione*. The death of the old man and the resurrection of the new is realizable only in the reality of the living Christ. It is not we who die and it is not we who are renewed, it is only in Christ that that can happen to us. Just in this teaching about rebirth, where we are most readily inclined to speak only of man, of his gifts and newness of life, Calvin's theology is strictly revelational. Here again he steadily holds in view the one Mediator who has all these gifts of life in perfection, and embodies what is imparted to us only derivatively.

This of course must not exclude the ideas which were expounded at the beginning. Christ is the Crucified and Risen One not in and for Himself. He does not remain aloof from us but He who once-for-all has experienced death and resurrection meets us to-day and really communicates to us those benefits which for our sakes He has obtained.[1] Our old man is seized upon and crucified by the power of the death of Jesus Christ. We are awakened into a new life by the power of His resurrection. This happens through the Spirit of Christ which binds us to Him and evokes in us faith and obedience.

At this point we must recall the eschatological character of Calvin's whole teaching about communion with Christ. Just as certainly as Jesus Christ alone will bring about the consummation, so certainly the change which He effects in our lives does not take place in a moment,[2] nor does it represent the beginning of a process of development by which man gradually attains the goal of perfection. It is rather that throughout our whole lives we must practise penitence.[3] We must ever anew make the decision to turn away from

---

[1] *In.* III, 3, 1.   [2] *In.* III, 3, 9.   [3] *In.* III, 3, 8.

ourselves to God. In this world where sin dwells within us, even though its dominion has been broken by Christ, we remain engaged in a constant struggle. Penitence, conversion, rebirth, brought about within us by the action of Jesus Christ, mean that He restores us men who are dead in our sins and summons us to militancy against sin. This state of affairs lasts our whole life long and only comes to an end with death.[1] No doubt in the struggle laid upon us there is the fact of progress. The process of sanctification is one of gradual growth. Christ really gains power over us. But all our advance is attended by tottering and limping and indeed crawling on the floor.[2] With time we are forced to recognize ever more and more our essential incapacity.[3] God exercises us daily in humility to prevent us from becoming proud and forgetting our dependence on grace.[4] We are to realize that the source and strength of the new life does not lie in ourselves, nor have we any security about the attainment of perfection. Such security is given us solely in Jesus Christ.[5]

It is for this reason that Calvin speaks in such a strange way about progress in sanctification. In this regard progress is properly the recognition of our lack of progress. Calvin says: "The more a man is marked by the spirit of holiness the more must he realize how far he is yet from the attainment of perfect righteousness, and is thus led to trust only in God's pure mercy."[6] Even in death we do not reach perfection,[7] which is not of course the fruit of any development inherent in ourselves but the gift of God. Death certainly frees us from sinful flesh. It signifies an important episode. After death we are released from struggle. Yet perfection is only granted to the faithful at the Last Judgment. After their bodily death they wait and watch for the return of their Lord[8] who will consummate their communion with

---

[1] *In.* III, 3, 8,   [2] *In.* III, 6, 5.   [3] *In.* III, 3, 10.
[4] *CR* 46, 360.   [5] *CR* 23, 36.
[6] *CR* 31, 317; see Alfred Göhler, *op. cit.* p. 52.
[7] Occasionally Calvin does say that God completes the work of salvation in us at death. Cf. *CR* 46, 360.
[8] Cf. Calvin's work: *Psychopannychia, CR* 5, 165 ff.

Himself and thus will bestow upon them the perfect life of heaven.[1] Both the beginning and the ending of the new life are at His disposal.

(b) Justification

We have already seen "that Christ who is given to us by the pure goodness of God is apprehended and appropriated by us in faith and that from our fellowship with Him two graces come to us: namely, that by His sinlessness we are reconciled with God and have in heaven a gracious Father instead of a Judge, and also that sanctified by His Spirit we aspire towards an innocent and pure life".[2] We have just been dealing with the second of these graces, that is, sanctification or regeneration. In his *Institutes* Calvin discusses this first, and only then writes his chapter on the other grace of justification. "For"—and this is his explanation of the curious sequence—"if we rightly acknowledge this truth (regeneration), it will be all the clearer how man is justified by faith alone and by nothing further than forgiveness, and how the holiness which is essential to the Christian life may not be divorced from that imputation of righteousness which is a gift of grace"[3]; that is to say (thus he adds in the French translation) "the two aspects are complementary: we are not devoid of good works and yet apart from good works are declared righteous".[4]

In other words: Calvin placed his doctrine of regeneration before his doctrine of justification in order from the start to forestall the objections of Roman theologians. To be righteous in the sight of God solely by faith—that was the message of the Reformation. But is not this doctrine of salvation by faith simply a soporific? Does it not make people careless and wanton? Calvin has already taught us that mere faith has no significance for salvation but that it acquires saving value only by reference to its object: Jesus Christ. But this Christ whom we receive in faith through the action of the Holy Spirit does not leave us undisturbed in our old manner of

[1] *CR* 33, 402; cf. Alfred Göhler, *op. cit.*, pp. 59 ff.
[2] *In.* III, 11, 1.   [3] *In.* III, 3, 1.   [4] *Ibid.*, cf. *In.* III, 11, 1.

life which was hostile to God, but attracts us into His own dying and rising again. Calvin emphasizes all this before speaking in detail about the fact that we are justified in the sight of God by faith alone. Thus he undermines the force of Roman Catholic polemic.

But at the same time the priority given to the doctrine of regeneration expresses something peculiar to Calvinistic theology. As we have shown, Calvin answers the question as to how we appropriate salvation by pointing to our communion with Christ. When such communion is actualized by the Holy Spirit, then we sinners are tensely confronted by the Crucified and Risen Lord. When Jesus Christ apprehends us we escape the bondage of death and are called to newness of life. Otherwise Jesus Christ would not be the Mediator of salvation. The fact that in all the gifts which we receive we are in the last resort always confronted by Christ the Giver is made especially plain by the order in which Calvin arranges these two doctrines of regeneration and justification. From this point of view there is no possibility of misunderstanding the doctrine of justification as a mere pious opinion about the relationship of man and God, leaving us unaffected ultimately in our inmost lives. It is not a question of a religious theory but of the living Lord Himself.

Provided this insight is safeguarded by the prior consideration of the doctrine of rebirth or penitence, it must certainly be said that the most important gift which flows to us from our communion with Christ is our justification in the presence of God. Calvin describes it as "the primary article without which religion cannot subsist".[1] Justification means that to us is imputed the righteousness which Jesus Christ has gained through His obedience unto death, and that thus "before the countenance of God we appear not as sinners but as though we were just".[2] That is possible because Christ bestows upon us communion with His life and we are members of His body. Thus God sees us in Christ and for His sake treats us as if we were righteous although we are not so

[1] *In.* III, 11, 1.   [2] *In.* III, 11, 2.

in ourselves.[1] Hence justification is not a question of making us righteous. It is rather an act of judgment on the part of God through which He recognizes the fact that we sinners have communion with the one righteous Man.[2] This judicial action of God can be viewed in two ways: as the forgiveness of our sins and as the imputation to us of the righteousness of Christ.[3] Of course it is not a question of two successive and diverse actions of God but justification as a whole is included both in forgiveness and in the imputation of righteousness. "God justifies by forgiving."[4] God removes from the accused the grounds of accusation.[5] Since in man himself there is no basis for such a judgment, God can only acquit him without condonation by attributing to him the righteousness of Jesus Christ.[6] He does not see us as we are, but causes us to become invested with the righteousness and purity of Christ.[7]

God declares righteous people who in fact are not so.[8] The ground of our justification "lies outside ourselves" "because we are just in Christ alone".[9] "This is a wondrous way of making just, so to clothe the lost with the righteousness of Christ that they are not afraid when faced by the judgment which they deserve, and while they themselves rightly condemn themselves, they find that they are declared righteous in virtue of some authority outside themselves."[10] The recollection of the fact that in Christ we are truly born again and in this life make progress in holiness does not help us at all in regard to the question how we can stand before God. We never achieve perfect obedience such as would enable us to appear just before God. On the contrary, we see that our sanctification discloses itself precisely in the fact that we realize how far we lag behind the ideal of true righteousness. Hence nothing remains for us to do "but to flee to Christ so that we may be declared righteous in Him—what we are not in ourselves".[11] Jesus Christ alone is the truly

[1] *In.* III, 11, 3.   [2] *In.* III, 11, 23; cf. W. Niesel, *op. cit.*, p. 426.
[3] *In.* III, 11, 2.   [4] *In.* III, 11, 11.   [5] *In.* III, 11, 3, 4.
[6] *In.* III, 11, 3.   [7] *In.* III, 11, 11.   [8] *Ibid.*; III, 11, 3.
[9] *CR* 7, 448; *In.* III, 11, 4; 14, 17.
[10] *In.* III, 11, 11.   [11] *CR* 7, 449.

righteous One. We are so only derivatively because God considers us righteous by virtue of our communion with Christ. Calvin's insistence that righteousness is to be found only outside ourselves, only in Christ, makes it clear that in his doctrine of justification, as in his doctrine of rebirth, his theology is through and through revelational.

This again becomes evident from the way in which Calvin describes the righteousness which is imputed to us. Here it is not a question of the eternal righteousness which Christ possesses in virtue of His divine nature. Calvin met that view in Andreas Osiander.[1] The righteousness which is attributed to us is rather that divine righteousness which Christ acquired for us by His obedience and especially by His death and resurrection.[2] Christ accomplished this work for us as the Mediator, that is, the incarnate Son of God. "For"—and this Calvin observes in his polemic with Osiander—"although Christ could neither have cleansed our souls with His blood nor reconciled us to the Father by His sacrifice, nor freed us from guilt nor have exercised the office of a high priest at all unless He had been true God—for the flesh would have been too weak to bear such a burden—yet it is certain that He did all that as man".[3] In any case the righteousness which Christ imparts to us cannot be divorced from His office as Mediator.[4] In order to illustrate this point Calvin refers to the sacraments, "which, although they focus our faith on the whole Christ and not merely on one aspect of the Christ, yet also teach us that the ground of our healing and salvation lies in His flesh; not that a mere man of himself makes us spiritually alive, but that it has so pleased God to disclose in the Mediator what in His own being was hidden and incomprehensible. Hence I am accustomed to say that Christ is like an open spring from which we may draw what otherwise in the hidden depths of that same spring which gushes out to us in the person of the Mediator would remain unavailable."[5] If on the other hand you adopt the view of

[1] Cf. W. Niesel, *op. cit.*, pp. 415, 411, 417.
[2] *In.* III, 11, 9, 7, 12.   [3] *In.* III, 11, 9.   [4] *In.* III, 11, 8.
[5] *In.* III, 11, 9.

Osiander that we are endowed with the eternal righteousness which Christ possesses in virtue of His divine nature, then we are missing the point of the revelation of God in Jesus Christ. In that case the God revealed in flesh and His saving work become insignificant. What Osiander says has the sole result of drawing simple souls away from Christ.[1] But the love of God towards us is not a fact that we could reckon with apart from Christ.[2] Hence a doctrine of justification which overlooks the God-man and His work imperils the foundations of Christian faith.

For this reason Calvin engaged in a fierce struggle with Osiander[3] and refused to have his attention diverted from the God revealed in flesh. The message of our justification is so comforting because the righteousness which is imputed to us by the verdict of God is not our own. Since God considers only the righteousness of Jesus Christ, we are completely, not partially, justified.[4] "We are without limit just before Him."[5] But the case would be quite different if God's verdict were to be based on the degree of new life existing in us. This would not help us at all. "For consciences are not quietened by any partial righteousness."[6] We would then remain before God in the desperate plight in which we find ourselves naturally.[7]

When Calvin, with the logical rigour of a revelational theology, teaches that the ground of our justification lies outside ourselves, we must not forget what we urged in our first section. The righteousness which lies outside us because Jesus Christ once gained it by His suffering and dying for our sakes would be of no use if it were not truly communicated to us in the present. We obtain righteousness in so far as the Righteous One is our Saviour. Thus, while the ground of our righteousness lies outside us in Christ, the Lord Himself "we do not regard as outside of and distant from us, in such a way that His righteousness is imputed to us in mechanical fashion, but we put Him on and are made members of His body, and

---

[1] *In.* III, 11, 5.   [2] *CR* 47, 342.   [3] *In.* III, 11, 6.
[4] *In.* III, 11, 11.   [5] *Ibid.*   [6] *Ibid.*   [7] *Ibid.*

He has deemed us worthy to be united with Him so that we may glory in being vitally linked with His righteousness".[1] We may not qualify the "outside of us" but He who once earned righteousness for our sakes is present in us by His word and spirit. By such union with Him we become clothed with His righteousness. Because we are sheltered by its authority we can stand as just without limit before God.

From the standpoint of this view of justification Calvin was able in his polemic with Roman Catholics to develop a special doctrine which we may not leave unnoticed. He was confronted with passages of Scripture which declare that "God is gracious and merciful to them that practise righteousness."[2] Such words seemed hardly compatible with the proof texts quoted in support of the Reformation doctrine of justification. Calvin did not leave them to his enemies but sought to understand them in the light of the Bible as a whole. He observes that divergent Scripture texts cannot be harmonized "if we fail to note that there is a twofold acceptance of Man with God".[3] We must distinguish justification granted to man in his estrangement from God and the justification which the believer needs during his lifetime. Hence there is a justification which pays no regard to the works of man and a justification in regard to which works are considered as the fruits of faith.[4] The grace of rebirth which man receives together with the grace of justification is a living reality. Although the sinner whom God accepts by grace is again and again in need of forgiveness, because he still lives in this world and bears the body of sin, yet in making a gracious judgment God beholds him in his ideally true situation. He does not forget the fact that the believer is being renewed by the Holy Spirit into the likeness of His Son. This reality is truer than the fact that sin still lives in him. "The Lord cannot fail heartily to love the good which His spirit brings to birth in believers."[5]

The works of the regenerate are acceptable to God in spite

[1] *In.* III, 11, 10.   [2] *In.* III, 17, 5.   [3] *In.* III, 17, 4.
[4] *In.* III, 17, 4, 5; cf. Göhler, *op. cit.*, pp. 93 ff.
[5] *In.* III, 17, 5.

of the ever necessary forgiveness of sins; but this does not mean that they are counted in the reckoning. It is the same with works as with persons. God cannot but be gracious to them, "because He looks not upon their intrinsic value but sees them as embraced by the merits of Christ".[1] Since even our best deeds are sullied by sin, they cannot count in the process of justification. "But after we have become sharers in the life of Christ, not only are we ourselves counted as righteous but our works also are reckoned as just in the eyes of God; for what is imperfect in them is covered by the blood of Christ."[2] The effect of our incorporation into Christ is so great that we are justified in our being as a whole, and thus our deeds become acceptable to God for Christ's sake.

By this doctrine of a twofold justification Calvin not only refuted the Scripture proofs of Roman theologians but also deepened his own view of the matter. He showed that not merely once but again and again we are thrown back upon the grace of God in Christ and that this grace really embraces us on every side. We have already explained, in discussing the law, the enormous importance for ethics of this doctrine of the "justification of works".[3]

Such, then, are the essential features of Calvin's doctrine of justification. It will have been noticed that we have hardly spoken of faith itself. Calvin treats of it in connexion with his account of our communion with Christ before he comes to deal with regeneration and sanctification. By contrast with the Catholic emphasis on works, Calvin certainly stressed the *sola fide*. But faith does not assume a central position in his description of justification. "For if faith by its own efficacy, as is said, made men righteous, it would do so only partially because it is always weak and imperfect. In that case righteousness would be mangled, giving us only a partial salvation."[4] It is dangerous to speak of faith with too much emphasis. It is always to be noted that faith justifies "because its effect is that we put on Christ, that He dwells in us and

---

[1] *In.* III, 17, 5.   [2] *CR* 49, 60; *OS* 4, 263, 7.
[3] See above p. 98 f.   [4] *In.* III, 11, 7.

that we become members of His body".[1] Christ is the ground for the divine judgment that we are righteous; faith is nothing more than an empty vessel, of which the purpose is to receive the decisive content—the God-man Jesus Christ.[2]

(c) The relation of regeneration and justification

It has been objected that Calvin simply juxtaposes the doctrines of justification and sanctification without setting them in immediate relation to each other. This criticism does not reflect upon Calvin so much as on the theologians who have expressed it and still do express it. They are over-looking the heart and centre of Calvinistic theology—namely, the fact that it is a theology of revelation, and hence all that he says is strictly concerned with the Mediator.

Of course it is not true that justification and sanctification have nothing to do with each other, or that we might even go so far as to dispense with one of these gifts of grace. When Jesus Christ bestows Himself upon us, then we receive salvation as a whole and a unity; we are made just before God without reservation, although we as men are and remain sinners. But when we thus reckon with the present reality of Christ, the other fact must not be forgotten—the fact that our old Adam must die daily and be resurrected as a new man who eternally lives before God in righteousness and true holiness. "He has been given to us for our righteousness, wisdom, sanctification, and redemption. Hence Christ makes no one just whom He does not also make holy. For these benefits are connected together by an eternal and indis-soluble bond."[3] "Just as Christ cannot be torn asunder in parts, so also these two things which we receive in Him simultaneously and together (*simul et coniunctim in ipso*), namely justification and sanctification, are never dissociated from each other."[4] Justification and sanctification are a reality in Jesus Christ and form in Him a living unity.[5] But

---

[1] *CR* 7, 599.   [2] *In.* III, 11, 7.   [3] *In.* III, 16, 1.
[4] *In.* III, 11, 6.   [5] *In.* III, 16, 1.

because "the Lord does not give us these benefits except in so far as He bestows Himself, He confers both of them simultaneously and never the one without the other".[1] Here it must be noted that we do not in the strict sense receive gifts, but the one gift, Jesus Christ Himself. If we do not appreciate and receive this gift in its full significance for ourselves, not only must our doctrine of sanctification or justification be perverse, but we destroy the value and meaning of that gift itself. When we attempt to separate sanctification from justification we are in fact seeking to break up the unity of the one Christ.[2]

But of course justification and sanctification are to be distinguished from each other,[3] and we shall be unable to distinguish them if our thinking does not stem from the Mediator but from one or other of those doctrines. When we try to establish a direct nexus between justification and sanctification, as did Osiander whom Calvin attacked particularly in this matter, the result is a fusion of the two which inevitably imperils the certitude of salvation. If God were to pronounce us just in consideration of the new life which is in us and will one day fill our souls completely, then we could not avoid asking whether we should ever be able to stand before God. "But God does not graciously accept us because He sees our change for the better, as if conversion were the basis of forgiveness; He comes into our lives, taking us just as we are out of pure mercy."[4] One basis and no other suffices for God's declaration that we are righteous. This one basis in which we can really take comfort is Jesus Christ. Also He alone is the guarantor of our sanctification. The two things—justification and sanctification—are one in Him but only in Him.

The teaching of Calvin that justification and sanctification are two aspects of the same process in our lives, and yet are not to be confused, has nothing at all to do with his gift for dialectics, as has been supposed; but rather it is deeply

[1] *In.* III, 16, 1.   [2] *Ibid.*; *CR* 7, 448; 49, 331.
[3] *In.* III, 16, 1; 11, 6.   [4] *CR* 39, 120.

138

grounded in the facts of spiritual experience. It is an indication that in his theology he is concerned to exalt the Mediator Jesus Christ. In this doctrine of justification and sanctification we are not simply faced by the general question: God and man; rather the fact is that here as elsewhere we have to do with the God revealed in flesh.

Chapter 10

THE LIFE OF A CHRISTIAN MAN[1]

THE fact that in Calvin's doctrine of justification and sanctification it is not a question of theoretical knowledge but of witnessing to the one living Lord, who adopts us as His own, becomes especially clear from one consideration. Calvin does not content himself with noting that our justification and sanctification flow from communion with Christ; rather he shows even in the texture of our daily lives what it means that we are disciples of Christ. Starting from a debate on dogmatics, he takes his sequences of thought right into the field of ethical reflections. Here again we find a good opportunity of noting what the ultimate concern of his theology is.

I. CHRISTIAN FREEDOM

Critics have usually failed to observe the significance of the fact that, in the *Institutes*, not only is the discussion of regeneration followed by a few chapters on "The life of a Christian

[1] Peter Barth: "Was ist reformierte Ethik?" (*Zw. d. Zeiten*, 10, 1932, 410–36). Peter Brunner: *Die Alkoholfrage bei Calvin. Ein Beitrag zum Verständnis der Ethik Calvins (Die Alkoholfrage in der Religion*, Vol. 4, no. 2, Berlin, 1930). Gall: *La vie de l'homme chrétien ou la vie sainte selon Jean Calvin*, Diss. (Strasburg, 1930). Alfred Göhler: "Das christliche Leben nach Calvin" (*Ev. Theologie*, 4, 1937, 299–325). H. Quistorp: *Die letzen Dinge im Zeugnis Calvins* (Gütersloh, 1941; Eng. trans. *Calvin's Doctrine of the Last Things*, London, 1955). Martin Schultze: *Meditatio futurae vitae: Ihr Begriff und ihre herrschende Stellung im System Calvins*, Leipzig, 1901 (*Studien z. Gesch. d. Theol. u. d. Kirche*, Bonwetsch & Seeburg, Vol. 6, no. 4); *Calvins Jenseits-Christentum in seinem Verhältnisse zu den religiösen Schriften des Erasmus untersucht*, Görlitz, 1902. K. Stokmann: "Das Leben der Christen nach Calvin Inst. III, 6–9" (*Reform. Kirchenztg*, 1908, pp. 162 ff.).

man",[1] but similarly the chapter on justification is followed by an ethical appendix[2] with the heading: "Christian Freedom".[3] Both justification and sanctification yield conclusions for ethics. The fact that we are accounted just before God is no less significant for practical life than the fact that in Christ we die and are made alive again as a new creation. Only when we pay heed to these points can the ethics of Calvin be rightly understood.

The thesis that the life of a Christian man is a life under the guidance of the Lord, which Calvin develops in connexion with his doctrine of regeneration, is so fully confirmed by the chapter on Christian freedom that the centring of Calvin's ethics on Christ can hardly be overlooked. It is barely understandable that from Calvin's discussion of "the life of a Christian man" it could be inferred that he preaches "a monastic outlook".[4] Such a misunderstanding becomes incomprehensible when we remember that in direct parallelism to the ethical appendix of the doctrine of sanctification he has written a chapter about Christian freedom as an adjunct to his doctrine of justification.

As those who in Christ are made just before God we are called to walk in the freedom of the sons of God. We are freed from the curse which strikes the transgressors of the divine command and can go through life fearlessly. We are free from the constraint of the divine law, and can go about our daily tasks in the comfort of the assurance that God does not judge us according to our achievement but after the perfect obedience which Christ has shown. We are free from the tyranny of things; we may thankfully use all gifts for the purpose for which the Creator gave them to us. Here we need only recall these three aspects of Christian freedom which inspire our life, because we have already enlarged upon them in our discussion of the divine law.[5]

In any case it must be made clear that in Calvin's opinion it is impossible to speak about the Christian life without at

[1] *In.* III, 6–10.   [2] *In.* III, 19.   [3] *Ibid.*
[4] Martin Schultze: *Calvins Jenseits-Christentum*, p. 30.
[5] See above, p. 98 f.

the same time referring to the freedom of the Christian. We must not lightly esteem what Christ has so dearly purchased for us.[1] Whoever supposes that his life must be dominated by principles forgets to glorify Christ, who has delivered us from all worldly authorities and has called us to Himself so that we may find rest in Him.[2] The rules according to which we propose to shape our lives may be never so important, they only lead us into bondage and idolatry.[3] On the other hand, if we interpret as caprice the freedom to which we are called and suppose that we can live our lives as our desires dictate, then we are forgetting that Christ has made us free so that we may serve Him and our neighbour.[4] With regard to the conduct of our lives it must therefore be laid down that if we do not remain in Christian freedom "neither Christ nor the truth of the Gospel nor inner peace of soul are properly understood".[5] By walking in freedom, we are bearing witness in the midst of the bondage and the lusts which rule this world to the Christ who is our Saviour and our Lord.

2. THE IMITATION OF CHRIST

Christ has freed us from the curse and the tyranny of the law and delivered us from the rulers of this world in order that we might be available for His service. As our Saviour, He reveals Himself also and in one unified process as our Lord. We have now to enquire about the meaning of this second aspect. We should be eluding the fact of Christ if we failed to see that our life is determined not only by justification but also by the second gift—sanctification. However essential be our persistence in Christian freedom, it is from this second point of view that Calvin has with particular attention mapped out the Christian life. He has given the ethical appendix to His account of sanctification the direct heading: "Of the life of a Christian man".

(a) Calvin's points are clearly and simply made. Because

---

[1] *In.* III, 19, 14. [2] *Ibid.* [3] *In.* III, 19, 7.
[4] *In.* III, 19; 1, 9. [5] *In.* III, 19, 1.

Christ has set us free, our daily life is moulded by the truth:
"We belong not to ourselves but to the Lord." [1] What this
implies is suggested to us by the Lord's commands. [2] But
Calvin does not content himself with merely expounding the
law. The Reformer who is branded as legalistic sketches out
the main outlines of his ethics in quite a different manner.
He views our life from the standpoint of the imitation of
Christ. [3]

By this he does not mean to supersede the instruction of the
law. On the contrary, he points out that the heavenly
Teacher Himself wished only the more carefully to direct our
lives by the rule of the law in calling us to be a living sacrifice
in discipleship to Him. [4] But by taking as his starting point
for ethics the insight that we are called to imitate Christ, he
makes quite clear the ultimate aim of the commands of the
law. We are not challenged to realize moral ideals but to
surrender ourselves to the God revealed in Jesus Christ.

"Only those can be called disciples of Christ who truly
imitate Him and are prepared to follow in His footsteps."
"He has given us a summary rule of discipleship so that we
may know in what the imitation of Him essentially consists:
namely, self-denial and the willing bearing of His cross." [5]
Thus in surveying the Christian life from these two
points of view, self-denial and the bearing of the cross, he
is holding fast to the rule of discipleship which Christ Himself
has given us in Matthew 16:24. In both passages of the
Institutes he expressly refers to this word of the Lord. [6] What
he says is nothing more than an exposition of this word of
Christ. If we fail to see this and try to explain Calvin's
arguments in a different sense, we do not understand them
at all.

(*b*) The first aspect of the imitation of Christ consists in
self-denial. "This self-denial has far-reaching implications.
We are to renounce our own point of view, turn away from
all covetous desires of the flesh, become as nothing in order

[1] *In.* III, 7, 1.   [2] *Ibid.*   [3] *In.* III, 7, 2; 8, 1.
[4] *In.* III, 7, 1.   [5] *CR* 45, 481.   [6] See note 3.

THE THEOLOGY OF CALVIN

that God may live in us and control us."[1] In this process it is a question of human initiative; but its negative character is to be noted. The substance of Christian ethics is in no sense the positive shaping of life by the initiative of the pious man. The essential action which we are called upon to perform is rather the renunciation of all that is our own, that we may give scope to the action of God. "If we are discussing the criterion of pious and holy living, we must always take as our starting point the fact that the Christian who is as it were dead in himself allows God to live within him, that he rests from his own works in order to give place to the work of God."[2] In the negative character of Calvinistic ethics which has been recognized but rejected[3] lies concealed the strongest positive force and inspiration. The fellowship with Himself which Christ bestows upon us forms the guiding line and inspiration of our life. We must fully accept the fact that He Himself wills to live and rule within us.[4] What could there be of greater consequence for our daily lives than just this? Hence Calvin has coined the epigram: "Man becomes happy through self-denial."[5]

All this makes it quite plain that the self-renunciation which we are called upon to exercise has nothing in common with self-denial in the usual sense. Firstly, it is not a question of resignation in itself but of a resignation which relinquishes the control to Christ. Secondly, such resignation means not merely passive self-denial but an active rejection of all our own willing and desiring. The Christian must not merely sacrifice himself peaceably and comfortably for the sake of Christ: "He must rather in the light of Christ come even to despise the most precious thing in the world."[6] This extreme devaluation of all things earthly we find also in the mystics; yet the self-renunciation which Calvin teaches is something quite different from the self-emptying which is extolled by the mystics as the way to the highest grade of being. It is a self-renunciation which is orientated to God, to Christ, and to

[1] *CR* 45, 481.　　[2] *CR* 55, 48.
[3] Martin Schultze, *op. cit.*, p. 28.
[4] *In.* III, 7, 1.　　[5] *CR* 55, 48.　　[6] *CR* 12, 259.

one's neighbour.[1] In the same direction point the two tables of the law[2]; they guide us to the same goal as does the call of Christ—to the path of discipleship. This self-denial finds its proper expression in love to the brethren,[3] and reaches its climax in the fact that we allow our whole life to be controlled by the will of the Lord.[4] This also precludes the mistaken notion that self-denial consists in a self-tormenting scrupulosity. The secret of its power lies in the Lord and not in us; it flows from the work of Christ and is poured out upon us from thence. "Christ died and rose again that we might have eternal Sabbath, i.e. that we might rest from our own human works and allow the spirit of God powerfully to work within us."[5]

(c) The other aspect of the imitation of Christ lies in *bearing the cross.* One cannot follow Jesus Christ "without being determined to hold fellowship with Him in His cross".[6] The Son of God Himself was not only tried by the bearing of His cross throughout His earthly life, but the whole of His life was shaped and dominated by the cross, so that in this fashion He should learn obedience.[7] Hence we cannot escape this destiny. God wills thus to test His own so that they become conformed to the image of His Son.[8] "By means of the cross He disciplines and tames the pride of our flesh, and that in manifold ways as is suited to the needs of each."[9] By sending us misfortune and sorrow God breaks our resistance to His will and trains us to obedience. The cross of circumstance which He lays upon us promotes our self-renunciation and brings us to cast ourselves wholly upon Christ.

Of course the life of man in general is subject to pain and sorrow. "God burdens both the evil and the good with the cross, and yet only those who gladly shoulder the burden can be said to carry it."[10] Misfortune and sorrow in them-

---

[1] *In.* III, 7, 4.   [2] *In.* III, 7, 3.   [3] *In.* III, 7, 7.
[4] *In.* III, 7, 10, 8.
[5] *CR* 37, 335; see Alfred Göhler: *Calvins Lehre von der Heiligung*, p. 37.
[6] *CR* 12, 169.   [7] *In.* III, 8, 1.   [8] *CR* 45, 482.
[9] *In.* III, 8, 5.   [10] *CR* 45, 482.

selves do not help man. They are rather to be seen as punishment for man's alienation from his Creator. If suffering contributes to our salvation it is only because we are in a communion with the Son of God.[1] When that is so, we can carry the cross, because we know that we participate in the sufferings of Christ.[2] The bitterness of the cross is thus softened for us; "for what could we wish for more than to share all things with the Son of God?"[3] The more we are harassed by hardship the more our communion with Christ is strengthened.[4] But, if we share the cross with the Son of God, then like Him we shall enter into heavenly glory through many afflictions.[5] He esteems us worthy of the cross only that we might be glorified with Him.[6]

This is our consolation in all sorrow. And this assurance must be sufficient for us. We must count as nothing all worldly success in comparison with the privilege of fighting under the sign of our Lord Jesus by bearing His cross.[7] It is the divine will that this struggle under the sign of the cross should be permanently our lot. "It does indeed happen that at times there is a truce or intermission, since God has regard to our weakness. Yet even though swords are not always drawn against us we must be prepared, because we are nevertheless members of Christ, always to share His cross of suffering."[8] In this world there is no escape from the cross. We may turn where we will, "the cross of Jesus Christ will always follow us".[9] When we have passed through many afflictions we must still be thinking of equipping ourselves to fight afresh.[10]

We are especially comforted "when we suffer persecution for righteousness' sake",[11] when we are burdened with the hatred of the world, because we champion among men the gospel and the law of God, His truth and His right. Then we must cling to the promises of Christ and not interpret our

[1] *CR* 50, 55.　[2] *In.* III, 8, 1.　[3] *CR* 45, 554.
[4] *In.* III, 8, 1.　[5] *Ibid.*　[6] *CR* 12, 169.
[7] *CR* 13, 145.　[8] *CR* 31, 447.　[9] *CR* 13, 296.
[10] *CR* 45, 482.　[11] *In.* III, 8, 7.

situation falsely in the light of our fleshly nature. "Hence it will come to pass that we, like the apostles, rejoice whenever he deems us worthy to suffer shame for His name's sake. For what harm can come to us thereby? If with an innocent and clear conscience we are robbed of our goods by the malice of wicked men, we are indeed impoverished in a worldly sense, but true riches accrue to us in heaven; the more we are expelled from our earthly home the more we shall be welcomed in our heavenly, the more we are tortured and despised the more we shall be rooted in Christ; the more we are slandered and reviled the higher will be our seat in the kingdom of God; and if we utterly perish, then the gates of eternal life will be opened to us." [1] It was in this way that Calvin exhorted the members of the persecuted church in France and illuminated for them the meaning of their suffering. He summoned them to sacrifice all for the sake of Christ; if it could not be avoided, even their fatherland and their own lives: "If you cannot restore your position, then rather become exiles from your country for a time than be excluded for ever from the eternal inheritance to which we are called. Whether we like it or not we must be aliens in this world. . . . Blessed are those who prove this in their lives and prefer to abandon their homes rather than to fall from the faith and surrender without hesitation their earthly welfare in order to remain united to Jesus Christ." [2] All this can only be frightening "to those who have not known the precious sweetness of Christ". [3] The Christian man is resolved to make the uttermost sacrifice for the sake of His Lord. [4] "There is no genuine fear of God in us if we do not carry our heart in our hands; that is, if we are not always ready to sacrifice our lives." [5]

This fellowship in the cross of our Lord Jesus Christ, which serves the end of slaying our old man, even includes our being buried with Him. "For there is no death without the grave." Hence those who have begun to die to the world

---

[1] *In.* III, 8, 7.   [2] *CR* 12, 646; cf. 12, 453 f.; 14, 741 f.
[3] *CR* 12, 646.   [4] *CR* 31, 447.   [5] *CR* 40, 632.

out of love to Him "must equip themselves to suffer even to the uttermost".[1]

Calvin did not suggest that we should take up our cross with stoic resignation. On the contrary, Christian patience and stoic calm are two very different things. "To carry the cross patiently does not mean that we should brace ourselves so as to feel no pain."[2] Christ Himself made that clear to us by His behaviour.[3] As long as we are in the flesh, we shall shrink from the cross. If we fail to realize this we are disastrously deceiving ourselves about our condition. We have not yet attained the state of perfection; we are still engaged in pilgrimage. Here below we are shaken by adversity and recoil from it. The point is simply that "if we wish to be disciples of Christ, our hearts should be filled with such fear of God and obedience towards Him as will subdue the resistance of our senses and enable us to submit to His decrees".[4] "Hence, when we are overcome by illness, we shall sigh and be troubled and desire health; when we are oppressed by poverty we shall be tormented by the sting of care and sadness, and vexed by the sense of disgrace, contempt, and wrong; and when we bury our dead we shall, as nature requires, weep; in all this the last word will always be: Thus has the Lord willed it, so let us be obedient to His will."[5] The ability to bear the cross patiently flows from God alone, just as does the capacity for self-denial. He it is who imparts to us this power.[6]

If we so strongly rebel against the bearing of the cross that in the end we cast it away from us, we shall be repulsing Christ at the same time. We cannot of course escape misfortune and pain but only the special trials which come upon those who confess the truth and the right of God in this world. For we must be clear about the fact that we can only escape the hatred of the world, and that suffering which strictly deserves to be called the cross, when we have already betrayed the Crucified. "Since the life that is a daily dying,

---

[1] CR 12, 86. [2] In. III, 8, 9. [3] Ibid.
[4] In. III, 8, 10. [5] Ibid. [6] CR 12, 86.

that is exposed to ridicule and unremitting stress, is too hard and too great a misery in the opinion of the backslider, he abandons and denies Christ in a shameful way in order to escape this fate."[1] Since Jesus Christ is the Crucified there can be no fellowship with Him which is not also a sharing of His cross.

(d) But our pilgrimage will one day have an end. We are called to imitate Christ so that one day we may reach the goal. If we share in Christ's cross of suffering, we shall also share in His glory. "God subjects us to unjust persecution that we may rejoice because, as we bear the cross with Christ, we shall also experience and share in the resurrection to a blessed immortality."[2] The imitation of Jesus Christ implies a looking forward to the eternal consummation and the bearing of the cross implies the aspiration towards future blessedness. The two things are indissolubly linked together. Also the word of the Lord about discipleship, to which Calvin referred as the basis for his ethical outlines, culminates in eschatological sayings. He felt that there existed an objective necessity to give his arguments about the imitation of Christ an eschatological bearing.[3]

He speaks from two points of view about the relation which exists between the bearing of the cross and the vision of eternity. Firstly, the painfulness of the cross which is laid upon us should startle us out of our concern with this transient life and direct our gaze towards eternity. "By whatever trouble we are vexed, we must fix our attention upon the one aim of accustoming ourselves to despise this present life, and of rousing ourselves to aspire to the next life."[4] We are only really making progress in the school of the cross when we learn to appreciate the fact that earthly life is full of unrest and trouble without any enduring good. In this world we have nothing but struggle to expect and we must

---

[1] CR 31, 447.   [2] Ibid.

[3] All other points with regard to the origin of Calvin's *meditatio vitae futurae* should be subordinated to this insight. Martin Schultze proceeds in a different way and hence to a large extent fails, *op. cit.*

[4] *In.* III, 9, 1.

"raise our eyes to heaven whenever we think of the crown of victory".[1]

Secondly, the carrying of the cross is eased for us if we look forward to the life that is to come. Jesus Christ, in whose cross we share, is the living Lord who has promised us that He will come again. "He will come for us as the Saviour who will deliver us from this unfathomable gulf of misery and sorrow, and lead us into the blessed inheritance of His glorious eternity."[2] Only as we reflect upon this can we learn truly to despise this present life.[3] We become willing to sacrifice all earthly goods, even the greatest.[4] The hope of leaving our exile and gaining our heavenly home enables Christians to overcome even the fear of death and makes them ready gladly to sacrifice their lives when necessary.[5] "The glory of God must be of more importance to us than a hundred lives."[6] The certainty that we shall become participators in it is the inspiration of martyrdom[7] and still more gives strength and patience to endure the shame and disgrace of the cross. "For however much the world exerts itself to bury Jesus Christ in infamy, His grave nevertheless brings glory not only for Him but also for the members of His body."[8]

All this suggests why we should long for the life of the world to come, and despise our present life; in fact—according to one expression[9]—trample it under our feet. But let us make the reason for this attitude still plainer. Earthly life is not really to be abhorred because it is full of pain and sorrow and culminates in death, "but we should hate it for the sole reason that it subjects us to the power of sin".[9] The transiency of our life springs from the fact of sin which destroys the value of all earthly things.[10] Yet we must not wantonly cast away this life. God has placed us in this world as in a military station, and hence we must abide here until

---

[1] *In.* III, 9, 1.   [2] *In.* III, 9, 5.   [3] *In.* III, 9, 4.
[4] *CR* 12, 542.   [5] *In.* III, 9, 5.   [6] *CR* 40, 633.
[7] *CR* 40, 633 f.   [8] *CR* 12, 170 f.   [9] *In.* III, 9, 4.
[10] *CR* 33, 661 ff.; see Alfred Göhler, *op. cit.*, pp. 42 f.

He calls us away.[1] But in the struggle by which God wills to try us,[2] we must ceaselessly long for the day when we are delivered from the dominion of sin and the prison of our flesh[3] and shall enjoy full communion with our Lord, to whom we now belong only in faith. In His unveiled presence we shall find the life[4] which we have trifled away by sin and by our alienation from God, the Creator.

Calvin does not teach us to despise the world in itself. Such an attitude would help us just as little as the fond fancy of men who "have forgotten their real estate and have taken to dreaming that there is an imperishable kingdom upon this earth".[5] Calvin preaches neither pessimism nor optimism but calls us inexorably to the imitation of Jesus Christ. The true situation of man is just as much misapprehended by the pessimists as by the optimists. It is far more worthless than the worst pessimist might suggest. But in so far as we recognize this in Jesus Christ and at the same time come to realize that in this world of sin and death we are called to follow Him, our earthly life receives a relative value. We must be grateful to God for this life, because He has placed us here so that through its sorrows we reach the life of eternity.[6] This world has no value in itself but receives value from the imminent outbreak of the kingdom of God. The present life, for those who belong to the Lord, is "a pilgrimage in the course of which they must strive to attain the kingdom of heaven".[7] Hence we can comfortably enjoy the values of this world, but in such a way "that furthers our course rather than impedes it".[8]

The ethics of Calvin are not negativist[9]; they are rather determined by the fact that we have a living Lord who was crucified and rose again and who will come again as our Saviour. In the strictest sense they stem from the principle of the imitation of Christ.

---

[1] *In.* III, 9, 4.   [2] *In.* III, 9, 3.   [3] *In.* III, 9, 4.
[4] *In.* III, 9, 5.   [5] *CR* 31, 399.   [6] *CR* 33, 508.
[7] *In.* III, 10, 1.   [8] *Ibid.*
[9] Thus Martin Schultze, *op. cit.*, p. 28.

Chapter 11

PRAYER[1]

1. THE NECESSITY AND THE ESSENTIAL CHARACTER OF PRAYER

THE fellowship which we experience with Christ through faith is not an objective permanent fact, but the gift of God which becomes a reality for us solely through the power of the Holy Ghost operative in response to our faith. We are always in danger of misunderstanding this. We are inclined to seek peace and satisfaction within ourselves instead of lifting up our hearts to the source of all life. "Our faith would quickly dissolve if God did not test it by manifold trials."[2] God sends us misfortune and affliction of all sorts so that we do not get entangled in a false self-complacency. The blows of fate which strike us are meant to make us flee to God and call upon Him in our distress. Since communion with Christ necessarily leads us into the participation of His cross, God provides that we shall not sink into a religious satiety but ever and again turn away from ourselves to the Author of our salvation. "The discipline of the cross is necessary in order that earnest prayer may be kept alive in our hearts."[3] Prayer is one of the fruits of the penitence which God has aroused within us.[4]

Calvin gives a very exact and simple definition of the essence of prayer. "Prayer is none other than an expanding

---

[1] W. Dahm: "Gebete Calvins" (*Reform. Kirchenztg.*, 82, 1932, 353 f.; 390 f.; 405 f.). A. Schneider: "Die Lehre vom Gebet bei Luther und Calvin" (*ibid.*, 85, 1935, 297 f.). Udo Smidt: "Das Gebet bei Calvin" (*ibid.*, 80, 1930, 97 ff.).

[2] *CR* 30, 482.   [3] *CR* 44, 359.   [4] *CR* 38, 595.

of our heart in the presence of God."[1] "When we pray, we do no other than pour out our thoughts and wishes before God."[2] Prayer is thus "a kind of conversation between men and God, by which they gain entrance into the heavenly sanctuary and personally address Him on the strength of His promises; with the result that in their distress they see that they have not vainly believed His word alone".[3]

2. CHRIST AND PRAYER

In the last quotation, taken from Calvin's *Institutes*, is to be found an important indication which gives us the key to Calvin's understanding of prayer. We sinful and mortal men are able to come before God and to speak with Him because He has first spoken to us and has given us His promises. Calvin repeatedly emphasizes this aspect of things.[4] God Himself has invited us to call upon Him.[5] Hence we must honour His Word by relying upon it implicitly.[6] We ourselves cannot by our own resources make a way to God. It is God Himself who prepares for us the way of approach. In His Word we draw near to Him.[7] It gives us the certainty that our prayer will be heard by Him.[8]

For the word of promise rests on the covenant which God has made with us. In every prayer we can take our stand upon this fact. We may come to God in confidence because in the founding of the covenant He has declared His will to be our God. No doubt is here possible; "for the blood of our Lord Jesus Christ seals the pact which God has concluded with us".[9] "Hence each one of us by trusting in the grace of Christ must have confidence in prayer and frankly dare to invoke God."[10] In Jesus Christ we find the true basis on which we can draw near to God in prayer. "For, even were we of our own accord to praise the name of God, we would only succeed in desecrating Him by our impure lips if

[1] *CR* 37, 402. [2] *CR* 49, 522. [3] *In.* III, 20, 2.
[4] *CR* 31, 603; 34, 472; 44, 359 f. [5] *CR* 44, 360.
[6] *CR* 26, 720. [7] *CR* 53, 368. [8] *In.* III, 20, 3.
[9] *CR* 28, 292. [10] *CR* 45, 218.

Christ had not once offered Himself as the sacrifice to make us and all that we do holy."[1] Hence it is not a question of somehow or other bestirring ourselves to prayer, but rather we must realize that we can lift up our voices to God in prayer because He Himself in His incarnate Son has taken action on our behalf. "God cannot be called Father except through Him."[2]

This does not mean that Christ by His atoning work has opened up for us the way to God so that whenever we wish we can tread it and pour out our concerns before God by our unaided initiative. For Jesus Christ is not only the Preparer of the way: He is the way Himself.[3] His atoning work is not merely a basis on which we can proceed to build, but it sustains and makes effective our prayer at every moment. The possibility of prayer does not really lie within our grasp. "For as soon as the terrible majesty of God strikes our mind, we inevitably recoil in fear and shrink in the knowledge of our own unworthiness, until Christ intervenes and makes the throne of glory which terrifies into the throne of grace which succours."[4] The priestly office of Christ which renders possible our prayer to God is fulfilled without intermission.[5] It is not simply that He has once by His sacrifice interceded between God and sinful humanity; it is rather that His intercession with the Father on our behalf continues day by day.[6] Because Christ intercedes for us, the prayers which we bring before God are not in vain.[7] Our own praying is nothing other than our uniting ourselves with the prayer of Christ; and we have no hope of being heard unless He precedes us with His prayer.[8]

3. THE HOLY SPIRIT AND PRAYER

No prayer is possible without the Word, without the incarnate Word, and the continuous intercession of this Word for us. In this connexion the bearing of Calvin's

[1] *CR* 31, 615.   [2] *CR* 37, 402; 27, 700.
[3] *In.* III, 20, 19.   [4] *In.* III, 20, 17.   [5] *CR* 31, 208.
[6] *In.* III, 20, 18, 19.   [7] *In.* III, 20, 18.   [8] *CR* 31, 208.

teaching on prayer becomes quite clear. But this observation does not take us far enough. Here, as elsewhere, the real issue is not the recognition of a point of doctrine but the recognition of Jesus Christ. "Until God has caused us to taste the sweetness of His mercy, we can have no access to Him and no one prays rightly who has not experienced His grace and is not convinced that God is graciously disposed towards Him."[1] In other words: "As we cannot pray unless the Word precedes us, so before we pray we must believe."[2] This does not imply that we must add something of our own to the Word in order to make prayer possible. On the contrary, the faith which is grounded in the work of Christ and supported by the word of promise does not spring up from the depths of our own hearts. It springs from the operation of the Holy Ghost within us.[3]

But such action of the Holy Spirit must take effect within us; this "yes" to the divinely given word must be spoken, if prayer is to be a reality. Christ furnishes the objective possibility of prayer, faith the subjective. Strictly speaking we should say the Holy Spirit rather than faith. Hence when Calvin comes to indicate the subjective presuppositions of prayer he emphasizes at times the work of the Holy Spirit instead of the power of faith. "Before we can utter a prayer we must have received the firstfruits of the Spirit. For he alone is the proper teacher of the art of prayer. He not only inspires in us the words but guides the movements of our hearts."[4] The work of the Spirit is thus not only faith but also the fruit of faith; namely, prayer. This fact is the guarantee that our prayer is grounded in the word of God. For the Spirit which makes itself manifest in our prayer is not some mysterious power which calls forth in us a certain religious awareness; but it is the Spirit which draws us to the Son, the Spirit through whose action God accepts us as His children for the sake of Christ.[5]

[1] *CR* 31, 69.　　[2] *CR* 55, 387; cf. 48, 654; 34, 472, etc.
[3] *CR* 48, 16; *In.* III, 20, 5.　　[4] *CR* 48, 16; *In.* III, 20, 5.
[5] Cf. *CR* 32, 418.

4. THE CHURCH AS THE SPHERE OF PRAYER

(a) The sphere in which prayer is properly exercised is the church. If a dialogue between the soul and God is only possible because Christ ever intercedes for us at His Father's side, then only those can truly call upon God who are aided by the priestly intercession of Christ. The body of Christ, the church, may pray to God because the Head, Jesus Christ, ceaselessly intercedes for it before the throne of the Father.[1] God cannot be called Father by all; "but it is a special privilege of the church that it can name God Father".[2] The sacrifice and the intercession of Christ are efficacious among the people of God; among them the Holy Spirit accomplishes its work to help their weakness. Hence at the heart of the world that miracle happens within the church by which sinful men draw near to the holy God and can pour out their hearts before Him.

(b) In his lengthy discussions about prayer in the *Institutes* Calvin deals especially with the question how prayer may rightly be made before God. He draws up rules for true prayer and explains the conception of prayer which Christ Himself imparted to His disciples in order to help them in their weakness. Thus in the *Institutes* Calvin gives instruction about prayer rather than a doctrine of prayer. And this has a good reason. It shows how practical is the purpose of his whole theology. If anywhere, it must become plain here when he considers prayer at the end of his teaching about man's appropriation of salvation, that faith is no dead thing but rather implies the absolute divine claim made upon man's whole being, because the truth which evokes faith demands full self-surrender. It is impossible to think theologically and to discuss God and His revelation in Jesus Christ if we do not realize that every moment we are thrown back upon prayer. If we fail to grasp this we are not speaking of the one truth, but of some truth or other and we are not really teaching theology; for the latter can only arise in the sphere of the church where prayer is practised. Calvin put this insight into

---

[1] *CR* 31, 207 ff.   [2] *CR* 37, 402.

practice by uttering at the beginning of all his lectures: "May the Lord grant us so to wrestle with the secrets of His divine wisdom that our piety truly increases to His honour and to our edification."[1] He similarly concluded every lecture, which was always appropriate to the previously discussed word of Holy Scripture.[2]

Here we only wish to draw attention to this fact without expounding the guide to prayer which Calvin gives in his *Institutes*. We have set ourselves the task of extracting the kernel of the various doctrines of Calvin. And, although it must be recognized that Calvin in his section on prayer wishes to give the reader, above all, guidance and advice in the art of prayer, it is obvious that his practical suggestions presuppose a clear view of the essence of prayer. We have already stressed the fundamental features of his interpretation of prayer and must now, in order to complete the picture, add to this what he says about the end of prayer.

5. THE END OF PRAYER

Prayer which proceeds from the Word of God is directed towards the Word as its true end. It is based upon the promise of God and takes place in the certainty that what is promised will be our portion. With this basis of prayer firmly fixed, it becomes clear that we cannot bring before God just as we please any chance desires. The basis of prayer determines its end. "The one true aim of prayer consists in the fact that the promises of God should have their way with us."[3] "In prayer those treasures are disclosed which lie at the heart of the gospel and which our faith has perceived."[4] The aim of prayer is not that we should carry through our own will but that we should allow God to bestow upon us what He has planned for us. The chief of our wishes should be above all things to be in harmony with the will of God.[5]

[1] *CR* 37, 463.

[2] Cf. W. Dahm, *op. cit.*, and his translation: *Johannes Calvin, Gebete zu den Vorlesungen über Jeremia und Hesekiel*, Munich, 1934.

[3] *CR* 32, 231.   [4] *In.* III, 20, 2.   [5] *CR* 52, 61.

This does not prevent us from freely pouring out our cares unto Him. We are in fact exhorted to do so; for by so doing we testify that our God is One who is sensitive to our dire need.[1] Hence submission to the will of God does not mean that we must give up prayer.[2] "Not in vain does the heavenly Father declare that our sole help and chance of rescue lies in calling upon His name; for when we do so we invoke the reality of His providence—the fact that He cares and watches over us; the power with which He sustains us in our weakness and near collapse, and the mercy with which He pardons us who are so heavily laden with sin; yes, by such invocation we seek to unite ourselves with Him wholly so that He offers Himself to us here and now."[3] The aim of prayer is communion with God. With that everything is given us, even that which each one of us most desperately needs for his journey through life; for when we belong to God, His providence is active on our behalf and we stand under the control of His power and mercy. It is the same point when Calvin says: "We must continue steadfast in prayer so that we daily grow in the power of the Spirit. I speak of growth, for before we can utter a prayer we must have received the firstfruits of the Spirit."[4] If we would understand this saying, we must remember that the Holy Spirit brings us to Jesus Christ. If, as a result of prayer, the Spirit is more richly showered upon us, then the aim of our prayer is that we remain in communion with the Lord by the power of the Spirit and grow ever more closely united to Him. And in Jesus Christ we find communion with God and every gift that we need.

Here at the close of these reflections on our appropriation of salvation we find as it were a circular argument. There is no prayer without the firstfruits of the Spirit, i.e. without communion with Christ. But then it is also true that we cannot belong to Christ and abide in Him without constant prayer.

---

[1] *CR* 31, 163. [2] *In.* III, 20, 3. [3] *In.* III, 20, 2.
[4] *CR* 48, 16.

Chapter 12

GOD'S ETERNAL ELECTION[1]

I. ELECTION IN CHRIST

U NTIL recently it appeared as if Calvin researchers had gradually reached the conclusion that the doctrine of predestination is not the central doctrine of the Reformer on which all his other doctrines are based, or which at least interpenetrates them all. But recently it has been said with regard to the theological system of Calvin that "the thought of predestination has overwhelming significance for the other parts of his dogmatic system".[2] Still more in secular literature on the subject is the principle maintained as though it were a matter of course: "Calvin's central dogma, as is well known, is that of predestination."[3] If this be the case, then all that we have so far said is false. Then Calvin's doctrines are not like so many signposts pointing through the far-ranging and complex fields of the Bible to the one incarnate God. It would rather be true to say that Calvin's theology is a system of thoughts about God and man proceeding from the one thought of the utter

[1] Karl Barth: "Gottes Gnadenwahl", *Theol. Existenz heute*, no. 47, Munich, 1936. Peter Barth: *Die Erwählungslehre in Calvins Institutio von 1536* (in *Theol. Aufsätze, K. Barth z. 50 Geburtstag*, Munich, 1936, pp. 432–42); "Die biblische Grundlage der Prädestinationslehre bei Calvin" (*Ev. Theol.*, 1938, pp. 158 f.). A. Bernel: *Calvin défenseur de la prédestination*, Diss. Genève, 1931. L. Boettner: *The Reformed Doctrine of Predestination*, Grand Rapids, 1931. H. Otten: *Calvins Theologische Anschauung von der Prädestination*, Munich, 1938.

[2] O. Ritschl: *Dogmengeschichte des Protestantismus*, III, 156.

[3] F. Schnabel: *Deutschlands geschichtliche Quellen und Darstellungen in der Neuzeit*: Part I: *Das Zeitalter der Reformation*, 1931, p. 51.

dependence of man on God. Metaphysical speculation about the ground of the world and its relation to the creature, however powerful and impressive, and revelational theology of which the only aim is to lead us to the Lord, are nevertheless mutually exclusive. We must now make a final decision as to how we are to understand Calvin's theological work.

But is not this question already answered by the mere fact that Calvin puts forward a doctrine of predestination in formal terms? In the *Institutes* the first chapter relating to this doctrine bears the title: *Concerning the eternal election of God by which He has ordained some to blessedness and others to damnation.*[1] These few words make it already plain that when Calvin speaks of election he means an eternal decree of God made before time and before the foundation of the world. But how is it possible that such an eternal counsel of God can be treated within the framework of a theology of revelation? When we speak of revelation we mean too, of course, the eternal God, but in so far as He has stepped forth out of His hiddenness, has revealed Himself in time, and still to-day declares His will. Thus does not Calvin betray, by the simple fact that he affirms an eternal election, that in the last resort he is not concerned about Jesus Christ but about metaphysical speculation?

Exactly the opposite is true. It is just Calvin's doctrine of election which proves that he is not primarily a speculative thinker.

(*a*) At the very beginning of his considerations about this doctrine in the *Institutes* Calvin warns us against a speculative approach to the doctrine. Those people who show such tendencies "ought first of all to realize that in seeking to investigate the idea of predestination they are trying to penetrate the depths of divine wisdom. If any one audaciously intrudes on that ground he will find nothing with which to satisfy his curiosity, but will fall into erroneous courses from which he will be unable to extricate himself. For it is not right that a man should with impunity enquire into those things which the Lord has willed to remain hidden in Him-

[1] *In.* III, 21.

self, and should seek to probe into that eternal ground of wisdom which God wills to be adored but not understood, that on account of it He may be feared by us."[1] God's eternal counsels are for us "a tremendous and unfathomable abyss". There is nothing there that we can explore to any profit; on the contrary, if we attempt to do so "all our understanding will be unavailing".[2]

Calvin's warning goes still further. Not only does he disallow all attempts to comprehend predestination by our human resources of thought as fruitless and dangerous. He considers it illegitimate that the question of predestination should even be formulated. "If the eternal counsels of God are in question, we, as people who are worthy of death, should be struck with terror."[3] "What should God have decided with regard to us His enemies except damnation?" If we seek our salvation in God's inscrutable will, we get involved in over-ingenious speculations.[4] "We should over and over again become entangled in and dazzled by our own ingenuity before being able to grasp the purpose of God."[5] Merely by enquiring about election in itself we fall into a labyrinthine maze of fancies in which we get completely lost. "Thus"—says Calvin—"this doctrine would not profit us at all."[6] Rather all mere thinking about eternal predestination as an idea in itself leads us into uncertainty and despair.

When we see that Calvin rejects any attempt to investigate the eternal purposes of God by the resources of human reason, and even forbids any enquiry into this idea in itself, then we are reminded that in another connexion he disallows the pseudo-theology of Turks and Jews because it is concerned to make affirmations about God in Himself and apart from revelation.[7] Hence we should not be surprised about Calvin's treatment of the question of predestination. If apart from revelation all access to God is barred to theology, then

---

[1] *In.* II, 21, 1.   [2] *CR* 44, 407.   [3] *CR* 54, 58; *In.* III, 24, 4.
[4] *CR* 48, 314.   [5] *CR* 54, 57.   [6] *CR* 42, 130.
[7] See above p. 33.

also it may not seek to grasp what God has determined in Himself before all time.

(*b*) But this must not be taken to imply here any more than elsewhere that for Calvin the only possible course is to keep silence. For God declares to us His eternal will in so far as that is necessary.[1] Hence at this juncture in the theological debate the implied answer to the question which naturally arises is: "We must pay heed to what we are told in the gospel."[2] "Those secrets of His will which God desires to disclose to us, He has revealed in His Word."[3] Theology cannot aim at being in part a theology of revelation and in part a theology of speculation. God has spoken. Therefore theology here as elsewhere must strictly adhere to His Word. "Then we shall understand that, as soon as we step outside the limits of the Word, we shall stray from the path of truth and wander in darkness, where we shall necessarily fall and stumble. Hence let us keep this well in mind: to aim at reaching some other knowledge of predestination than what is offered to us in the Word of God is no less nonsensical than to wish to go by an undiscovered way or to see in the dark."[4]

But what does it mean when Calvin requires that in regard to the doctrine of election we should gain our knowledge of the divine purpose solely from the Word? Certainly he is thinking of Holy Scripture. But the very fact that in this connexion he can substitute Gospel for Word suggests in what sense he is using the phrase. In referring to the Word he is not simply expressing the opinion that along with other doctrines the Bible also contains this doctrine of election and that we have only to extract it. To be sure, we find expressed in the Bible the idea of God's choice, yet we must consider that in Holy Scripture it is not a question of the Word only but of the Word which in the last analysis apprehends us, as indeed we have already seen; the concern of the Bible is not with doctrines as such but with the one joyful message which claims our total obedience. As once with the people of Israel, so now with us God has in Christ concluded with us the

[1] *CR* 51, 282.   [2] *CR* 54, 57.   [3] *In.* III, 21, 1.
[4] *In.* III, 21, 2.

covenant of life; in fact, in Christ He has chosen us before the foundation of the world. When we grasp this message of the Bible, when we encounter Jesus Christ at the heart of it, then we know ourselves to be members of His chosen people; we know that our salvation is grounded uniquely and solely in God.

If theology is to testify to the God who reveals Himself to us in Jesus Christ then it may and must at the same time bear witness to the fact that "some have been allotted eternal life, others eternal damnation".[1] But only for this reason may it speak of the eternal choice of God. "Hence it must be said that God has not chosen those whom He has accepted as His children because of their intrinsic worth, but because He sees them in Christ (Ephesians 1:4); because only in Him does He love them, nor could He reward them with the inheritance of His kingdom until He had made them joint-heirs with Christ. Seeing then that we are elected in Christ, we cannot find the assurance of our election in ourselves nor even in God the Father in so far as we see Him in Himself apart from the Son. Hence Christ is the mirror in which we must and certainly may behold the fact of our election. For as He is the Person in whose body the Father has determined to incorporate those who from eternity He has willed to regard as His own, recognizing as His children all those who are members of His Son, we have an open and sure witness that we are written in the book of life, provided that we are in communion with Christ."[2]

When Christ confronts us in His Word and we become His own, then there is no longer for us any mysterious counsel of God which might become the object of our brooding and the source of our uncertainty. It is certainly not the will of God that by the process of our thinking we should seek to raise ourselves to Him in order to become clear about our destiny. "But look, God condescends to our level. He shows us the reason for this in the person of His Son, as though to say: here I am to be found; behold me

---

[1] *In.* III, 21, 5.   [2] *In.* III, 24, 5; *CR* 8, 318.

and recognize that I have adopted you as my children."[1] In addressing us thus He gives us also the certitude of our salvation. "For our Lord Jesus Christ is the ground of both things—of the assurance of our salvation and of our election which was determined by grace before the foundation of the world."[2] He is "the mirror to which we must lift up our eyes if we desire to attain the certainty of our election",[3] "the mirror in which the will of God becomes visible to us and in fact the pledge by which it is sealed".[4] But Christ is not merely the ground of our recognition of the truth of our election; He is also its objective ground. In the *Institutes* Calvin goes as far as this insight; Christ is the Author of our election.[5] If that were not so, then it would not be God who declares Himself to us in Jesus Christ. "Because Christ is the eternal wisdom, the unchangeable truth, and the abiding purpose of the Father, we need not fear lest anything which He proclaims to us in His word deviates in the smallest degree from the will of the Father, whom we desire to know; but He reveals the Father to us faithfully, as He was in the beginning and ever will be."[6]

Because Christ assures us of our election to salvation we not only can and must speak of God's eternal counsel, but we can do so, too, without being terrified at the thought of our guilt and lost condition. "If we have Jesus Christ as our Guide, we shall be able to rejoice in good comfort, since we shall know that He possesses sufficient authority to make all the members of His body pleasing to His Father."[7] For we must bear in mind: Jesus Christ is not only the Son of God who as such can alone give us a true disclosure of the will of His Father, but He is also true man, and in the unity of His divinity and humanity the Mediator who walked on this earth for our benefit and experienced death for our sakes. When Jesus Christ addresses us in the word of Holy Scripture, then we are no longer mere onlookers who take from the Bible what they please: we can no longer worry

[1] *CR* 8, 114. [2] *Ibid.* [3] *CR* 51, 282; 42, 127, 131.
[4] *CR* 5, 333. [5] *In.* III, 22, 7. [6] *In.* III, 24, 5.
[7] *CR* 54, 58.

our heads as to whether we are elected or rejected; nor can we remain of the doubtful opinion that nothing certain can emerge in these matters. When Jesus Christ really calls us and we hear Him, when we are united to Him by faith through the Holy Ghost, then our lot is decided, then all speculation and all fear is ended.[1]

Just in this discussion about God's eternal choice Calvin proves himself to be a theologian of the Word, but not simply in the sense that he derives his doctrine of election from the Bible but in the sense that he points to our connexion with the Word; with Christ manifested in the words of the Bible. Certitude of salvation in Christ is also certitude of election, and vice versa: certitude of election is only to be found in Christ.

(c) That Calvin even in treating the doctrine of election adheres to his principle of disallowing all speculation on the matter, in fact all discussion of election as such, is confirmed by the way in which he has fitted the doctrine into the structure of his theology as a whole. The first edition of the *Institutes* contains no special section on the question of divine predetermination. Only within the framework of the doctrine of the church, which is described as the number of the elect, does the matter emerge.[2]

No doubt here the essential considerations on the point are already mentioned. But the doctrine first receives special treatment in the Genevan catechism of 1537.[3] Yet even here it does not stand first in the catechism; important aspects have been already dealt with—the doctrine of God, of man, of free-will, etc.; in fact, it has already been said that we possess Christ only by faith, before the mention of the doctrine occurs. It is not only the case in the Genevan catechism of 1537 that fundamental doctrines are expounded without mention of election, but also in the later editions of the *Institutes* where the doctrine of election receives special consideration.[4] But there, as contrasted with the catechism, it stands in a still later position until in the last, the chief

[1] *CR* 51, 281 ff.; 53, 152.   [2] *OS* 1, 86 ff.   [3] *OS* 1, 390 ff.
[4] *OS* 3, XIV, XXI.

edition of the *Institutes*, it is deferred almost to the end of the treatment of salvation. It is followed only by the chapter on the resurrection of the dead. Everything else that Calvin has to say about God, Christ, the appropriation of salvation, has already been said without any mention of election. Thus it is not surprising that the second and final Genevan Catechism of 1542 [1] again includes no special treatment of election, thus returning to an arrangement similar to what we find in the first edition of the *Institutes*. Calvin could not express more plainly from a formal point of view that the doctrine of election has no intrinsic significance for theology in the sense that other doctrines might stem from it. It must be considered at the appropriate point within the total structure of a theological system; but no more than other questions. Indeed, Calvin's reserved treatment of the problem is rather to be seen as a warning against a too diffuse discussion which might easily degenerate into mere speculation. If we refuse to see that—and, as far as externals are concerned, it is already clear from the place which Calvin has allocated to this doctrine in the total structure of his theology—then it is because we refuse to see it and because here as elsewhere we are adapting the theology of Calvin to suit our private views just as we please.

(*d*) But within the total structure of his theology Calvin does develop the doctrine of God's eternal election in its dual aspect, speaking of God's election and rejection. It is not merely that some whom the message of the Bible grips come to recognize their election in Christ, but there is the further surprising fact "that the covenant of life is not preached to all men in the same way and that even among those to whom it is preached it does not in all cases fall on the same ground nor always retain its hold".[2] Such is the problem which Calvin necessarily comes up against when his consideration of the question how we are to appropriate the salvation wrought by Christ has reached the point at which he recognizes that we must always rely on prayer, and must ask

[1] *OS* 2, 88, 24.   [2] *In.* III, 21, 1.

God to strengthen us and keep us in communion with Christ. God's promises, which, as we have seen, are the foundation of our prayer, "do not concern everyone; but how can it be that they are not similarly efficacious in the lives of all?"[1] How are we to account for the distinctions among men which arise when God reveals Himself to us in His word? Are we to suppose that Christ is so powerless as not to be able to win over to Himself and preserve all who resist Him, just as He has conquered us? Certainly not. The distinctions which thus arise among men are grounded in the fact that "God has not made manifest His mighty arm to all."[2]

We are here confronted by something incomprehensible, by "the inscrutable judgments of God".[3] In other words: as we know that in Christ we are chosen by God Himself when we receive the gospel in faith, so also the refusal of the good tidings is in the last analysis rooted in the divine will itself. In face of God, man is in such a lost condition that he possesses neither the power to say "yes" to the gospel which has been preached to him, nor to utter a defiant "no" to it. The independence of man is crushed into the dust in the presence of the majesty of God.

The will of God, which triumphs over the will of man, is not of course capricious; it is His righteous will. Hence Calvin speaks of the judgment of God which is reflected in the fact that some accept the gospel and others reject it. The justice of this divine disposition remains a mystery to us. But Paul himself confessed "that the essence of divine righteousness is too transcendent for it to be measured by human standards or understood in the poverty of man's understanding". "At least", says Calvin, "the apostle admits that the divine judgments are so unsearchable, that the mind of man must be engulfed in those depths if it would attempt to sound them."[4] Calvin shows how sincerely he is inspired by this insight in that he says very little about the damned. He keeps strictly to what the Bible teaches on the subject.

[1] CR 14, 417. [2] Ibid. [3] CR 9, 263; In. III, 21, 1.
[4] In. III, 23, 4.

167

(e) Yet the question may urge itself upon our minds, why Calvin does not confine himself to the simple fact that Christ finds both belief and unbelief. Why does he carry the theological debate to the point of asserting that election and rejection take place through the action of God? As we have seen, Calvin's point of departure is the observed fact that the Word of God is not everywhere preached, and that where it is preached it does not always fall on the same ground. In view of these facts of experience Calvin accepts the witness of Holy Scripture that the divisions brought about by the declaration of the Word to man are grounded in ultimate divine determinations. He develops a doctrine of election because he feels constrained to do so obediently to the word of Scripture. But he was also clear about the fact that the Bible not only offers a number of indications about the choice of God, but in so doing wishes to communicate something of decisive importance.

Firstly, the doctrine of election is the ultimate and essential expression of the evangelical doctrine of grace. It magnifies the honour of God and reduces us to a status of true humility.[1] For once more it gives pointed expression to the fact (which was already implied in the doctrine of justification and sanctification) that the ground of our salvation in every respect lies uniquely and solely in God and nowhere else. It is an effectual antidote to every attempt on the part of man to evaluate himself in terms of religious significance; it is the spearhead of the attack on the Romish doctrine of grace in whatever form and wheresoever it may raise its head. For it causes the merit of Christ and the working of the Holy Ghost, in virtue of which we are made members of Christ—hence grace in its objective and subjective aspect—to be seated exclusively in the mercy of God.

This implies a second point: the doctrine of election alone makes the certitude of salvation a living efficacious reality; for when we see that God gives to us what He refuses to others, then we come to realize that our salvation truly flows

1 *In.* III, 21, 1.

from the spring of His pure mercy.[1] "It is impossible", says Calvin in the first *Institutes*, "that those who really belong to the elect people should finally perish or sink unsaved. For their salvation is founded on such sure and firm bases that, even if the whole structure of the world tottered, that certainty itself could not dissolve. Firstly, it stands or falls by divine determination, and thus could be changed or disappear only as that eternal wisdom decides. The elect can no doubt sway and fluctuate, nay even fall; but they will not perish because the Lord will always stretch out His arm to save them." "Further, the Lord has committed those whom He has chosen to the guardianship of His Son, so that He should lose none of them but raise them up at the Last Day (John 6:39). Under so good a Guardian, while they may err and slide, they certainly cannot be finally lost."[2] Thus Calvin considers that the assurance of salvation only becomes real and effective as the assurance of election.[3] And yet the latter—as we see particularly well from the words of the Reformer just quoted—is not to be divorced from the security of Christ, that security which Christ as the Good Shepherd ever affords us.

The orientation of Calvin's theology towards the Incarnate God is unmistakable precisely in regard to election, where the flood-gates to speculation seem to be opened; although it must be admitted that the Reformer has not always consistently maintained this direction of his thoughts, especially in his polemical writings about predestination.[4] But this does not alter the fact that Calvin's doctrine of election is intended to be nothing more than an expression of the glad tidings: in Christ God has elected us before the foundation of the world, so that we may be holy and blameless before Him in love.

2. THE QUESTION OF ASSURANCE OF SALVATION

The question of assurance of salvation, which we have just touched upon, needs more precise consideration because it

[1] *In.* III, 21, 1.   [2] *In.* III, 24, 6.   [3] *CR* 8, 260.
[4] Cf. *CR* 9, 713 f.

169

has played a great part in Calvin research and in fact is of no small importance for our judgment of Calvinistic theology. How can one chosen of God be assured of his salvation? May he rely upon the promises of God, thus ultimately upon Christ, or must he seek tangible signs of the divine election? For instance, must he, in order to become clear about his relation to God, discover from his inner attitude and his conduct whether he is elected or rejected? To a large extent this opinion has been maintained and it has been supposed that the starting point for the later doctrine of the *Syllogismus practicus* is to be found in Calvin.

In order to elucidate this matter we must especially note that it is not here simply a question of justification and sanctification, or faith and works, nor is the point how far the attitude and conduct of another person allow one to make a judgment about his state of grace. The question is simply and solely whether works have any sort of significance for one's personal assurance of salvation.[1]

(*a*) In order to find an answer we propose to turn first to Calvin's major work, the *Institutes*.[2] If the truth is that, according to the doctrine of Calvin, works are helpful in permitting the believer to attain a secure knowledge of his election, then somewhere in the section on predestination—which extends to four long chapters—Calvin must have said so.

But if we look for such an expression of opinion, we shall not find it in the least. In one passage he certainly mentions the fact that if we would be certain of our salvation we must cleave to the "*signa posteriora*".[3] What does he mean by this? Since he disallows any speculative approach to the doctrine of election as fruitless and dangerous, he prefers to rely on the "*signa posteriora*" of our election. But by this he means not our attitude or our works—the latter are never mentioned—

---

[1] This is overlooked in the detailed thesis which Klingenburg has devoted to this question. Cf. G. Klingenburg: *Das Verhältnis Calvins zu Butzer, untersucht auf Grund der wirtschaftsethischen Bedeutung beider Reformatoren*, Diss. Bonn, 1912, pp. 64–77.

[2] Cf. *In.* III, 2, 38 also.   [3] *In.* III, 24, 4.

but God's "objective Word",[1] "His calling",[2] which means in the last resort, Christ,[3] whom we encounter in the Word in virtue of the Holy Spirit. If we wish to be assured of our election, then we must cling to the Word which the revelation of God in Jesus Christ attests to us and which brings near to us the Mediator Himself. Calvin is alluding to this Word when in that one passage he speaks of the "*signa posteriora*" of our election. The fact that within his exposition of the doctrine of predestination he never by one word supports the opinion that we can recognize the fact of our election by what we are or do, but rather flatly rejects that idea,[4] ought to give pause to all those who assert that Calvin teaches the *Syllogismus practicus*.

(*b*) But does he nowhere else in the whole of the *Institutes* support this doctrine? In the section on justification Calvin quotes at the end of a polemic against the Roman doctrine of merit 2 Peter 1 : 10. He says, "See, we justify man not by his works in the sight of God, but say that all those who are of God are born again and become new creatures, so that from the realm of sin they may enter the realm of righteousness and thus secure their calling by the witness they bear and as trees become recognized by their fruits."[5] The object of Calvin in this context is to show the Roman controversialists that he does not exclude works, that he teaches not only justification but sanctification. When in this connexion he simply quotes the exhortation of 2 Peter that we should make assured our calling, without adding any comment, we have no grounds for asserting that he is countenancing the *Syllogismus practicus*. Moreover we shall soon see that his exegesis of this text is quite different.

His real opinion on this point is expressed in another section of his account of justification. In the *Institutes* III, 14, 18 ff. he goes into the question of the *Syllogismus practicus*. It is the only place in which he does so in the whole work. For a right judgment of what he says it is of the greatest importance to note that he is not here concerned positively

---

[1] *In*. III, 24, 4.   [2] *Ibid*.   [3] *In*. III, 24, 5.
[4] *Ibid*.   [5] *In*. III, 15, 8.

to develop his own doctrine, but that the occasion is a debate with the Roman theologians on the significance of works.

The serious objection raised against Calvin is that the saints of the Old Covenant "often think of their innocence and uprightness and are comforted and strengthened thereby, even at times not refraining from self-praise".[1] What answer is he to make? He suggests that in this regard two possibilities arise. In many of such Old Testament passages the pious were comparing their own good conscience with the bad conscience of the godless, and were inferring from it hope of an eventual triumph. Hence they were not so much concerned to praise their own righteousness as to curse their adversaries.[2] These passages can be eliminated for the consideration of what is in question. Calvin has only to consider the second group of texts which imply that for the pious "the purity of their conscience, when they examine themselves in the sight of God, brings to some extent consolation and joy".[3] How are such passages of Scripture compatible with Calvin's own doctrine "that in the judgment of God we have no authority to rely upon our own works or to rejoice in the conceit of them"?[4] What is his reply to the Roman controversialists when they quote such Old Testament texts?

It is for him a matter of course that "the saints, when it is a question of the basis and security of their salvation, should fix their attention without any regard to their works solely upon the goodness of God. And they not only turn to it above all things as the source and fountain of their blessedness but rest in it as the fullness of life".[5] The mercy of God is the sole foundation of our bliss. Hence it alone can afford us assurance of our salvation; and, if it does afford us such certainty, then we need no other assurance. Calvin first establishes this principle; but he has not thereby answered the Biblical objections of his opponents. Then he continues in the following terms: "When our good conscience is thus firmly based and secured, it is further consolidated by a

---

[1] *In.* III, 14, 18. [2] *Ibid.* [3] *Ibid.* [4] *Ibid.* [5] *Ibid.*

consideration of our works in so far as they witness to the indwelling of God in us." "For just as all the gifts which God has given us are, if we think of it, like so many rays shining upon us from the divine countenance, to enable us to behold the glorious light of His mercy, so the good works which He has permitted us to do should serve still more the same end; for they show us that the spirit of adoption has been bestowed upon us." [1]

Thus Calvin concedes to the Roman theologians that our works may have a certain significance for the conviction that we are saved, but only when we have first of all fully and sufficiently recognized that it is through the sole mercy of God that we are saved. It is in this sense that Calvin desires to interpret the Old Testament texts in question. Their purpose is not to discuss the basis of our assurance of salvation. [2] But because the saints of the old covenant see in the fruits of their regeneration signs that the Holy Spirit dwells within them, "they are not a little encouraged thereby to wait for the help of God in all their distresses, because they feel Him to be, in the great passages of their life, a heavenly Father". [3]

This point of view is worked out by Calvin with greater precision in the sentences which follow. He makes quite plain what significance the *Syllogismus practicus* has: "And they cannot even do so unless they have first apprehended the goodness of God which is confirmed to them solely by the secure promises. For if they once begin to estimate it on the basis of their own good works, there is nothing more uncertain and unconvincing, seeing that the works when considered in themselves show no less the anger of God by their imperfection than they testify to His goodness by the purity which marked their commencement." [4] As it has already been argued that the mercy of God alone affords us full assurance of salvation and that our works can come into consideration only in a subordinate sense, so now Calvin reminds us that the divine mercy on which all our certitude

[1] *In.* III, 14, 18.   [2] *In.* III, 14, 19.   [3] *Ibid.*   [4] *Ibid.*

is based is attested to us in the promise of God in His Word. It is the will of God to reveal Himself to us in the Word. This Word as a testimony to our salvation has thus quite a different authority from that of our works, which can also be an indication to us that we are the children of God. The Word alone makes us truly confident of salvation in that it discloses to us the mercy of God. The works, as indications that we are in a state of grace, do not possess the same weight as the word of promise, but they can be added after the Word has already fulfilled its task. Works in themselves have absolutely no power to assure us that we are saved. One might interpret them as tokens of God's wrath as much as of His mercy. Their authority as witness depends entirely on that of the Word. In fact it is more likely that on account of the multitude of our sins "the conscience on examining its works will feel fear and despair rather than confidence".[1] This observation concludes the debate with the Roman controversialists, after Calvin has once again firmly pointed to the source of all our certitude which is contained in the Word. This source is the free grace of God, our Mediator Jesus Christ.[2]

Only if we fail to read carefully what Calvin writes at this point, or tear sentences from their context, can we assert that he is here expounding the doctrine that our works serve to confirm us in the assurance of salvation. The position is rather, broadly speaking, as follows: Calvin is not here establishing any principle of doctrine but is making a concession to the Romanists. Just here he is not developing his own teaching but is answering a serious Biblical objection raised by his opponents. In so doing he concedes that our works can be for us signs that we are in a state of grace, provided that we have first assuredly and sufficiently recognized our salvation to lie in the Word of God and in Christ. And in conclusion he really cancels the small concession which he was able to make to his opponents. For what else does it mean when he says that our works, because they are so intertwined with

[1] *In.* III, 14, 20.   [2] *In.* III, 14, 19, 20.

our sins, arouse in us despair rather than certainty? This is not what is usually meant by espousing a doctrine.

This is the clear finding which emerges from Calvin's major work, the *Institutes*. We now pass on to consider, from the point of view of our problem, his Scriptural exegesis. So far as we know, only two commentaries come seriously into consideration.

(*c*) In the commentary on 1 John there would have been in several places occasion to champion the *Syllogismus practicus* if that had been Calvin's intention. But only in two passages does he speak of it in any detail. Firstly in connexion with 1 John 3 : 14 : "We know that we have passed from death unto life because we love the brethren." Calvin comments: "In a striking statement the apostle commends to us the virtue of love because it is a testimony of our transition from death unto life." But two possible misunderstandings must here be set aside. The text does not mean "that man is his own saviour". The apostle "is not here speaking of the cause of salvation. But since love is the necessary fruit of the Spirit, it is also a sure sign of our regeneration." Hence it would be false to draw the conclusion "that by love we gain life, for love stands here in second place".

Equally false would be the further—and at first seemingly more justified—conclusion: "If love assures us that we have gained life, then the assurance of salvation rests upon works." "Although, of course, faith is strengthened and supported by the tokens of God's grace, yet it does not cease to have its sole basis in the mercy of God. For example: when it is bright around us we are certain that the sun is shining. If the sun irradiates the place in which we happen to be, we have a clearer field of view; but even if no visible rays reach us we are still satisfied that the sun bestows its light on us. Similarly after our faith has been rooted in Christ other things can be added in support of it. Yet, in spite of all that, it rests on the grace of Christ alone." [1] Our works, Calvin means, are not the real foundation of our salvation, nor are

---

[1] *CR* 55, 339.

they—and this concerns us more closely—the ground of our recognition of it; for it is not the tokens of God's grace, which include our good works, which assure us of salvation and of our being in a state of grace; that is the work of the grace of Christ alone. However much our works as tokens of the grace of God contribute to our certainty of salvation, its sole and sufficient ground is in Christ alone.

We have seen that Calvin expresses this point of view in the *Institutes*. But if we consider his exegesis of 1 John 3:14 in isolation we might suppose that here, as distinct from in the *Institutes*, Calvin really teaches the *Syllogismus practicus* even though he assigns to it less significance. But if we read on a little in the commentary, we shall have occasion to think otherwise.

On 1 John 3:19 Calvin comments as follows: "But let us always remember that it is not love which gives us the conviction of which the apostle speaks, as though from love we were to gain assurance of our salvation. In truth we know that we are the children of God for no other reason than that by His Spirit He seals in our hearts His free adoption of us as His children, and in faith we grasp this sure pledge which is offered to us in Christ. Love is thus an auxiliary of subordinate significance, given to us for the strengthening of our faith; but it is not the foundation on which faith rests."[1] Thus Calvin speaks here. He does not invite us to use the *Syllogismus practicus* in order to strengthen our faith, but he begins with the warning that we are not to place any false emphasis on such a proceeding. And it is very important to note that he also concludes his exegetical arguments with a similar warning: "Although a good conscience cannot be separated from faith, yet no one could rightly infer that we should examine our conduct in order to gain a firm assurance such as faith gives."[2] After his conclusion with such an observation it is impossible to assert that Calvin teaches here the *Syllogismus practicus*. His concluding point plays only a subordinate role in his previous considerations and at the

[1] *CR* 55, 341 ff.   [2] *CR* 55, 342.

close he almost annuls the exegetical concession which he has made.

With regard to this commentary on 1 John, we are thus faced with the question whether we are to place the greater emphasis on the exegesis of 1 John 3:14 or on that of 3:19. After all that we have heard Calvin urging, there cannot be the smallest doubt that we should understand the notes on 1 John 3:14 in the light of his exegesis of v. 19. His comment on this verse goes further than that on v. 14, and the amplification fits in with what we have seen to be Calvin's opinion in the *Institutes*. The expansion consists in a warning against the *Syllogismus practicus* and is at the same time a firm reference to Christ as the One who alone can assure us of salvation when we encounter Him in the power of the Holy Spirit.

The second commentary in which Calvin has occasion to say something about our problem is that on the second epistle of Peter. It is a question of the text 2 Peter 1:10, which we have already found mentioned in the *Institutes*: "Thus, dear brethren, give the more diligence to make your calling and election sure."

Calvin is aware that this verse is misused by Roman controversialists in support of their teaching. But the point surely is as follows: "Because God calls us and chooses us to the end that we should be pure and unspotted before His countenance, purity of life is not wrongly regarded as a sign of election and a proof whereby believers are not only made manifest to others as the children of God, but also are themselves confirmed in this faith, though they know that its sure foundation lies elsewhere."[1] This adds nothing new by contrast to what we have already found in Calvin. But the remark which he adds to these words is important for us: "Yet the assurance which Peter speaks of is in my judgment nothing to do with a good conscience, as though believers should recognize themselves in the sight of God to be the elect and the called. But I simply understand it to mean that

[1] *CR* 55, 450.

our calling should appear as certain from the holiness of our life." Calvin considers therefore that the Greek text may be translated thus: "See to it that your calling becomes assured." However this may be, "the main point is that the children of God are distinguishable from the damned by the sign that they live in piety and holiness".[1] Thus Calvin thinks that this text is not an allusion to the *Syllogismus practicus*. It does not invite believers to strengthen their assurance of salvation by a consideration of their good works, but it requires that they should contrast with others by the manner of their life. In this sense, too, Calvin adduces this Petrine text in the passage of the *Institutes* mentioned above. This is also shown by the fact that he places it alongside the other one about believers, like trees, being recognized by their fruit.[2] For the latter says simply that faith is not without works and that therefore the believer can be recognized by his works. But it does not say that works are of significance in answering the question whether I am a partaker of salvation or not.

(*d*) We will now summarize the result of our enquiry. Nowhere does Calvin teach the *Syllogismus practicus*. So much could only be asserted if from his own theological insights or in combating the errors of his opponents he had developed a special doctrine on this point, and—since it is a question of a *Syllogismus practicus*—were to encourage us to use this method of deduction. He does neither. If of course we wrest expressions of Calvin out of their context or bring together everything which has any sort of bearing on the *Syllogismus practicus*,[3] then it is possible that we may easily reach a different conclusion; by such a procedure we could find anything in Calvin that we wished to find. Conclusions reached in this way could make no claim to scientific scholarship. What we have found as a result of detailed and exact investigation is confirmed by the fact that neither Genevan

---

[1] *Ibid.*   [2] *In.* III, 15, 8.

[3] Cf. for example the explanation of the fifth petition of the Lord's Prayer. *In.* III, 20, 45; *CR* 6, 103 ff.; 45, 201.

Catechism mentions by so much as a syllable at any appropriate point this doctrine of the *Syllogismus practicus*.

Calvin's theology is too closely dependent on the Bible for him to be able to dismiss the texts which were quoted to him by opponents or which confronted him in exegesis. He concerned himself seriously with them. But he did not feel it appropriate to generalize from occasional apostolic observations, such as he found in 1 John, and to build upon them dogmatic definitions, however much the latter might have appeared the necessary consequence of a theology which, like that of Calvin, laid no less emphasis upon sanctification than upon justification.

Calvin felt able to admit that our works may become a sign of our godliness provided that in Christ we have previously gained assurance of salvation. But he emphatically called attention to the great danger of the *Syllogismus practicus*. We have already seen how grave were his doubts: Our "conscience feels upon consideration of our works more fear and despondency than confidence".[1] Or, as he says in another place: "When a Christian looks into himself he finds cause to be afraid or even to despair; but since he is called to communion with Christ he must, in so far as assurance of salvation is concerned, regard himself as a member of the body of Christ so that he is in a position to appropriate all the benefits of Christ's passion. Thus he will win a sure hope of eternal perseverance when he considers that he belongs to Him who cannot fall or fail."[2] Our salvation is grounded solely and exclusively in the mercy of God, which is to say in Christ. Hence we recognize that He alone is the Author of our salvation, who gives us the certainty of final deliverance.

But this is not meant to suggest that we tarry here in our wretchedness and uncertainty of deliverance while in the remote past looms the cross of Golgotha, bearing the figure of Him in whom all our hopes are anchored, and that we must look backwards, linking ourselves with the Crucified, in

---

[1] *In.* III, 14, 20.   [2] *CR* 49, 313.

order to gain assurance of being saved. No. He in whom God uniquely revealed His goodness takes the initiative in order to bring us into union with Himself. In Him, the Crucified and Risen Lord, God reveals Himself to us also to-day. Christ ever confronts us in the power of the Holy Ghost and bestows Himself upon us. Then we do indeed gain a sure hope; for He, our salvation, becomes our own.[1]

The means by which Christ the Risen and Ascended Lord wishes to encounter us to-day is the Word which bears witness to Him. Hence, when the question of salvation arises, Calvin not only refers to the mercy of God and to Christ but just as rigorously requires that we trust in the Word alone, because it is this Word which according to the will of God mediates to us the fullness of divine mercy in Jesus Christ.

There are certainly, according to the theology of Calvin, ancillaries to the Word which seal its promise and thus consolidate our faith and hope. But this function is performed not by our works but by the sacraments which Christ has instituted to this end. Calvin held fast to these commands of the Lord. Hence he did not invite us to use the *Syllogismus practicus* to strengthen our hope of salvation. But he did require the Christian society to celebrate the Holy Communion on Sundays because of the "great comfort which believers receive therefrom"; for in that service our faith receives the promise confirmed by visible signs "that we truly participate in the Body and Blood of Jesus, in His death, His life, His spirit, and all the benefits which He has procured for us".[2] And Calvin admonished every Christian to adhere loyally to the Word and Sacraments in order to become firm in the faith.[3]

The position which Calvin thus takes up makes it clear that his theology is something very different from a predestination system of thought concerning the relation of God and man, in which the *Syllogismus practicus* is assigned an important place. It becomes clear that Calvin is strictly con-

---

[1] *In.* III, 2, 24.   [2] *OS* i, 370.   [3] *CR* 13, 64.

cerned with the theology of revelation and that his teaching is wholly centred on Jesus Christ. For this reason he warns us against the *Syllogismus practicus*; for the latter implies that our view is deflected from God, who is to be found in Christ alone, and is turned towards man. By such a proceeding the hope of salvation is not increased but rather imperilled.

Chapter 13

THE CHURCH[1]

I. THE CHURCH AS THE MOTHER OF BELIEVERS

GOD provides the means whereby we ignorant slothful men, who are disobedient to truth, are called into fellowship with Christ and sustained therein. He Himself has made all the necessary arrangements for the faith which unites us to Christ "to be born in us and to grow unceasingly until it reaches its appointed end".[2] For this purpose God has committed the gospel which awakens faith to the keeping of the church. Calvin says very characteristically that God has deposited this treasure in the bosom of the church.[3] Just as a man invests his capital, so that it may work for him and bear fruit, so God has committed the gospel to the church. The latter, however, has no control over the gospel and may not exploit it to suit its own convenience, to influence men and bring them under its own authority. Rather it is God alone who remains Lord of the Gospel and who has entrusted it to the church, in His pure mercy, although the church is not worthy of such a treasure.

---

[1] Peter Barth: "Calvins Verständnis der Kirche" (*Zw. d. Zeiten*, 8, 1930, 216–33). J. Bohatec: *Calvins Lehre von Staat und Kirche mit besonderer Berücksichtigung des Organismusgedankens*, Breslau, 1937. P. J. Kromsigt: "Calvins Lehre von der Kirche" (*Bibl. Zeugnisse*, 22, 1924, 45–76). A. Lecerf: "La doctrine de l'église dans Calvin", (*Rev. de Théol. et de Philos.*, 1929, 256–70). Th. Werdermann: *Calvins Lehre von der Kirche in ihrer geschichtlichen Entwicklung* (*Calvinstudien*, Reform. Gemeinde, Elberfeld, 1909, pp. 246–338).

[2] *OS* 5, 1; 4, 12. Part of what follows is to be found in similar form in my essay: "Wesen und Gestalt der Kirche nach Calvin", *Ev. Theologie*, 3, 1936, pp. 311 ff.

[3] *In.* IV, 1, 1; 3, 1.

THE CHURCH

By the gospel Calvin understands the witness of the law, the prophets, and the apostles of Jesus Christ.[1] The church has not received this deposit from the Lord in order to preserve it with veneration and as a mass of pious tradition to hand it on from generation to generation. Of course the books of the Old and New Testaments compose Holy Scripture; but this does not mean that they are there to arouse pious admiration. They are not there to enable individuals to bury themselves in them for their own private edification. Rather the fact is that the church is in a supreme degree mastered and claimed by the gospel entrusted to it. The proclamation of the Messiah who is to come and has come makes of men, who would wish to use the gospel like any other truth as they please, servants who stand at the bidding of their Lord. In proportion as the good news is imparted to the church it claims the church for its service.

The Word of God is of such a character that it is not possible to treat it as though it were a piece of ancient religious tradition; but it requires to be spread abroad with audible speech so that it may have its way with men. God has committed this precious gift to the church so that the preaching of the gospel should remain a live and efficacious force.[2]

The good news of Jesus Christ orally proclaimed by the church captures our attention and arouses in us the response of faith. Calvin refers those who despise this mission of the church to the word of Paul: faith comes by hearing, by preaching.[3] "It is not without reason", he says, "when it is written that Jesus Christ shall smite the earth with the rod of His mouth and with the breath of His lips slay the wicked. The means by which He wishes to subdue us is the destruction of all that stands in His way." "God wills to make bare His sovereign power by means of the spiritual sword of His Word whenever it is preached by the pastor."[4] Although Christ no longer lives on this earth He rules by His Word. He overcomes and wins us by His Word which His preachers and

[1] *In.* IV, 1, 5.   [2] *In.* IV, 1, 1; *CR* 8, 412.   [3] *In.* IV, 1, 5.
[4] *CR* 13, 72.

servants declare. Christ has not left the world "in order to cast away all concern for us".[1] The very fact that He has set up His rule in the church is proof "that He is concerned about our salvation. Yes, He has borne witness that He will remain with His own and guide them to the end; and He continues to be objectively present through His ministers."[2] Jesus Christ is with us to-day in the word of His witnesses. By this orally declared Word we enter into communion with Him through faith and so come to share in the salvation which He has won for us.[3]

After the resurrection and ascension of Jesus Christ there did not dawn, as the ecstatics of all times have supposed, an aeon of the spirit in which we were allowed to enjoy an immediate and so-called spiritual relation with God. "It is always characteristic of God"—Calvin constantly admits this—"that He works and creates by spiritual means, but as He uses the servant of the Word as His instrument He inspires in the latter His own spiritual message; for He unites with the efforts of man the Power of the divine spirit."[4] It must not be forgotten that in order to draw near to the world God revealed Himself in the disguise of human flesh in the one man Jesus of Nazareth. And therefore both before and after the incarnation of His Son He does not act upon men otherwise. But parallel to that unique event He uses earthly means in order to approach mankind. He offers us His gifts in earthly vessels.[5] He wills to speak to us Himself through the mouth of men[6] and through visible elements—water, bread, and wine—to work upon us and within us. No pure reality of the spirit has been promised us apart from the work of the Incarnate Son of God nor in independence of the message which, obediently to His command, His witnesses spread abroad, or apart from the earthly sacraments which He has instituted. At this important point the teaching of Calvin is precisely the same as that of the Augsburg Confession—art. 5: "He has ordained pastors and teachers in order through their words to instruct His own, has invested

---

[1] *CR* 48, 3.   [2] *Ibid.*   [3] *In.* IV, 1, 1.
[4] *CR* 50, 235.   [5] *In.* IV, 1, 5.   [6] *CR* 48, 109.

them with authority, and in fact has left nothing undone which might serve the cause of the sacred unity of the faith and good order. Above all He has instituted the sacraments of which we in fact know that they are extremely useful means to preserve and strengthen our faith." [1]

There is a divinely ordained institution in this world; namely, the church. The church is the means by which the exalted Christ accomplishes His work among men. By the services which He has bidden it perform and by the earthly signs which He has entrusted to it He continues His action upon us and within us. "The Lord does not merely signify that it pleases Him when we are instructed by His servants, but He has committed that task to us as a holy ordinance which He has instituted." [2] "Since He is the Author of the ordinance, He wills that His presence should be recognized in the arrangements which He has made." [3] The church is the sphere of the self-revelation of God and of the encounter between Christ and ourselves.

God is not of course fettered by His own ordinances; but He has bidden us use the regular channels of preaching and instruction [4] and therefore we must obey His command and not enquire whether God could not also take over avenues of approach to us. That institution is authoritatively and permanently binding upon us. "God could no doubt in one moment perfect His saints; but He wills that they should not grow to maturity apart from the discipline of the church." [5] Since we live in a world which is hostile to God, our faith, the very moment it is born, is threatened on all sides. Christ must constantly call us and guide us by His word; He must again and again bestow Himself upon us if we are not to sink in this world of death. Hence the church as the sphere of Christ's presence is not only the point of departure for our life in faith, but because in it the living Lord confronts sinful men we are meant to abide within it throughout our earthly lives. "Those who despise the spiritual food of the

---

[1] *In.* IV, 1, 1; *CR* 20, 421 ff.   [2] *CR* 48, 204.   [3] *In.* IV, 1, 5.
[4] *Ibid.*; *CR* 18, 414.   [5] *Ibid.*

soul which Christ offers to them in the church deserve to perish from terrible hunger."[1]

For these reasons Calvin has characterized the being of the church by a single word which was applied to it from earliest times; the church is our mother. This name is fitting for it "because there is no other means of entry into life except that it should receive and bear us in its womb, feed us at its breasts, and then preserve us under its guardianship and guidance until we have put off this mortal flesh and have become like the angels. For our weakness does not permit that we should be dismissed from this school until we have spent our whole life therein. Consider further that outside its bosom there is no hope of either forgiveness of sins or of any felicity, as Isaiah and Joel declare, Jeremiah agreeing with them." In their words "the fatherly mercies of God and the special witness of the spiritual life are so bound up with the people of God that separation from the church always spells destruction".[2] Because the church is placed in the service of Christ, because it has His promise that He desires to meet us there and only there in human earthly guise, Calvin can—nay must—repeat the ancient saying that outside the church there is no salvation.[3] This truth is not grounded in the church as such, but solely in the will of its Lord. What is at stake in the ministry of the church is the realization of the presence of Jesus Christ in Word and Sacrament and thus something momentous and decisive— life or death. The fact that Calvin sees in the church such a mystery, divinely ordained to serve our salvation, is strikingly confirmed by the consideration that he has headed the decisive first chapter of his section on the church in the *Institutes*: *Of the true church, with which we strive to be at one, since it is the mother of all the pious.*[4]

Many will suppose that in this characterization of the essence of the church considerable vestiges of the Roman doctrine of the church are visible. On this point we must observe that in fact, here as elsewhere, Calvin is quite

[1] *In.* IV, 1,5.   [2] *In.* IV, 1, 4.
[3] Cf. also *CR* 11, 25; 36, 578.   [4] *In.* IV, 1, 1.

consciously dependent on the teaching of the early church and takes seriously the testimony of the church fathers. But in the last analysis he does so because he must agree with them in so far as he recognizes that, according to the divine will, we are made integral to an institution against which the pride of the godless but also that of the pious and religiously satisfied man rebels.[1] A "yoke of humility" is laid upon us.[2] We must surrender all our own religious resources, all our so-called points of contact with the knowledge of God, and simply accept the word of another, confronting us authoritatively. "God searchingly tests our obedience when we hear His servants not otherwise than if He Himself were speaking."[3] But this ordinance was created and made efficacious by God's merciful regard for us. "Because we are so ignorant, slothful, and vain that we need these external helps to allow faith to be born in us and to grow unceasingly to its appointed end, God has given us the same as a means of grace to help us out in our weakness."[4] God graciously condescends to us so that there may be an encounter between Himself and ourselves. He draws us to Himself by speaking to us in human fashion through His servants. Were He to speak to us directly, His majesty would terrify us and repel us.[5] Thus in the ministry of the church there takes place a condescension of God to our world similar to that implied in the incarnation of the Word in Jesus Christ. The condescension of God in the institution of the church is a type of the former original condescension.

2. THE CHURCH AS THE BODY OF CHRIST

But the church by tending us ceases to be an institution which is set over against us. We have seen that it is the sphere where Christ comes into our lives. By the fact that the Lord offers Himself to us in this His instrument "there arises an integrated structure of the congregation of the faithful, the

---

[1] *In.* IV, 1, 5.   [2] *In.* IV, 1, 6.   [3] *In.* IV, 1, 5.
[4] *In.* IV, 1, 1.   [5] *In.* IV, 1, 5.

Body of Christ is built up, and we grow in every part in adhesion to Him who is the Head and become at unity among ourselves".[1] Because the church acts upon us and within us we are drawn into its bosom. That very sense of confrontation, in which the ministry of the church is enacted towards us, works itself out in such a way that we become one body with Christ, and by our union with Him are drawn into a fellowship with each other which is distinguished from all earthly and religious fellowships by the fact that it rests, not upon a conviction and a decision of men, but solely upon the saving work of Christ exerted towards us. Because the Risen Lord claims men as His own, in order through them to complete His work, we belong together as those who serve as a congregation in which each is dependent on the help of others. Thus the church is not a rigid institution but a living organism, a fellowship of mutual service and help-fulness.[2] The thought of the Body of Christ, of the communion of saints, is necessarily bound up with the view that the church is the mother of believers.

This brings out very clearly the fact that Christ alone is the Lord of the church. Neither one individual nor individuals as a collective body may rule over the church; Jesus Christ alone is its ruler and head. As compared with Him we are all nothing but unprofitable servants.[3] In order that we may serve Him, as He wills, He must impart to each of us the gifts of His Spirit. Each receives from Him a special gift with which He is to work for the edification of the whole.[4] Even the outward goods of this life are given to us by God that we may bear the burden of the bodily needs of our brethren. "It cannot but be that those who are convinced that God is their common father and Christ their common head are united together in brotherly love and share their goods in common."[5] According to the gifts which Christ imparts, and the services which He expects from individuals so endowed, the various members of the church are dependent on each other. Such mutual interdependence

[1] *In.* IV, 3, 3.   [2] *In.* IV, 1, 2; *OS* 1, 466.   [3] *CR* 50, 235.
[4] *CR* 49, 238; 51, 192.   [5] *In.* IV, 1, 3.

precludes any government by individuals which would be destructive of church unity. Certainly there is in the church the fact of superiority and subordination. There is also the task of church government. Calvin has expressly drawn our attention to this and emphasized how necessary but also how difficult this task is.[1] But God places men in office over us only in order to keep inviolate His right.[2] Once this is overlooked, once the brotherly fellowship in mutual service of the members of the church is lost, then it is not just any sort of harm which results, but the church is most deeply damaged in its innermost being as the church of the one Lord. If we fail to see that the order and the government of the church spring from its very essence, we know little about the church as the body of Christ. "The right method of governing the church can be learnt from no other source but from Him alone, the Lord."[3] Of course the attempt is made again and again to plan a church which is governed in a manner alien to and completely dissociated from Christ. "But"—so Calvin exclaims—"what is that but a wanton and wicked attempt to separate the body from its head?"[4] The question of the order and the government of the church is for Calvin not indifferent nor secondary, but utterly central, because just there the sovereignty of Christ is at stake. It must be confessed, and the confession must be put into practice, that we as individuals and as a community are subject body and soul to Jesus Christ our Head in order that we may serve Him alone.

3. THE CHURCH AS THE ELECT PEOPLE

Calvin also described the church as "the congregation of elect people".[5] It was above all in the first edition of his *Institutes* and in his Catechisms that he stressed this aspect of its being. It is "the total number of the elect, whether angels or men and of men, whether dead or yet alive".[6] Calvin does not speak thus in order to detract from the significance of

---

[1] *CR* 11, 281, 168. [2] *CR* 48, 109 [3] *CR* 13, 284.
[4] *CR* 13, 283. [5] *In.* IV, 1, 2. [6] *OS* 1, 86.

those ideas which we have had in view so far. On the contrary, they receive from this new thought their most serious purport. "The secret choice of God is the foundation of the church"[1]; this thought at once severs at the root all self-praise of man, howsoever and wheresoever it may arise and spread in the church. In the church we really are confronted by the sovereignty of God and the glory of Christ. As a totality we are of just as little importance as individuals. As a church too we are nothing before Him, He is all. He has the first and last word over the church. He alone can separate the wheat from the chaff in the church. "He knows his own."[2]

But this knowledge must not lead us to idle speculations or drive us into a sense of insecurity and fear. "It is not enough that we with our understanding and heart should apprehend the church as the body of the elect, if at the same time we do not realize its utter unity, believing that we ourselves are incorporated into it."[3] We must not speculate idly but must cling to Christ if we are not to be lost eternally. The thought of God's election is pointed like a sharp sword against all who allow themselves to be complacent about their religious possessions, who exult in the historical development and impressive structure and exclusiveness of the church, but not against those who know they are utterly dependent on the grace of Christ. Those who realize that by faith they are made members of the body of Christ must not be afraid at the doctrine of election by divine grace, but rather strengthened in the assurance that faith gives. The church of the Lord, that body of poor and needy souls, must be comforted by this conviction: "Our salvation rests upon sure and firm foundations, so that even if the whole round world were to collapse, it could not itself dissolve. For first it rests upon God's own election and can just as little totter or vanish as His eternal providence."[4] Because the doctrine of election takes everything out of our hands, in reality it leaves us securely abiding in the ultimate certainty of God.

[1] *In.* IV, 1, 2.   [2] *Ibid.*   [3] *Ibid.*   [4] *In.* IV, 1, 3.

THE CHURCH

The thought of election by divine grace deprives the church of all self-security and power, but precisely in so doing strengthens it to accomplish its work in the world. It robs it of all false props and precisely so leaves it invincibly facing all the attacks of the powers of this world. According to Calvin's theory of the church, the fact of its election gives to the church its peace and certainty and the impetus which it needs for its ministry in this world.

4. THE VISIBLE AND THE INVISIBLE CHURCH

In connexion with the thought of election Calvin speaks at times of the invisible church.[1] After all that we have had occasion to say about his doctrine of the church, this cannot mean and does not in fact mean that he intended thereby to loosen in any sense our connexion with the church in which we live and whose cult we attend. The momentous statement that outside the church there is no salvation is found precisely in his arguments about the visible church which is the mother of us all.[2] If Calvin makes use of the Augustinian distinction between the visible and invisible church, it is not in order to withdraw the visible church partly or wholly from the rule of Christ and to hand it over to other powers. He does not intend his description "visible church" to be taken as a cloak behind which human weakness and sin, and the deliberate disavowal of the Lordship of Christ, may undisturbedly work themselves out. We do not see the church in its totality; for to it belong men who have gone before us and such as will come after us.[3] Again, not all whom we now see to be members of the church belong to it in reality. Much chaff is mixed with the wheat.[4]

But it does not lie within our province to make judgments about this, and hence Calvin does not lapse into idle and dangerous speculations. He takes over the ideas of Augustine, not in order to develop a doctrine of two churches, but rather in order to confront the empirical church which we know

[1] *In.* IV, 1, 7.   [2] *In.* IV, 1, 4.   [3] *In.* IV, 1, 2, 7.
[4] *Ibid.*

with the concept of the invisible church. All this play of ideas is intended to show clearly that God is really the Lord of the church and that therefore the church in which we live is not simply identical in its empirical reality with the Body of Christ. In this sequence of thought Calvin is moving on strictly Biblical lines.

Again, the fact that in his major work his arguments about the elect church, visible only to God, form an integral part of his consideration of the church as the mother of believers also suggests that he is using the ideas of the visible and invisible church in this sense. What he says about the truth that God alone knows His own is strictly concerned with the empirical church in which here on earth we live and from which, Calvin declares, we cannot separate ourselves without denying God and Christ.[1]

5. THE TRUE AND FALSE CHURCH

Let us remind ourselves that he has entitled the first decisive chapter of the *Institutes*: *Of the true church, with which we strive to be at one, since it is the mother of all the pious.* The next chapter, which is intended to support his arguments against the Roman church, bears the heading: *Comparison of the false church with the true.* Here Calvin introduces, as a further criterion, an antithesis which does not occasion such common misunderstanding as does the expression visible and invisible church. Here it becomes plain that there is not one church in the world which must make its peace, well or ill, with the powers of this world and over and above this in the beyond, the true and pure church; rather there is only one church which is distinguished from the spurious church by the fact that it exists to serve Jesus Christ. In spite of the very relevant distinction between the true and the false church, Calvin cannot give up the usual critical antithesis of visible and invisible church. For he is obliged to use the critical idea of the invisible church precisely with regard to the church which serves Christ in this world, and proves its

[1] *In.* IV,. 1, 10.

truth by this service, and is also on account of its activity in the world a visible church. Precisely if it is the true church of its Lord it will be ready to undergo the test of that critical idea and so will witness to the glory of its Head.

The true church, in so far as it is an empirical reality in this world, is visible for every one. The same considerations apply to it as to its Lord when He tarried upon the earth. Against the background of the world the church emerges as a despicable thing.[1] Just as the world in its enmity to God did not allow that Jesus was His Son, no more is the church recognized as the body of the Son who as Head of His communion is also the Lord of the world. But by faith we can "come to know which is the true church of God; namely, that which follows the pure truth, i.e. which allows itself to be guided by the teaching of Moses and the prophets and of our Lord Jesus Christ".[2] The church which realizes by Holy Scripture that Christ accepts its service is the true church. It cannot but be that the church which rightly bears that name becomes visible for us "where Christ is manifest and His living Word is heard".[3] For where the Head is, there is also the body.

Since Jesus Christ—as we have already seen—comes face to face with His own in the Word that is preached and the sacramental signs which are added, Calvin like the Augsburg confession specified as the marks of the true church the unadulterated proclamation of the Word and the due celebration of the sacraments.[4] "We must maintain that the church is not otherwise edified than by oral preaching, and that believers are held together by no other bond of union than their adherence to the divinely prescribed order of the church, their hearing of the Word in unity, and their constant expansion and growth"[5]; for He wills that in the words of His witnesses His own voice should resound.[6] In doctrine, that is to say, in the preaching of Jesus Christ, the countenance of God shines forth upon us.[7] It is reflected in

[1] *CR* 43, 361.　　[2] *CR* 41, 482.　　[3] *CR* 7, 31.
[4] *In.* IV, 1, 9; *CR* 10b, 275, 309.　　[5] *In.* IV, 1, 5.
[6] *Ibid.*　　[7] *Ibid.*

the mirror afforded by the preaching of His Word.[1] Hence true and pure preaching of the Word which Scripture testifies to us is the one sign of the true church. Still more powerfully than the orally preached Word the sacraments proclaim to us the presence of Jesus Christ. Where in the midst of the world of visible and tangible things the signs chosen by Christ Himself appear in due operation, we can be certain that there Christ and His flock are to be found. These earthly elements—water, bread, and wine—have the effect, so to speak, of making it impossible for the world to overlook the church.

Since Christ has commanded us to preach the Word and to administer the sacraments as the means by which He wills to act upon us and within us, we may be sure that these instruments are never void and without fruit.[2] Whenever the Word is preached and the sacraments are administered according to His will, Christ Himself confronts us in His living reality, and where He is there also are His own. These appointed tokens of the presence of Christ guarantee for us the existence of the church at a specific "locus", even though false brethren be found within it.[3]

On the other hand we cannot deduce from an assembly of pious men as such, neither from its size nor from its character, whether we have before us the congregation of the Lord. The true signs by which the church can be recognized lie as it were within the disposal of the church, but they are not contained within the fellowship of believers itself. They are the means of grace but not the results of grace.

Calvin's objection to all who wished still to recognize the Roman Church as the true church was that it could not in any case be the church of Jesus Christ "who makes His own flock recognizable by other tokens when He says: My sheep hear my voice".[4] The institution as such does not constitute the signs, nor does the fact of an existing notable religious body. The question arises whom that body worships. "The church of God is distinguished from all corrupt sects by the

[1] *In.* IV, 1, 5. [2] *CR* 53, 308. [3] *CR* 38, 228.
[4] *CR* 10b, 149.

fact that it alone hearkens to His word and is willing to be guided by His counsels."[1]

Nor does Calvin consider that the fruits of piety in the church are a sure sign by which it can be recognized. How in such matters could we make a confident judgment? It is a dangerous temptation to refuse to believe in any church which does not evince perfect purity of life.[2] Calvin rejected in an impassioned way the delusive ideal of a spotless church.[3] For in church life it is not a question of striving to attain an ideal community but of accepting the life in fellowship which Christ bestows upon us. What is at issue is the living reality of Christ; not the formation of a circle of pious men.

The fact that Calvin accepts as valid signs of the true church only the Word and the sacraments strikingly shows that his doctrine of the church is a testimony to God's revelation in Jesus Christ, and not a characterization of the essence of religious fellowship.

6. THE DANGER OF SCHISM

Because the true church only exists where the pure Word is preached and the sacraments are rightly administered, there is constant need for every church to examine itself.[4] The preaching of the Word is unceasingly threatened in this world. Satan himself is at pains to silence the authentic proclamation of the Word.[5] Hence it behoves the church to watch in all earnestness. But even here the adversary intrudes himself, and attempts to seduce us into applying false criteria so that we turn our backs on the church without sufficient reason.[6] Hence we must bear in mind that when the question of the true church is raised—as it must be raised—Satan ever lurks in our path.

In regard to this perilous situation Calvin issued the most serious warning against a premature secession from the church for some doctrinal reason or other. We have already

[1] *CR* 48, 569.　　[2] *CR* 49, 307.　　[3] *In.* IV, 1, 13.
[4] *In.* IV, 1, 11.　　[5] *Ibid.*　　[6] *Ibid.*

heard him affirming that he who abandons the church, his mother, without sufficient cause, is denying God and His Christ.[1] For His body must not be torn asunder. Its unity should find expression even on this earth. Anyone who sees in Calvin the author of all modern centrifugal tendencies in church life shows that he has not read a single line of him. When the Reformer had been expelled from Geneva his followers refused any longer to take part in the Holy Communion service as celebrated by pastors who were hostile to him. On this occasion Calvin absolutely implored his friends to desist from their intention, so that the unity of the church might not suffer harm.[2] There is no reason to leave the church simply because the preaching contains some false elements and strange doctrines are disseminated; "for there is probably no church which is not marred by some degree of ignorance".[3]

This does not mean that Calvin defended or indeed extenuated error.[4] Calvin has acquired the reputation of being a schismatic because of his sharp break with Rome.[5] But the schism can only be made responsibly when "the church has completely lapsed from the adoration of God and the preaching of the Word".[6] When the message of salvation is no longer heard and the sacraments are perverted or set aside, then Christ is no longer preached and His church no longer exists in such circumstances, whatever appearances may be. In such a case the only possible course is secession.[7] Calvin attempted to specify the fundamental points of Christian doctrine which the church must unconditionally hold.[8] He means of course those aspects of doctrine which are essential to salvation.[9] But such an enumeration must always remain inadequate, because in the last resort the one essential doctrine of the church which may never be impaired is nothing other than its testimony to the prophets and the apostles of Jesus Christ.[10] Once that foundation is abandoned

[1] *In.* IV, 1, 10. [2] *CR* 10b, 309 [3] *CR* 10b, 275, 309.
[4] *In.* IV, 1, 12. [5] *In.* IV, 2, 5. [6] *CR* 10b, 310.
[7] *In.* IV, 2, 2. [8] *In.* IV, 1, 12. [9] *CR* 10b, 354.
[10] *In.* IV, 2, 1.

it can no longer be called a church. When Christ ceases to be known as the living Lord, then, in spite of its outward forms and ordinances, the church no longer exists.[1] But even so Calvin's reserve in passing judgment is clear from the fact that in the Roman church itself he perceived traces of the true people of God, because it held fast to the sacrament of baptism.[2]

On this whole question it is to be noted that those who believe in Christ are not in danger of schism.[3] They are convinced of the unity of the body of Christ into which they are incorporated. If they are compelled to secede, there is no break up of church unity but a discrimination of the true and the false.

7. CHURCH DISCIPLINE

Implicit in the church's task to preach in purity the Word of God and rightly to administer the sacraments is not only the clear necessity of unremitting vigilance in self-examination, and the dangerous possibility of schism, but also the disciplinary duty of the church with regard to its individual members. In Word and sacramental sign Jesus Christ wills to meet His own as they experience the inspiration of the Holy Spirit. Hence it is impossible that those should take part in the assembly of the congregation who show by word or deed that they live a life of impenitence in open rebellion against the word of the preacher. In order to obviate contempt of the Word it is imperative that pastor and elders should care for each individual member of the flock and admonish each in particular by the solemn message of the divine Word.[4] Such admonition of the individual forms the basis of church discipline. If any one refuses to hear the special warnings thus addressed to him, and openly rejects the Word of God, then in the last resort he must be excluded from the fellowship of the faithful so that Christ who dwells in its midst be not blasphemed and dishonoured.[5] Thus

[1] *In.* IV, 2, 3. [2] *CR* 10b, 308; *In.* IV, 2, 11. [3] *CR* 45, 665.
[4] *In.* IV, 12, 2. [5] *In.* IV, 12, 5.

exclusion from the Holy Communion does not mean that a specially severe punishment is administered to the one concerned after other attempts to reform him have failed. It implies rather that the notorious sinner may not present himself at the service where Christ offers His presence to His own. "For it is assuredly true that any minister who wittingly admits to the sacrament a person whom he should properly refuse is as guilty as if he were to cast the body of the Lord away to the dogs."[1] Such church discipline is necessary for the sake of the Lord of the church. By seeking to preserve the honour of Christ in the church this disciplinary action serves to call the sinner to repentance, and that with the utmost seriousness, while at the same time it secures others against the temptation to lapse.[2]

Thus church discipline does not exist in order to promote moral conduct in the church, or in order to attain purity of church life. We have seen how sharply Calvin disallows such endeavours. But his criterion that the true church is to be recognized solely by the purity of its preaching of the Word and by its due celebration of the sacraments does not mean that he did not think the inner life of the church important. This is not the case provided that the church has already been summoned to obedience by the preaching of the Word. But whether the church is a true church or not cannot be decided by the moral condition of its life; it must be decided solely by asking whether it preaches the Word. That is an important consideration for us; for the sake of our salvation we must be clear whether a church, be it the local church or the church in its totality, is genuine or not. Hence God has given us the two infallible tests we have mentioned that we may recognize the truth.[3] The degree of spirituality which the church evinces is not an indubitable sign. "For those who seemed lost and utterly abandoned are by the mercy of God brought back into the way of life, and such as seemed most advanced often fall."[4] Hence in regard to individuals we can make no certain judgment whether they

[1] *In.* IV, 12, 5, cf. *CR* 13, 76; 14, 606; 17, 452.
[2] *In.* IV, 12, 5.   [3] *In.* IV, 1, 8.   [4] *Ibid.*

are Christians or not; we can only judge them in love. We must "regard as members of the church all such as testify to God and Christ by their confession of the faith, the example of their lives, and their participation in the sacraments".[1]

The knowledge, both necessary and consoling to us, that the church exists where Christ is preached, in spite of all shame and weakness, does not, however, release us from the task of discipline, from vigilant attention to the life of the church and of every single one of its members; not with a view to achieving some sort of moral standard but for the sake of Christ and His honour. If in any church His name is proclaimed, while His Lordship is denied, and nothing happens to those who rebel against Him, then the Church is endangered in the extreme. Calvin did not include the fact of the exercise of church discipline among the signs by which the true church may be recognized. Here again the Christocentric direction of his theology becomes clear. The reality of the church depends not upon our standards, even though they may have been commanded us, but solely upon the work of Christ accomplished towards us and within us through Word and Sacrament. Yet Calvin maintained that the existence of the church can hardly be preserved apart from the exercise of discipline.[2] "As the saving message of Christ is the soul of the church, so its discipline is like the sinews by which the members of the body each in its place are held together."[3] If the church allows each member to behave as he pleases, if it permits the government of man to be established in its midst, then it is threatened as a community of the Lord and its complete dissolution is imminent.[4]

8. THE ORDER OF THE CHURCH

In Calvin's description of the essence of the church it becomes at once plain that the church has an order. This is not due to the fact that it lives in this everyday world and of

---

[1] *In.* IV, 1, 8.   [2] *CR* 10b, 154.
[3] *In.* IV, 12, 1; *CR* 13, 76.   [4] *In.* IV, 12, 1.

necessity must adopt something of the forms of its social life. Rather the church has an order because it is the mother of believers and the body of Christ here below. We have sketched out the fundamental thoughts of Calvin on this point in the two first sections, and propose now to call attention to one or two matters of detail.

The order of the church is implicit in the service which it is called upon to fulfil. Both as a local church and as a totality it is not built up from powers inherent in its common life, but from the functions which devolve upon it. The life of the church is ordered from above, from Christ, who acts through His Spirit and His gifts. Neither a single individual nor the society as a whole has any controlling power over the organization of the church. Calvin thinks that the assembled believers have just as little to say about the matter as any single member. The right order is imparted when all even to the least are obedient to Christ as sovereign King[1]; when they are guided by His Spirit[2] and the church thus manifests itself as His body, as the communion of the saints in which each serves the other according to the gift which is given him. The order of the church is the true one when it expresses the fact that Christ is the sole Lord and Master of His own.[3]

What are the marks of such an order? In answering this question Calvin refers us to Scripture and says that we must adhere to its precepts.[4] He followed his own injunction, but not in the sense that he deduced from Scripture principles for the ordering of church life. Hence he did not project a church order on the basis of such guiding principles and put it into practice at Geneva. Calvin was far removed from so misunderstanding the Bible and from the reliance on works which such an approach would imply.

Yet, of course, Calvin appreciated as a result of his Scriptural studies that various offices are necessary for the proper organization of the church. All these offices have the one purpose of proclaiming Christ and His reign; for only so is the church truly edified. The most important office is

[1] *CR* 48, 357.   [2] *CR* 10b, 308.
[3] *CR* 52, 147; 48, 188; 52, 95, 172.   [4] *CR* 11, 281.

that of the pastors to whom is entrusted the duty of preaching and of administering the sacraments.[1] Closely allied to it is the office of the doctors.[2] Their duty is constantly to test the preaching of the church by the norm of Holy Scripture and to train future ministers.[3] The function of the pastors and doctors is the most essential because Christ Himself wills to speak to us out of the mouth of those who bear these offices.[4] "Without pastors and doctors there is no guidance in the church."[5] But the function of the elders who together with the pastors—to be sure Calvin sees in the latter not merely preachers but, as the name implies, shepherds of the flock[6]— exercise discipline,[7] proclaims the Lordship of Christ; for its effect is to restrain evildoers. Finally the deacons in the performance of their duties show that Christ is merciful towards the wretchedness and weakness of our body and satisfies our earthly needs.[8]

It should already have become clear from this short account of the offices of the church that Calvin by distinguishing these four functions did not attempt to construct a system of orders and to base it upon Scriptural references. But he recognized from Holy Scripture that these various functions must be permanently fulfilled if the church is to expand and be preserved. In this connexion it is to be noted that for Calvin an order of the church is not a given prerogative but, in the New Testament sense, a ministry.[9] Hence at times he refers to the various modes of service[10] or functions[11] to be fulfilled in the church rather than to offices.

How little rigid is Calvin's doctrine of order can be seen from the fact that he recognizes special powers and functions to be characteristic of special seasons in the church; and hence he allows for extraordinary offices,[12] as, for example, the apostolate or the prophetic office or the gift of healing

---

[1] *In.* IV, 3, 4.   [2] *In.* IV, 1, 1; 4, 1; *CR* 51, 198.
[3] *In.* IV, 3, 4; *CR* 51, 198.   [4] *In.* IV, 1, 1.   [5] *CR* 51, 198.
[6] *CR* 10b, 154.   [7] *In.* IV, 3, 8; *CR* 52, 315.
[8] *In.* IV, 3, 9; *CR* 48, 96, 265.   [9] *In.* IV, 3, 2.
[10] *Officia*: IV, 3, 8; *CR* 51, 198.   [11] *Functiones*: IV, 3, 4; 46, 23.
[12] *Ibid. CR* 49, 506; *OS* 5, 50, 17.

the sick. But it must especially be noted that as regards the permanently necessary offices Calvin affirmed as self-explanatory that more than one of these can be exercised by the same person. The pastor must in any case fulfil also the duty of an elder, while that of the doctor is also open to him,[1] and similarly the doctor can serve as a preacher and pastor.[2] In the final edition of his *Institutes* even, Calvin speaks in one important passage of three rather than of four orders in the church, reckoning the office of pastor and that of doctor as the same.[3]

Of course it must be said that offices may not arbitrarily be accumulated in the hands of one person. The pre-requisite for the bestowal of an office is that the person concerned shall have the necessary capabilities.[4] And in this respect we have already seen, in discussing the church as the body of Christ, that the Lord does not bestow all gifts on one individual but distributes the gifts of the Holy Ghost in such a way that each member is dependent on others, so that the coherence and the unity of the church are promoted.[5] Human ambition and desire to rule must be checked. "We must therefore realize that in the church we are assigned our places by the Lord in such a way that we must serve each other under the one Head; we must realize also that we are so endowed with a manifold diversity of gifts that we serve the Lord in all modesty and humility and bear in mind the honour of Him who has given us all that we possess."[6] This is why Calvin so much stresses the fact that the ministry of preaching in its varied aspects should be undertaken by variously gifted persons; the gifts which Christ has imparted to each individual are to be respected and thus "the sole Lordship and pre-eminence of Christ"[7] must be secured and His position as Head of the church recognized. For Calvin's doctrine of orders the New Testament vision of the church as the body of Christ is fundamental, while the thought of the

[1] *In.* IV, 3, 4.   [2] *CR* 51, 198.   [3] *In.* IV, 4, 1.
[4] *CR* 51, 196; IV, 3, 12.
[5] *CR* 51, 192; 49, 497 f., 238, 367, 503; 48, 186; *In.* IV, 6, 10.
[6] *CR* 49, 367.   [7] *CR* 48, 186.

priesthood of all believers, which only too easily can be understood as a common possession of all the necessary gifts, plays no part in his doctrine. Here again the strong Christo-centric tendency of his theology becomes clear.

Although the ministry and especially that of the preacher remains always a service, and its members are servants and unprofitable instruments of God,[1] yet its authority must be recognized and it must be had in honour of men. This is so because God Himself, as we have already seen, wills to act towards us mediately through the agency of men.[2] Naturally the dignity of the individual minister varies according to the character of the gifts and offices; but it is always a fact.[3] Calvin declares that the Lord wills that His servants should be regarded plainly as His messengers.[4] "To them is applicable the word: Whosoever hears you hears me: whosoever despises you despises me."[5] The preachers of the Word "represent the Person of the Son of God".[6] Hence Calvin could dare to say that by his ministry Christ ruled His flock.[7] He knew, of course, that the authority and dignity of the office did not spring from the man to whom it is committed. This authority and dignity are rather inherent in the office itself, or better still in the Word of God, to serve which the person concerned is called.[8]

No one should presume of himself to seize the authority and dignity of any office.[9] For the exercise of any office it is indispensable that one should be truly called.[10] This calling is decided by election.[11] For an understanding of Calvin's doctrine it is extremely instructive to observe how he conceives this election. It does not mean that by the will of a majority is to be decided what person is to hold any particular office in the church, whilst the independent power of the individual wishing to hold such office must be repressed. The choice does indeed take place through the agency of men; but it is not they who properly speaking decide

---

1 *CR* 49, 350; 50, 235.   2 See above.   3 *CR* 50, 190.
4 *CR* 10b, 352.   5 *In.* IV, 3, 3.   6 *CR* 27, 688.
7 *CR* 11, 121.   8 *In.* IV, 8, 2.   9 *In.* IV, 3, 10; *CR* 55, 59.
10 *In.* IV, 3, 10.   11 *In.* IV, 3, 15; *CR* 48, 120.

anything in the matter. Their own wishes are just as much excluded as the initiating impulse of the individual who considers himself to be the right man for the duty. The decision concerns the Lord of the church in that He distributes the gifts which are requisite for the offices in question.[1] The choice is nothing other than the recognition of this decision, seeing that the one who possesses the necessary suitability for the post concerned is only described and indicated.[2] This state of affairs is confirmed by the fact that the choice is only undertaken after prayer. Since the electors are not in a position to discover the right man whom they need, they ask God for the Spirit of counsel and understanding.[3] If this method is not followed, if they do not proceed to elect the bearer of office with the greatest care but prefer to appoint any one to the service of the church as they please, then a great injury is done to God Himself.[4] In particular it is implicit in Calvin's idea of the church that it is impossible for any one individual to appoint to office in accordance with his own discretion. The choice fundamentally concerns the church as a whole, that is, the community of Christ.[5] But in order that it should not simply be a triumph for the will of the majority but a real choice of the church, Calvin states in regard to practical procedure that there should be co-operation between the existing pastors and the congregation as a whole.[6]

It is also incumbent upon the church to see that the one thus elected to office rightly exercises his functions.[7] Only he can claim obedience who proves himself to be a faithful servant of Christ.[8] Appointment by the church does not in itself guarantee this. If we wish to know who is a servant of Christ, we must consider both aspects—calling and fidelity in the conduct of office.[9] But it is with the utmost reserve that Calvin speaks of the possibility that the church may depose those servants of whom it becomes persuaded that

---

[1] *In.* IV, 3, 11.   [2] *In.* IV, 3, 15, 12; *CR* 12, 296.
[3] *In.* IV, 3, 12.   [4] *CR* 48, 121.   [5] *CR* 48, 120.
[6] *In.* IV, 3, 15.   [7] *CR* 49, 361.   [8] *Ibid.*
[9] *CR* 49, 305, 362; 52, 172.

they have insinuated themselves into office without possessing the inward conviction of a divine call. In such action the risks are too great that the sacred dignity of the office and in the last resort the honour of its Giver may be violated.[1]

In no case may anyone be removed from office "or the recommendation of some other authority" without the rightful judgment of the church.[2] If without cause we compel a man to leave the church, then we are doing wrong not only to a man but to God Himself; for the person concerned was called to his office not merely by men but through them by God Himself.[3] Calvin required the servants of the Word to be fully answerable for the right exercise of their office: "It would be more than infamous if we pastors who exhort the flock to shed their blood as a testimony to Christ are made unsteady by any kind of fear. For what could be said if we, in order to maintain our power and prestige, were to fall away from Christ and the gospel?"[4] If anyone, however, relinquishes his post deliberately, he is a traitor. "If we are subjected to compulsion it is not our duty to resist unless the church requires us expressly to expose ourselves to every danger; for then it would be better to die a hundred times than to fail to respect the counsels of those who are prepared to follow Christ."[5] Because the holder of an office has not taken that office by his own exertions, but has received it by invitation of the church, it is not only he but the whole Christian society which is concerned to defend and secure it.

Whoever subverts the order of the church is fighting against God.[6] "The church should realize this for its comfort but also for its admonition. If a member of the church is not content with the position assigned to him and presumes to undertake further tasks, then, like the giants, he is declaring war on God."[7] The threat to church order by attacks from without or by encroachments on the part of individual members within is something of momentous import. The church order

---

[1] CR 55, 59.   [2] CR 15, 213; 10a, 223.   [3] CR 11, 295.
[4] CR 12, 689; cf. 11, 625, 707.   [5] CR 13, 156, 194.
[6] CR 49, 238.   [7] CR 49, 503.

which Calvin outlines rests upon the divine command.[1] We refer to the order which arises from the fact that God wills to act towards us through human agency, and which gains articulation and unity because God imparts varied gifts for manifold functions and thus binds us to each other through our mutual service.

9. CHURCH CEREMONIES

From what precedes it should have become clear that Calvin understands the organization of the church wholly in the light of Jesus Christ its Head. This decisive orientation of his thought is suggested also by his discussion of other questions concerning the structure of the church. If he warns us against secession on the ground of doctrinal disagreements, still less, he thinks, should there be divisions arising from differences about the forms of church life and worship. It is not necessary for the unity of the church that everywhere the same ecclesiastical rites and customs should prevail. Because the members of the church are Christ's own flock, they enjoy freedom in this matter.[2]

But this does not mean that occasionally a question of form and rite may not become a decisive issue. It is well known that Calvin opposed any co-ordination of Genevan sacramental usage with that of Berne—it was a question of baptismal fonts and wafers—and preferred to leave the city rather than give way on the point. But he was not primarily concerned about the use of fonts and wafers. "That is an indifferent matter which each church is free to decide."[3] Rather it was a question of the freedom of the church over against the state, which insisted on this degree of co-ordination.

For another reason Calvin did not so keenly defend the sacramental usage of Geneva. He says for example in regard to the celebration of the Lord's Supper: "As for the outward details of the action, whether believers should take the bread

[1] *CR* 49, 238.　　[2] *CR* 14, 285; 15, 538.　　[3] *CR* 10b, 189.

in their hand or not, should distribute it among themselves or whether each should eat the portion just as it is given to him, whether they should hand back the cup to the hand of the deacon or pass it to their neighbour, whether the bread should be leavened or unleavened, whether red or white wine should be used—all this is of no importance. These things are merely material instruments about which we can decide freely." [1] Under no circumstances must we idolize what are after all simply the forms of worship. Otherwise we are no longer serving the Lord of the church in the freedom of the children of God but are serving idols in the spirit of bondage. "It would be extraordinary indeed if in those matters in which the Lord has granted us freedom, in order that we might have greater scope for the edification of the church, we were to strive to attain a slavish uniformity without really caring about the true ordering of church life. For when we appear before the judgment seat of God in order to give account of our deeds we shall not be asked about ceremonies. In any case, such uniformity in outward matters will receive no consideration; we shall rather be asked about the right use of freedom. But the right use will be that one which has contributed most to the edification of the church." [2] Such is the opinion of Calvin who has been branded as legalistic. The church does not live and grow by strict conformity with specific forms. It does not live at all by our works, but solely by the Word of God. Now and then it is even good if complete uniformity does not prevail "so that it may be manifest that the Christian faith does not consist in such matters". [3] Every structure of church life can only have the purpose of contributing to the strengthening of the church through the power of the Word. That is the decisive viewpoint which should determine our use of ecclesiastical custom, and ritual.

This consideration too should prevent us from arbitrarily creating new forms of church organization and worship as we please and making innovations. The church is free in such

---

[1] *In.* IV, 17, 43.   [2] *OS* I, 432.   [3] *CR* 14, 285; 15, 538.

matters because it is bound to its Head, Jesus Christ. Everything must serve Him.

10. THE PERILS TO WHICH CHURCH ORDER IS EXPOSED

However true it is that the mission of the church implies an order according to which its worship should be carried out, and important as it is that it should be properly organized and governed, Calvin realizes nevertheless that the shape of the church is not always evident.[1] The church is, of course, not at home in the world, it is on its pilgrimage and has not yet attained its goal; it is therefore threatened by every sort of danger and enemy without and within. It may be the case that in certain periods of history the church can find expression only in the form of house-communities.[2] God often marvellously sustains the church in hiddenness and obscurity.[3] This imposes a severe test on its members. God wishes at times to teach them that it is He alone who protects the church with His power and apart from all human aid.[4] In fact when it seems on the point of perishing "it is wonderfully preserved as in a tomb" though it is no longer visible.[5] Even in the destruction of church order Christ manifests His sovereignty, even when in the opinion of men the church is declining His name is praised. In such circumstances the church will again emerge one day because it has God as its ever watchful Guardian.[6] He will "miraculously gather it together after it has been scattered, that it may grow up again as one body".[7] God so upholds the church "that He maintains it even when the whole world is perishing".[8]

These considerations of Calvin show that for him the being of the church is not dependent on any specific form or structure of church life. If we wish to judge by the appearance of things and "to believe the evidence of our eyes, we shall soon come to think that the church is finished. Since the Lord visits His own with the greater punishment all

[1] OS 3, 23, 38; CR 38, 597.   [2] OS 1, 326.   [3] CR 40, 237.
[4] CR 12, 552, 513.   [5] CR 40, 387.   [6] CR 12, 25.
[7] CR 38, 597.   [8] CR 12, 525.

attempts at rescue appear impossible; and since the various sicknesses of the church seem to us incurable, we should soon be comfortless if the promise of God did not come to us."[1] Where the Word of God is living, there we are called into the church in spite of the wretchedness and apparent hopelessness of its plight. There the church of Jesus Christ comes alive.

II. THE CHURCH MILITANT

Calvin was under no illusions about the fact that the church is committed to warfare in this world and must always be militant. In its own strength the church cannot win through. The power of endurance is not promised to the church as such, but only to the church in so far as it abides in Christ.[2] In Him alone will it be able to overcome its enemies.[3] Because under the ensign of Christ we fight as victors, confident in His strength, we may aspire to be triumphant.[4] And if the church appears to succumb: "it will remain healthy even in the valley of the shadow of death, and in ultimate despair it will nevertheless be freed by the power and help of God".[5] Calvin set no store on so-called extensions of the front in battle,[6] but trusted wholly in the promise of God and based all his hopes on Christ alone: "One thing alone will suffice to strengthen us, namely, the fact that we have a leader who is so invincible that the oftener he is attacked the more he emerges victorious."[7] Yet at times Calvin sighed about the protracted and severe nature of the struggle. He had no desire to evade it in order to enjoy rest and peace. "We shall not grow weary of fighting under the sign of the cross of our Lord Jesus Christ; for that is more valuable than all the victories of this world."[8] But Calvin saw that the church was engaged in eschatological warfare,

---

[1] CR 42, 578.   [2] CR 48, 194.   [3] CR 48, 277.
[4] CR 13, 597.   [5] CR 41, 289.
[6] CR 27, 614. Cf. also his statement: "quam perversum sit multitudine ecclesiam metiri, ac si in turba consisteret eius dignitas" (CR 15, 199).
[7] CR 13, 286.   [8] CR 12, 561, 659, 552, 513.

and hence longed for the end which God will bring in when the church, delivered at last from all strife, will rest in its Lord as one who has overcome. This longing stirred in him daily.[1] This is shown by the prayers which at the close of each lecture he offered up in the presence of the students. Usually they end by looking forward to the consummation, "to the coming glory of the kingdom of God in Jesus Christ".[2]

[1] *CR* 21, 161; *In.* III, 9, 5.
[2] J. Calvin, *Gebete zu den Vorlesungen über Jeremia und Ezechiel*, trans. W. Dahm, Munich, 1934. The publishers of *CR* have unfortunately published the lectures on the books of the Bible without these prayers.

Chapter 14

THE SACRAMENTS[1]

WHEREAS the fifth article of the *Augustana* reads: "To win such faith God has instituted the order of preaching and has given the gospel and sacraments as means by which He imparts the gift of the Holy Ghost",[2] Calvin begins his doctrine of the church with the observation that God has instituted "shepherds and teachers in order to instruct His servants by their words" and then continues in characteristic fashion: "Above all He has instituted the sacraments, of which we know in fact that they are efficacious means of grace—means of maintaining and consolidating our faith."[3] The administration of the sacraments

---

[1] Joachim Beckmann: *Vom Sakrament bei Calvin: Die Sakramentslehre Calvins in ihren Beziehungen zu Augustin*, Tübingen, 1926. D. J. Groot: "Het effect van het gebuik der sacramenten voor ongeloovigen volgens Calvijn" (*Vox Theol.*, 7, pp. 144–49). Jean de Saussure: "La notion réformée des sacremens" (*Bull. de la Soc. de l'Hist. du protest. français*, 84, 1935; pp. 243–65). W. Boudriot: "Calvins Tauflehre im Licht der katholischen Sakramentslehre" (*Ref. Kirchenztg.*, 80, 1930, pp. 153 f.). Alfred de Quervain: "Der theologische Gehalt von Calvins Taufformular" (*ibid.*, 84, 1934, pp. 261–3). W. Boudriot: "Calvins Abendmahlslehre" (*ibid.*, 79, 1929, pp. 90 ff.). Wilhelm Niesel: *Calvins Lehre vom Abendmahl*, 2nd edn., Munich, 1935: "Das Calvinische Anliegen in der Abendmahlslehre" (*Ref. Kirchenztg.*, 82, 1932, pp. 49–51). E. Pache: "La sainte cène selon Calvin" (*Rev. de Théol. et de Phil.*, N.S. 24, 1936, pp. 179–201). Ernst Pfisterer: "Calvins Stellung zum Krankenabendmahl" (*Ref. Kirchenztg.*, 85, 1935, pp. 268).

[2] *Die Bekenntnisschr. d. ev. luth. Kirche*, Göttingen, 1930, p. 57, I; see esp. Lat. text, "institutum est ministerium docendi evangelii et porrigendi sacramenta".

[3] *In.* IV, 1, 1.

is not simply placed in the hands of the pastors as something ancillary to preaching (despite the fact that Calvin regards them alone as having authority to administer the same)[1] but they are stressed as something of particular importance. The focus of church life, that upon which the act of worship depends, is not simply the Word of God proceeding from human lips, but also and above all the sacrament in its objective reality independent of man. Whereas the Word can and must be preached to individuals also, the celebration of the sacrament requires absolutely the presence and the participation of the congregation.[2] It is an act of worship in which the whole community engages, even though the distribution of the sacred elements is entrusted to the servant of the Word alone. Calvin regards the church as essentially a Eucharistic fellowship. "It is certain that a church cannot be regarded as well ordered and governed if the holy meal instituted by our Lord is not often celebrated and well attended."[3]

I. THE MEANING OF THE RITE

Seeing that Calvin lays such emphasis on the sacrament, we must at once ask what he means by the rite. It is a "token of divine grace towards us confirmed by an outward sign".[4] Hence the Eucharist does not consist only of its earthly species. Rather its fundamental nature is determined by the divine word of promise spoken by Christ when He instituted the service. His word alone lifts the sacramental tokens out of the mass of earthly things which form our material environment. He declares to us for what purpose He has set aside the elements of water, bread, and wine.[5] In themselves and apart from the divine promise of grace

[1] *In.* IV, 3, 4; it is typical of Calvin's strict idea of the ministry that he definitely disallows baptism by private persons or women (cf. *CR* 45, 822). Baptism by women is invalid: *CR* 17, 453; 10a, 54; cf. 11, 625, 706.
[2] Cf. *CR* 15, 265, and next note.   [3] *In.* IV, 17, 43, 44.
[4] *In.* IV, 14, 1.   [5] *In.* IV, 17, 11.

these signs mean nothing. No efficacy is inherent in them as such by which they might acquire for us sacramental significance and be of use.[1] In fact it must be said: "If the visible symbols are offered without the Word, they are not only powerless and dead but even harmful jugglery."[2] "What meaning could it have if the whole assembly of the faithful were to pour out a little bread and wine without proclaiming aloud that heavenly truth which says that the flesh of Christ is meat indeed and His blood drink indeed?"[3] Let us recollect the fact that to-day Christ reveals His will through the words spoken by men. Thus it is not sufficient that in the celebration of the sacrament His words should be read out. The latter must be interpreted in a sermon,[4] for only the real preaching of the divine promises "leads the people as it were by the hand to those heavenly places which the symbols shadow forth and whither they are intended to guide us".[5] For faith—and just in this connexion Calvin stresses the point—comes by preaching.[6] When the promise of God rings out, when a voice from heaven is really heard, when God Himself speaks to man, then faith is made steady, comforted, and strengthened.[7] Thus the certitude of salvation is not grounded in the sacraments in so far as by these we mean earthly signs and tokens.[8] The Word of God alone is the foundation of our faith.[9]

But what is the purpose of outward signs if the Word itself secures our salvation? "Because our faith is slender and weak, it is soon shaken, tottering unsteadily, and finally falls if it is not supported on every side and held upright in every possible way. And so in this respect the merciful Lord according to His unfathomable goodness adjusts Himself to our mode of apprehension: since we are fleshly and ever creep on the earth, cling to the things of sense and think of nothing spiritual, far less understand it, He is not vexed to lead us to Himself precisely by means of these earthly elements, and even holds before us in the things of flesh a

---

[1] *In.* IV, 14, 3.　　[2] *CR* 9, 21.　　[3] *CR* 9, 21 ff.
[4] *In.* IV, 14, 4.　　[5] *Ibid.*　　[6] *In.* IV, 14, 5.
[7] *OS* 1, 137.　　[8] *CR* 7, 693, 702; 12, 728.　　[9] *In.* IV, 14, 6.

mirror of spiritual values."[1] God knows that we are not naturally inclined to seek Him, and hence He confronts us just in this earthly world here below which we love so much. Not only does He call us by His word but He offers us as media tangible palpable things. In speaking His word He claims for Himself our faculty of hearing, but through sacramental signs He claims also our other senses,[2] so that we cannot possibly escape His gift. We have seen that in the human word of preaching God condescends to us sinners. In the Eucharist His merciful condescension to the measure of our everyday realities attains its utmost extent. If we refuse His gift in the face of such kindness we are piling a very heavy load of guilt upon ourselves.[3]

These earthly elements—so we have understood—are like a mirror in which we see reflected spiritual values. They have this advantage over the word that as in plastic art they hold before our very eyes the promises of God.[4] Water, bread, and wine are tokens, figures, and symbols, of what is promised to us in the word.[5] Of course this does not mean that they should induce in us a mood of pious contemplation. During the celebration of the sacrament they are not merely visible; they are put into operation and in that process exert their due effect upon us. These symbols have a specific purpose. They express to us the promises in such a tangible way that we are as certain of them as if they were before our very eyes.[6] Their role is to seal for us and to make effectual within us God's promise of grace and salvation.[7] Hence Calvin compares the sacramental signs with a seal affixed to an original document in order to confirm its contents.[8] The elements render valid for us and make effective this divine promise.[9] Thus, strictly speaking, we should not say that the tokens authorize and make effectual the promise itself. "The truth of God is sufficiently firm and assured in itself not to require confirmation from any other source than its own

[1] *In.* IV, 14, 3; *CR* 6, 114; 28, 251.   [2] *CR* 46, 679.
[3] *Ibid.*   [4] *In.* IV, 14, 5.   [5] *In.* IV, 17, 1, 11.
[6] *In.* IV, 17, 1.   [7] *In.* IV, 17, 4; 14, 2.   [8] *In.* IV, 14, 5.
[9] *In.* IV 14, 3; *CR* 20, 423 f.

authority."[1] It is not the Word of God which in itself requires the service of these earthly things; but *we* need them in view of our ignorance and dullness and weakness. The sacramental signs must plastically represent to us what the words say, in order to arouse in us effective belief.

From this it is clear that the earthly tokens do not possess any intrinsic value. It is not the case that alongside the proclamation of the Word there is another mode of proclamation by signs. Rather it is that from the start the signs gather all their value from their vital connexion with the divine promise. They are nothing more than appendices to the Word,[2] or, as Calvin says in commenting on Augustine, "visible words".[3] Their purpose is in the service of the Word to preach the same thing as the latter.

The sacraments have this appointed part to play and it must not be denied. Their task is not simply "to maintain faith but also to increase it". Of course it must be noted that they do not fulfil this purpose by means of any power residing within them. In comparison with the divine grace imparted to us they are nothing more nor less than "instrumental causes".[4]

It is just here that Calvin joins issue with the Reformers of Zurich and their friends. Zwingli refused to entertain the notion that faith receives anything through the sacraments. He thought that such a doctrine violated the honour of God and implied a false view of faith. The Holy Spirit alone can generate faith, and it will not do to connect the reality of the spirit with material things. And as far as man is concerned he has everything if he has faith. But if he does not believe, the sacraments cannot help him.[5] Zwingli thinks that the Lord's Supper has merely the significance of enabling the believing congregation through the use of the signs to remember vividly the saving work of God, to confess its faith thereby and vow to pursue a Christian manner of life.[6]

---

[1] *In.* IV, 14, 3.   [2] *Ibid.*   [3] *In.* IV, 14, 6.
[4] *CR* 7, 494.   [5] *CR Zw. opp.* 3, 760 ff.
[6] Cf. my essay: "Zwinglis 'spätere' Sakramentsanschauung" (*Theol. Blätter*, 11, 1932, 12 ff.).

Calvin, of course, admitted that faith is the proper effect of the Holy Spirit. "But instead of the one benefit wrought by God on our behalf which they praise we count precisely three: For first, the Lord teaches and instructs us by His word; then He confirms our faith through the sacraments, and finally He sheds into our hearts the light of the Holy Spirit, and so opens them to the power of Word and sacrament."[1] We are dependent on this regular channel of hearing and instruction,[2] and are referred to the sacraments which the Lord has instituted for our soul's health,[3] although it is undeniable that God retains the freedom to accomplish His saving work towards man if it so pleases Him without any of these means. This freedom of God does not give us permission to wait for secret inspirations of the Holy Spirit.[4] We must hold fast to the means by which Christ wills to be present with us to-day. In this connexion it is wrong altogether to reject the sacraments as means of grace. Calvin pointed out to Bullinger that "the word of man too is an instrument of God for the promotion of our salvation, although in itself it is just as dead as the sacramental sign".[5] The human word of the preacher as such has no advantage over the earthly element. Neither can it intrinsically help us. The word of man is an instrument of God in so far as it testifies to the one Word, and the sacrament is a means of grace inasmuch as it expresses the word of promise and seals it for us,[6] and both channels can only be of any avail to us if the Holy Spirit makes them effectual within us.

But if the revelation of God in flesh implies that Christ wills to act towards us to-day through word and sacramental sign, then the second objection of the Zwinglians falls to the ground. There is no such thing as a faith that in itself is firm and complete. Faith is utterly dependent on the word of preaching and the use of the sacraments. Apart from the means of grace it would not arise within us and remain alive; for in this world it is threatened on all sides. Calvin

[1] *In.* IV, 14, 8.   [2] See above, p. 214, note 2.
[3] *CR* 9, 29; 15, 227.   [4] *CR* 9, 29.   [5] *CR* 7, 704.
[6] *Ibid.*

reminds us of the word: "Lord, I believe, help Thou mine unbelief",[1] and says that the fact that we are all sinners is sufficient proof of the imperfection of our faith.[2] Placed as we are in the midst of the temptations and assaults of this world, we need too just those sacramental means of grace which God has given us which confirm for us the favour of God and "in this way support, maintain, consolidate, and increase our faith".[3]

2. THE OPERATION OF THE SACRAMENTS

After hearing about the meaning of the sacraments as expressed in the words of promise, we must now turn to consider the nature and effect of the sacraments themselves as implied in the word of promise and sealed by the signs. Here we come to the heart of the Calvinistic doctrine of the sacraments, and are faced by the question whether the sacraments really convey a gift to us or whether they merely exercise an effect upon our faith—as has mostly been supposed. Anyone who has the remotest idea of Calvin's teaching about our appropriation of salvation must know straight away how he answers this question: "In proportion as by the ministry of the sacraments the true knowledge of Christ is implanted, strengthened, and increased in us, and in proportion as we attain perfect fellowship with Himself and enjoy the benefit of His gifts, so is their effect upon us."[4] The operation of the sacraments depends entirely on the fact that they bring us into relationship with Christ and bind us to Him. For Calvin believes that all spiritual effects have their ground in the one Mediator, and thus can be experienced by us only in so far as we stand in vital relationship with Him.[5]

But this insight does not only flow from the whole system of Calvinistic doctrine; it springs above all from the words of promise which are joined to the sacraments. If in the Last

---

[1] *In.* IV, 14, 7.   [2] *Ibid.*   [3] *Ibid.*   [4] *In.* IV, 14, 16.
[5] *OS* 1, 507.

Supper we are told that we must take the body of the Lord, then in fact this means that the Lord is really our Lord; and if we are further told that we must eat it, it means that He becomes fully one with us. The Word of the Lord cannot deceive us falsely. What God says takes effect. Because in the Last Supper a promise of God is declared, we must know that what is promised us will really be conveyed to us "not otherwise than if Christ Himself were present to our view and taken in our hands".[1]

The same applies to the sacramental signs themselves. God does not intend to deceive in them either.[2] Because it is the Lord who has given them to us they are completely different from all other signs in this world. For example, bread and wine do not symbolize to us the presence of Christ as the picture of a man brings the latter visually before us.[3] The material species do not merely suggest to us the spiritual reality in order to strengthen our assurance and faith; they also effectually convey it to us. If the breaking of bread is intended to show forth plainly that we are made participants in the body of Christ, we must not doubt that the Lord truly bestows on us His body.[4] If He causes the visible token to be presented to us, then He gives us also His living body. We are made to share no less truly in His life than in the bread which is put in our mouths.[5] By the symbols of bread and wine the real presence of Christ is conveyed to us.[6] They are not the thing represented, and must be carefully distinguished from the latter; but they are instruments and organs by which the Lord gives us His body and His blood.[7]

Just as certainly as the words and the species of the Lord's Supper do not promise us an accession of vaguely conceived spiritual strength, but rather certify to us our communion with the body and blood of Jesus Christ, so the substance of the meal is the crucified and risen Christ, or "His body and His blood with which He perfected His

---

[1] *In.* IV, 17, 3.   [2] *In.* IV, 17, 10; *CR* 12, 728.
[3] *CR* 49, 486.   [4] *In.* IV, 17, 10.   [5] *CR* 49, 486 ff.
[6] *In.* IV, 17, 11; *CR* 9, 30, 182, 195; 29, 226.
[7] *OS* 1, 508; *CR* 9, 17 ff.

obedience in order to win righteousness for us."[1] The gift
of the Lord's Supper is not therefore the spirit of Christ or His
divine nature. Nor does it consist in His human nature as
such, but in His humanity in so far as it was given over to
death for our sakes.[2] There lies the crux of the matter. The
crucified body would, of course, avail us nothing if Christ had
not thereby overcome death and passed into eternal glory.
For us Jesus Christ is for ever the two things—the Crucified
and the Risen One. Our salvation depends upon the fact that
He is both. But in this connexion Calvin avoids speaking of
the heavenly or glorified body of Christ.[3] What is in question
in the Eucharist is not the imparting of a heavenly substance
but communion with the Mediator. This is what Calvin is
concerned to express, whether he speaks of the body of the
Son of God delivered up for us, or whether in allusion to the
gospel of John he speaks of the flesh of Christ in which for
us lies embodied eternal life, so that we have not to seek it
in some remote sphere but can find it quite near to us, nearer
than hands and feet.[4] Through the Eucharist we truly receive
the body and the blood of Christ, and grow with Him into
one body, so that He dwells in us and we in Him.[5]

This recognition is the living heart of the Eucharistic
doctrine which Calvin develops in the framework of his
revelational theology. If anyone supposes that Calvin made
such statements only in order to be at one with the Lutherans,
let him read what he writes, about the sacramental teaching of
à Lasko, to someone like Vermigli to whom he really did not
need to prove that his own view of the presence of Christ in
the Eucharist was beyond suspicion. In this letter he deplores
the fact that the arguments of à Lasko always end up in the
assertion "that the natural body of Christ is not given us to
eat. As though we could gain life from any other source
than the natural body of Christ".[6] If we did not gain

---

[1] *OS* 5, 354; 7, 21.   [2] *CR* 9, 9 ff., 188 ff.
[3] Once in debate with Sadolet: *In.* IV, 17, 11.
[4] *In.* IV, 17, 8.   [5] *OS* 1, 509; *CR* 49, 487; 12, 728. *In.* IV, 17, 11.
[6] *CR* 15, 388.

communion with the God revealed in flesh, then all would be in vain. With reminiscences of the New Testament, Calvin describes this communion by means of various metaphorical expressions, all of which are meant to express the closeness of the union between Christ and His own. He even compares the communion between Christ and ourselves to the unity of the divine Son with the Father.[1] So important is to him the fact that the whole Christ in His spiritual and also in His bodily reality becomes our own.[2]

For the sake of clarity in exposition we have so far spoken only of the substance and theme of the Lord's Supper, but must now add that for Calvin what is at issue in baptism is equally the reality of the same Jesus Christ. "Baptism is the sign of our adoption, of our reception into the communion of the church, so that incorporated in the body of Christ we may be numbered among the children of God."[3] Calvin mentions three gifts which are imparted to us in baptism: forgiveness of our sins, our dying and rising again with Christ, and our communion with the Lord Himself[4]; but the first two of these gifts depend wholly upon the third.

Baptism is in the last resort symbolical of the fact that we are incorporated in the body of Christ. Christ is the real Subject of baptism.[5] This is the correct view of the matter, although Christ Himself it is who has commanded us to baptize in the name of the Father, the Son, and the Holy Ghost. For "although we receive the mercy of the Father and the grace of the Spirit only through Christ Himself, we rightly describe Him as the real aim and end of baptism".[6] It is for this reason that according to Calvin the New Testament at times speaks of baptism in the name of Christ alone. "If we wish to summarize the power and inspiration of baptism we name Christ alone."[7]

To sum up: "Christ is the matter or rather the life-blood

---

[1] *CR* 9, 31.   [2] *In.* IV, 17, 9.   [3] *In.* IV, 15, 1.
[4] *In.* IV, 15, 1, 5, 6.
[5] *In.* IV, 15, 6; *CR* 6, 119; 9, 718; 48, 600; 51, 407.
[6] *CR* 49, 318.   [7] *Ibid.*

of all the sacraments." [1] In this respect we must keep well in view the fact that not only the spirit but also the very body of Christ is promised us and must be bestowed upon us through the sacraments. "Although they direct our faith to the whole Christ and not to a mere part of Christ, yet they also teach us that the cause of our righteousness and salvation lies in His flesh; not that a mere man could make us just and spiritually alive, but that it has pleased God to reveal in the Mediator what in Himself lay unfathomably concealed." [2]

3. THE EFFECT OF THE SACRAMENTS

When through the sacraments we attain communion with the Mediator we receive everything which He has gained on our behalf. "We receive a share in the body and blood of Christ, that He may dwell in us and we in Him, and that thus we may enjoy all the benefits of His passion." [3] It must not be overlooked that from Christ who has performed His saving work for us there flows out upon us a decisive effect. We must now consider this in order to give a complete representation of the spiritual reality of the sacraments.

"Baptism testifies to us that we are purified and cleansed, the Eucharist that we are redeemed. The water symbolizes for us the washing away of sins, the blood the satisfaction wrought to redeem us from sin. We find both in Christ who, as John says, came with water and with blood; that means, to cleanse and to ransom." [4] The language of the symbols not only speaks to us about the theme and the meaning of the sacraments but also about the fruit which they are to bear in us. In virtue of the divine institution there exists an analogy between the earthly sign and the thing symbolized in regard to the effect which the sacraments exert upon us. [5] By the

---

[1] *In.* IV, 14, 16; *CR* 5, 437; 6, 114; 9, 718, 728; 29, 414. For the idea of "substance", cf. Niesel, *Calvins Lehre vom Abendmahl*, pp. 50 f.

[2] *In.* III, 11, 9; *CR* 10a, 159.

[3] *CR* 12, 728; *In.* IV, 17, 11; *CR* 9, 81, 165.

[4] *In.* IV, 14, 21.   [5] *In.* IV, 17, 3.

water of baptism we are meant to experience that in Jesus Christ we obtain the forgiveness of our sins, by the offering of bread and wine that the body and blood of Christ feed and sustain in us true life.[1]

All this is implied too in the words of promise which are uttered when the sacraments are celebrated. The words of the Eucharist especially make clear to us that Christ did not receive and sacrifice His human body for His own advantage but for our salvation.[2] Hence Calvin, following Luther, says: "It must be carefully noted that the most conspicuous, indeed almost the whole power of the sacrament resides in these words: 'which is given for you', 'which is shed for you'. For otherwise it would be of no avail that the body and the blood of the Lord should be administered, had they not once for all been sacrificed for our redemption and salvation."[3] Calvin's view of our communion with Christ is far removed from all mysticism of being. The sacraments do not effect our union with divinity as such, but with the Mediator, and we thereby attain the salvation which He has won for us by His suffering and death: "Redemption, righteousness, sanctification and eternal life." [4]

Just as certainly as the question of the effect of the sacraments is not a subsidiary one, since the work of Christ may not be separated from His person, so it must also firmly be believed that "the benefits of Christ would not reach us if He were not from the start willing to bestow His life upon us".[5] He Himself in His person is the substance and the foundation of all other gifts.[6] Without the matter of the sacrament there is no effect, and apart from fellowship with the divine-human Jesus Christ there is no salvation.[7] This teaching discloses the roots of the whole theology of Calvin. If anyone supposes that he expounded such a sequence of ideas only in order to achieve unity with the Lutherans, then he has understood nothing of Calvin.

---

[1] *In.* IV, 17, 3; 345, I, 4.   [2] *Ibid.*   [3] *Ibid.*
[4] *In.* IV, 17, 11.   [5] *Ibid.*   [6] *OS* 1, 508.
[7] *CR* 9, 88.

THE SACRAMENTS

4. THE ACTION OF THE HOLY SPIRIT

The communion with Christ which is assured us and bestowed upon us through the sacraments remains a mystery which we cannot pierce by our understanding nor describe in human speech.[1] Hence Calvin refrained from answering the question how the sacraments can mediate such communion. But he could not ignore what Holy Scripture declares to us on the subject. He observed that the Scriptures always refer to the Holy Spirit in answer to the question how it is possible for us to be united with Christ.[2] The distance between ourselves and Christ, who has really overcome and departed from this world and now dwells in the world of eternity, can only be overcome by an act of God Himself. Such action is effected by the Third Person of the Holy Trinity, "by the secret and incomprehensible power of the Holy Spirit".[3] By the action of the Spirit Christ condescends to our level and at the same time lifts us up to Himself.[4] By the Spirit our hearts are opened to the penetrating power of Word and Sacrament.[5] The Spirit links and unites us with Jesus Christ,[6] so that in body, mind, and soul we become His very own.[7]

Only so is it possible that by the word of man and earthly elements we become sharers in the living reality of the Christ. This statement does not mean that Calvin wishes to render acceptable to our human understanding the mode of Christ's self-communication to us.[8] The reference to the Holy Ghost is rather to be construed as the recognition of sheer divine miracle.[9]

His teaching is a protest against the idea of the inherence of Christ in the Eucharistic species as such, since it is legitimate to speak only of Christ as becoming inherent for us through word and sign and the power of the Holy Ghost.

[1] *In.* IV, 17, 7, 9; *CR* 9, 31.   [2] *In.* IV, 17, 12; *CR* 16, 678.
[3] *CR* 16, 677, 430.   [4] *CR* 16, 677; *In.* IV, 17, 24, 16.
[5] *In.* IV, 14, 8.   [6] *In.* IV, 17, 12, 24.   [7] *In.* IV, 17, 12.
[8] *CR* 16, 678.   [9] *In.* IV, 17, 24; *CR* 10a, 157.

THE THEOLOGY OF CALVIN

Two deviations of Lutheran sacramental doctrine are thus avoided.

Firstly: sign and gift of the sacrament are not confused. If we affirm, like the Lutherans, an inherence in the sacraments themselves of the reality they convey, we are violating the glory of the exalted Lord who has really overcome this our world.[1] But more important for Calvin is the fact that the true humanity of Christ is threatened if we suppose that Christ, invisibly omnipresent, corporeally indwells the bread and wine. Certainly the humanity of Christ enjoys pre-eminence through the resurrection[2] but assuredly not that immeasurability which the Lutherans ascribe to it in order to be able to maintain their Eucharistic doctrine.[3] For by glorification a body loses only those characteristics which arise from the corrupt and decadent state of this world, but not such as belong inseparably to its essential being.[4] If we describe the body of Christ in such a way as to cancel out the community between His body and ours, then we are endangering God's self-revelation in our flesh. Calvin said that he quarrelled with the Lutherans only on this ground. Because they substituted a reality of infinite extension for the flesh of Christ, he defended as against them "the truth of the human nature in which our salvation is grounded".[5]

We have already emphasized the fact that Calvin wished to see the symbol and the reality of the sacrament strictly distinguished but not separated from each other. We are bound to the sacraments in virtue of their divine institution. We do not indeed possess Christ in them; but the Holy Ghost bestows Christ upon us not otherwise than through word and sacramental sign. In the church which gathers around word and sacrament we stand face to face with the divine decision upon us. We may not seek it elsewhere because we have no promise that we shall find and receive Christ elsewhere.

It must, of course, be observed that the connexion between sign and reality which Calvin asserts is not only non-spatial

---

[1] *In.* IV, 17, 19, 32.   [2] *CR* 9, 79 f.   [3] *CR* 16, 429, 677.
[4] *CR* 14, 333; *In.* IV, 17, 24.   [5] *CR* 9, 208; 16, 678.

but also non-temporal in our sense of the words.[1] When the sacramental rite is completed, at that moment the sacramental gift is imparted, as certainly as God is true and His word and sign do not lie. But the connexion of sign and thing signified is grounded solely in the Holy Ghost.[2] The expression "at that moment", as far as this connexion is concerned, implies a divine reality. The divine moment in which the Holy Ghost fulfils His action of rendering effectual to us the ministry of the signs is not interchangeable with the earthly moment of the completion of the sacramental rite. The divine moment can—humanly speaking—be situated before or after the celebration of the sacrament.[3] Also it outlasts this action.[4]

Secondly, Calvin objects to the idea of a natural physical assimilation of the life-giving reality of the sacrament by the communicants. If a spatio-physical connexion exists between the reality and the sacrament which embodies it, the same connexion necessarily exists also between the reality and the sign on the one hand and the communicant on the other. The latter is implied in the former. In that case the reception of the body and blood of Christ takes place through the mouth in physical fashion[5] and a fusion of the underlying reality of the Eucharist with the communicants is an unavoidable thought. But this idea must be rejected[6]; for everything depends on this—that if Jesus Christ the God-man is to help us, then in His union with us He must remain what He is. In spite of the emphasis which Calvin places on the communion of the whole Christ with us, he is strictly concerned to note that there must be a distinction between Christ and ourselves. Hence he says: "It is enough for us that Christ out of the substance of His flesh brings life to our souls, indeed pours out His own life into us, although the flesh of Christ itself does not enter into us."[7]

---

[1] *CR* 7, 704; 9, 29. [2] *CR* 48, 180. [3] *CR* 9, 118.
[4] *CR* 9, 232 ff. [5] *CR* 9, 187, 183; *In.* IV, 17, 33.
[6] *CR* 15, 388; *In.* IV, 17, 32.
[7] *In.* IV, 17, 32. Thus also is to be understood the passage in the 1st *Institutes* (*OS* 1, 142, below), which does not appear in the later editions.

Let us note well that Calvin contrasts this point with the assertion that the body of Christ is received directly by us through our mouth. He does not by any means intend in all this to cancel his fundamental thesis that we really receive through the Eucharist the true body and blood of Christ. But it is just that we receive it by the agency of the Holy Ghost, which means that we are united with Christ but not fused with Him. The Holy Spirit guides us and preserves us as an integral personality. The fellowship with the divine which He procures is real fellowship and not fusion. "Christ in His body is far from us, but by His spirit He dwells within us and draws us upwards to Himself in the heavens in such wise that He pours out upon us the life-giving power of His flesh."[1] Christ is the gift of God to us and not a given power of which we can avail ourselves as we please. After His ascension He is not simply there for us but He comes to His own as their Lord. This implies too that Calvin rejects the doctrine of the enjoyment of the body and blood of Christ by the unworthy. This doctrine is a necessary consequence of the idea that we receive Christ directly through our lips, and shows very plainly its untenability. What sort of Christ is that which in the opinion of the Lutherans even unbelievers receive through the Eucharist? Is he not a dead thing? For with Christ dwells always His life-giving spirit.[2] If Christ is bestowed upon a man, it cannot be other than that at the very heart of this world of unbelief faith arises and goes on increasing. Because the living Lord in His sovereign ascendancy is the gift of the Eucharist, the saving effects of the rite cannot be separated from this gift. It is impossible that the unworthy should really receive Christ in the Eucharist.

This does not mean that the validity and efficacy of the sacrament are dependent upon man. What the words and the sacramental signs of the Lord declare to us is and remains true. "The Lord intends the bread as His body to be there for all."[3] "Christ with His gifts of grace is offered to all in the same way, and the truth of God remains unaffected by

---

[1] *CR* 9, 33.   [2] *In.* IV, 17, 33.   [3] *CR* 16, 678.

the unfaithfulness of men, so that the sacraments always retain their power." [1] In fact, Calvin can go so far as to say "that the body and blood of Christ are as truly given to the unworthy as to the elect faithful of God".[2] But this happens to the godless as when rain pours over a rock. The result of their hardness of heart is that divine grace does not penetrate their being. They are not worthy to receive so precious a gift.[3] In other words, Christ passes them by and does not cause His spirit to move within them in the way in which it accomplishes its work on the elect of God, incorporating them into Christ. The doctrine of Calvin preserves the objectivity of the sacrament on which the Lutherans set so much store; but he distinguishes it from the objectivity of a thing [4] by exalting the sovereign freedom of the Lord who in word and sign wills to bestow Himself upon us by the working of His Spirit. By the preaching of the gospel and the use of the sacraments the Holy Ghost as it were bridges the gulf between Jesus Christ and ourselves. Just as certainly as Calvin objects to a fusion of the sacramental gift with the communicants themselves, so here again he has no intention of teaching a reception which is not based on an inward spiritual relation. He wishes to distinguish but not to separate. If the Holy Spirit accomplishes His work, the receptive faculty of faith is created and strengthened in us [5]: for we ourselves are intrinsically incapable of receiving Jesus Christ into ourselves. Neither our soul nor our physical lips are capable of receiving the Lord who died and rose again for us. Christ Himself must by His Spirit open our hearts to His coming. This accessibility to Himself which He creates is called faith. But Calvin draws our attention to the fact that faith is not the reception of Christ, the eating and drinking of His body and blood itself.[6] When we receive the gift of Christ then that means not only that by the power of the Holy Spirit our hearts are turned towards Him, but that we receive life-giving fellowship with Him.[7] The Holy Spirit creates within

[1] CR 7, 719; 49, 74.　　[2] In. IV, 17, 33.　　[3] CR 16, 678; 7, 719.
[4] In. IV, 17, 33.　　[5] See p. 217, note 1.　　[6] In. IV, 17, 5.
[7] In. IV, 17, 5, 11; CR 9, 75.

us the relationship to Christ which we describe as faith; but He also crowns faith with that which consummates it.[1] The establishment of a relation between Christ and ourselves cannot take place apart from a relation at the deepest level of being. Our faith as such is always an empty vessel; but the Holy Spirit which creates and strengthens it through word and sacrament imparts to it in so doing its true content: Jesus Christ. That content leaves no part of our being untouched. Body and soul we become united with Christ.[2]

Calvin said that he clung to his particular form of sacramental doctrine not from obstinacy but because he believed himself to be bound by the authority of Scripture.[3] In defining his doctrine by contrast with that of the Lutherans he has no wish to cast doubt upon the fact that the Christ who died and rose again for us is the essential gift of the Eucharist. By his differentiations from the Lutheran doctrine he secures precisely the truth that the very body and blood of Jesus Christ are bestowed upon us in that sacred rite.

[1] *In.* IV, 17, 5.   [2] *In.* IV, 17, 12; *CR* 9, 208.   [3] *CR* 16, 430.

Chapter 15

SECULAR GOVERNMENT[1]

THE last chapter of the *Institutes*, in which Calvin considers the question of secular government, has the effect of an appendix to the rest of the work. It follows immediately upon his exposition of sacramental doctrine. And Calvin at once observes "that the spiritual sovereignty of Christ and the civil order are two quite different things".[2] Hence the possibility is excluded that, for example, Calvin might have wished to show in conclusion how his conception of the God revealed in flesh, and His eternal kingdom, finds its realization in this world and in human society and culture.

[1] Hans Baron: *Calvins Staatsanschauung und das konfessionelle Zeitalter*, Munich, 1924. Peter Barth: *Calvins Lehre vom Staat als providentieller Lebensordnung* (*Aus fünf Jahrh. Schweiz. Kirchengeschichte. Festschrift für Paul Wernle*, Basel, 1932, pp. 80–94). Gisbert Beyerhaus: *Studien zur Staatsanschauung Calvins mit besonderer Berücksichtigung seines Souveränitätsbegriffs*, Berlin, 1910. Hans Hausherr: *Der Staat in Calvins Gedankenwelt*, Leipzig, 1923. V. H. Rutgers: "Le Calvinisme et l'état chrétien" (*Bull. de la Soc. de l'histoire du protest. français*, 84, 1935, 151–71). Paul Wernle: "Zwinglis und Calvins Stellung zum Staat" (*Verhandl. des Pfarrvereins des Kantons Zürich*, i, J, 1916). Eduard Bähler: "Der Kampf zwischen Staatskirchentum und Theokratie in der welsch-bernischen Kirche im sechzehnten Jahrh." (*Zeitschr. f. Schweizer Geschichte*, 5, 1925, pp. 1 ff.). Josef Bohatec: *Calvins Lehre von Staat und Kirche mit besonderer Berücksichtigung des Organismusgedankens*, Breslau, 1937. Karlfried Fröhlich: *Gottesreich, Welt und Kirche bei Calvin*, Munich, 1930. H. E. Hess: "Kirche und Staat bei Calvin" (*Reform. Kirchenztg.*, 84, 1934, pp. 37 ff.). Ernst Pfisterer: "Die gesetzliche Regelung des Verhältnisses zwischen Kirche und Staat in Genf zur Zeit Calvins" (*ibid.*, 85, 1935, pp. 153 ff.). Alfred de Quervain: "Der theologische Gehalt des Genfer Pfarrereides" (*ibid.*, 88, 1938, 68–72). E. Chenevière: *La pensée politique de Calvin*, Paris, 1938.

[2] *In.* IV, 20, 1.

Rather his interpretation of their connexion is just the opposite. Calvin regards the state as fulfilling its appointed role in the service of Christ's dominion. When he speaks of the secular government he is not concerned about the state as such, nor even about the Christian state; but about Christ and about the significance which the civil power has for our life in fellowship with this Lord. "It is the will of God that so long as we are striving to reach our true fatherland we must be pilgrims on this earth; during the time of our pilgrimage, however, we imperatively need such help."[1]

In the fourth book of the *Institutes* Calvin treated of the Church, the Word, and the Sacraments, and he now proposes to show that among these "outward aids or instruments by which God calls us to and maintains us in communion with Christ",[2] the secular government also belongs. The latter is not the same thing as the spiritual reign of Christ; but neither does it function merely in juxtaposition with it, but it exists for the good of those who in this perishable world belong to Christ and His eternal kingdom. There can be no decisive separation between state and church because the state has the same Lord as the church. Christ as the Head of His church is also precisely the Lord of this world. The fundamental section containing those reflections which Calvin devotes to the subject of civil government in his *Institutes* received therefore in the first edition the title: *The civil order is necessary for the well-being of the church.*[3]

I. THE DIVINE INSTITUTION OF THE STATE

"Secular government rests upon God's providence and sacred prescription."[4] But the authorities of this world have not their origin in God "in the same way as plague, hunger, war, and other punishments for human sin flow from His righteous will"; the fact is that "He Himself has instituted them in order that they may govern the world according to law and righteousness."[5] Magistrates "have a commission

[1] *In.* IV, 20, 2.   [2] *In.* IV, 1, 1.   [3] *OS* 1, 283.
[4] *In.* IV, 20, 4; *CR* 29, 306; 55, 244.   [5] *CR* 49, 249.

from God, they are equipped with divine authority, in fact they stand in the place of God and in a certain sense conduct His affairs".[1] They occupy a place midway between God and man.[2] Calvin points out with emphasis that in Holy Scripture they are even called gods (Psalm 82:6) "not indeed in regard to their person but in regard to the office they hold".[3]

Yet as the representatives of God[4] they enjoy no independent power but are entirely His servants[5] and officials.[6] "God needs, of course, subordinate executives in order to govern the world; but that does not have the effect of diminishing His own authority, nor does it happen because He wishes to have co-rulers; for He remains at all times Lord over all. What are the greatest kings but the hands of God? And He makes use of them as He pleases."[7]

This mode of the divine government of the world is grounded in the fact that God exercises His sovereign power only mediately. He has exalted Jesus Christ as the eternal king and now reigns with His help.[8] Christ is, as it were, the vice-gerent of God and all earthly rule is like "a symbol of the kingly authority of our Lord Jesus Christ".[9] Thus, when Calvin teaches that civil government was instituted of God, he is not thinking of an ill-defined supernatural foundation of human rules but of the one Lord Jesus Christ. The kingdoms of this world are grounded in Him and maintained by Him.[10] His throne is erected among us "so that His heavenly voice both for governors and their subjects is the one rule for living and dying".[11] All magistrates and princes are therefore bidden to subject themselves in all humility to the great king Jesus Christ and to His spiritual

---

[1] *In.* IV, 20, 4.   [2] *CR* 36, 626.

[3] *CR* 7, 83; 24, 609 f.; 31, 46, 769.

[4] *Lieutenants*: *CR* 7, 83; 14, 342; 49, 637 ff.; 53, 138, 140, etc.

[5] *Ministri, servi*: *OS* 3, 11, 30; *CR* 7, 84; 29, 555; 38, 544; 39, 243; 53, 134, etc.

[6] *Officiers*: *CR* 25, 645; 26, 315; 53, 138 ff., etc.

[7] *CR* 35, 152; 25, 645.   [8] *In.* II, 15, 3, 5.

[9] *CR* 53, 132.   [10] *CR* 13, 17.   [11] *CR* 13, 282.

sceptre.[1] Their government can be nothing other than a service under this one Lord. It can have no other aim but that this One should tower far above all others and exercise His sovereign sway over all.[2] When the magistrates fulfil their obligations "what they do is harmonious with the order of the kingdom of our Lord Jesus Christ"[3] although the latter kingdom is a spiritual one and the rule of the magistrates an earthly rule.

2. THE TASKS OF THE CIVIL GOVERNMENT

We appreciate more clearly the fact that the character of the civil government does not in any sense bring it into conflict with the spiritual rule of Christ when we enquire into the nature of the tasks which are incumbent upon secular rulers. It is their duty "to look after and protect the outward side of church worship, to defend the pure doctrine appertaining to the true worship of God and to secure the stability of the church, to establish social harmony, to shape our conduct as citizens according to the law, to bind us to each other and to maintain the common peace".[4] Although the civil authorities have a secular duty, yet it is not their proper task to care for the physical well-being of men—nevertheless they must be to some extent concerned about it[5]; rather their main concern must be "that in a Christian society religion receives public and official recognition and that humanity prevails among men".[6]

---

[1] *CR* 13, 69; 17; 14, 342.

[2] *OS* 5, 476, 5; *CR* 13, 69. Hence the teaching about civil government belongs not simply to the doctrine of divine providence: it is rather to be viewed in the light of the doctrine of the royal Lordship of Christ. The powers of this world are not so much grounded in the general providence of God as in His special decrees (see p. 230, notes 4, 5). Their office is founded on the fact that Jesus Christ sits at the right hand of God.

[3] *CR* 53, 137.

[4] *In.* IV, 20, 2.   [5] *In.* IV, 20, 3.   [6] *Ibid.*

SECULAR GOVERNMENT

The task of secular authority in the strict sense has therefore two aspects. But the one cannot be separated from the other.[1] Peace in a country is threatened when God is not worshipped and His commands are not heeded, and the public worship of God is imperilled when strife prevails among men. This connexion must not be lost sight of. If Calvin more often speaks of the fact that the duty of the civil power is to preserve and protect the lives of citizens,[2] this is not because for him human life as such has ultimate worth which the civil government is called on to serve. But ordered human conditions are the ground on which the Christian community can live in peace.[3] Already in our exposition of the doctrine of divine providence we have heard that God sustains the world and humanity for the sake of His church.[4] Humanity does not exist in its own right but because it has been called to the service of God. Calvin has left us in no doubt about the fact that the pre-eminent duty of the secular power is to secure the right worship of God.[5] The other duty, which is concerned with peace and the exercise of the human virtues among the subjects, is clearly subordinate to the former. We must not suppose "that God has instituted magistrates in His name solely to bring to an end earthly disputes, as though He had forgotten the most important point, namely, that He Himself should be purely honoured according to the precepts of His law".[6]

The foremost duty of the secular power, which is concerned with the first table of the divine law, consists of two parts. First, it is obliged to protect the pure preaching of the gospel and therewith the church which has this service to perform. It must take care lest "idolatry, taking the name of God in vain, blasphemy, and other troubles subversive of religion openly break out and spread among the people".[7] If need be, the magistrates must take action with the sword

---

[1] *CR* 29, 532; 41, 377.   [2] *CR* 52, 266, 426; 53, 143.
[3] *CR* 52, 266.   [4] See above pp. 73 f.
[5] *In.* IV, 20, 9; *CR* 29, 532; 52, 267; 53, 135.
[6] *In.* IV, 20, 9.   [7] *In.* IV, 20, 3; *CR* 37, 211; 40, 650, etc.

against open despisers of the divine name.[1] If God commands the civil ruler to punish all rebellion in earthly things, it must be noted that an open contempt of God, a wanton slandering of His Word, is much less to be borne.[2] "If the authorities were to overlook such evil deeds, they would themselves incur a degree of guilt which God would by no means leave unpunished."[3]

Then the government has the duty of caring for the church which preaches the pure unmixed gospel. It is not enough for the civil power to secure and protect the church. Rather it must further the cause of the church which is the proclaimer and servant of the Lord to whom the civil power itself is subject. It is even obliged to support the church in its endeavours to establish the ascendancy of true doctrine. It must promote the work of that church which preaches the pure gospel, and is therefore alone entitled to be called the church; and it must recognize ecclesiastical decisions and discriminations. In this connexion Calvin has often pointed to the word of Isaiah: "And kings shall be thy nursing fathers" (Isaiah 49:23).[4] The holders of civil office are responsible in part for the spread of the gospel. This means in detail: "They are to provide for the pastors and servants of the Word everything needful for their maintenance and for church worship; their duty is to care for the poor and not to allow the church to find itself in a position of disgraceful and oppressive poverty; they are to erect schools and to furnish emoluments for the teachers; they must build houses for the poor and for travellers and arrange all other matters concerning the protection and maintenance of the church."[5] In particular they must be concerned about the spirit prevailing at the universities. Those seed-beds of future servants of the Word must be places where the gospel is supported.[6]

---

[1] Calvin explains in detail the reasons for this duty in his treatise against Servetus: CR 8, 461 ff.　　[2] CR 27, 688, 246.

[3] CR 27, 688.

[4] In. IV, 20, 5; CR 7, 82; 8, 478; 14, 288; 24, 357; 27, 246; 29, 532; 37, 210; 43, 135; 53, 138, etc.

[5] CR 37, 211.　　[6] CR 14, 40.

Whether the government does these things is another matter. It is its duty to do them, just as every man, even the heathen, is called to confess Christ as Lord. "That ruler is deceiving himself who expects his kingdom lastingly to prosper when it is not ruled by God's sceptre, that is, by His holy Word, since the sacred proverb cannot remain without effect which says that where there is no vision the people perish." [1] If the government does not decide for Christ, then it decides against Him. There is no other alternative. Whether or not it recognizes and furthers the cause of the true church is in any event a decision for or against faith.

When the secular authorities obediently do their duty to advance the kingdom of Christ, the spiritual character of that kingdom is not impaired,[2] just as it is not impaired by secular government in general.

It is in general true of all this-worldly ordinances and laws that they have no authority over the inner life of man.[3] God alone can search man's heart and call him to account with regard to his most secret thoughts.[4] He alone is the spiritual Lawgiver whose law disposes both of our bodies and our souls.[5] Human laws have no power to constrain consciences. When Paul says that we must be subject to the powers that be for conscience sake (Romans 13:5), according to Calvin it does not mean that secular law is binding on the conscience of man, but is simply a reminder that the divine law in general bids us honour civil authority, since it rests upon the ordinance of God and there must be social harmony among us.[6] Hence with regard to all human laws it must be precisely and carefully noted that "the judgment seat of God which is spiritual and the earthly judgments of men" are by no means the same thing.[7]

That is the position with regard to the law of secular governments as distinct from the divine law. Still less, of course, has it the duty of itself preaching the gospel. That is the business of the church alone. Christ wills that His

---

[1] OS 3, 11, 32. [2] CR 24, 357. [3] In. II, 8, 6.
[4] Ibid. [5] Ibid. [6] In. IV, 10, 5. [7] In. IV, 10, 3.

ministers should openly preach the gospel even though the power of the whole world be against them, and for this purpose He equips them alone with the inspiration of the Word. But this does not prevent Him from leading earthly rulers into the way of obedience to Him and causing them to fulfil their duties towards the church.[1] Only it must be strictly noted that they fulfil their good offices towards the church precisely as holders of civil authority. Calvin strongly criticized the fact that in the Germany of his day the princes encroached too much on the spiritual sphere. If the magistrates do not keep within their proper limits, but try to usurp ecclesiastical control and constitute themselves judges both in matters of doctrine and in those of spiritual government, their service to the church becomes a disservice.[2]

3. THE RESPONSIBILITY OF THE SECULAR GOVERNMENT

We have already seen that rulers are bound by the Word of God. Hence Calvin protests against the opinion that the civil power functions within a sphere of life which is not affected by the claim of God. Guided by his Biblical insights, he refuses to surrender the world utterly to impiety and the powers of darkness. Since Christ is the Lord of all there can be no sealing off of the civil power from His universal dominion. If the rulers of this world are to bow before Him, they are also called to recognize the truth and authority of the Gospel.[3] No doubt they would like to be free from all law and from every kind of yoke; but they are subject to the Word of God[4] and must allow themselves to be enlightened by the preachers of that Word.[5] They depend ultimately on the Word of God and are bound to the law of God.[6] They are obliged to be obedient, and therefore have constantly to ask whether their action is in harmony with the divine Word.[7] In the school of God they learn how to fulfil their tasks rightly,[8] and in particular the law of love to God and

[1] *CR* 24, 357.   [2] *CR* 43, 135.   [3] *CR* 27, 246 ff.
[4] *CR* 38, 322.   [5] *CR* 43, 79.   [6] *CR* 29, 555.
[7] *CR* 40, 622.   [8] *CR* 25, 645.

neighbour is applicable to their fulfilment of their functions.[1] In teaching that the supreme duty of the civil power is to foster the fear of God and peace among men, Calvin considers that this twofold duty is laid upon it by the two great commands of the divine law.

This does not mean that rulers must control the life of their peoples according to particular laws prescribed in Holy Scripture. The Mosaic ceremonial and judicial law had its special function to fulfil in the economy of the life of Israel[2]; but now after the appearance of Jesus Christ it is superseded and cannot be relevant for the ordering of the life of other peoples.[3] But, within the requirement of the twofold law of love to God and neighbour, rulers have freedom to issue such laws as seem to them necessary and useful.[4] In virtue of their office they are authorized by God to do so.[5] The civil laws valid in any particular state are thus altogether the work of man.[6] They are in the strictest sense laws governing the life of citizens; yet they must be compatible with the abiding law of love which is the divine requirement.[7]

Rulers stand in a position of responsibility before the Lord who is the Author of this eternally valid law. Since they are not private citizens, but rule the peoples at the bidding of God, their responsibility is particularly heavy. They must constantly "consider what is permissible to them and what God allows. For as they may now simply issue commands, they have also to remember that one day they will have to give an account to the King of kings."[8] This applies to all who hold any official post in the state. Their responsibility is not of a vague and indefinite character; but they must know "that they will have to appear before the Lord Jesus Christ in order to give a reckoning of the way in which they have acquitted themselves in their office".[9] He is the sovereign Lord in whom all authority on earth is grounded. Hence all must give account to Him. Those, too, who refuse to

---

[1] *In.* IV, 20, 15, 9.   [2] See above, p. 101.   [3] *In.* IV, 20, 14.
[4] *In.* IV, 20, 15.   [5] *CR* 25, 645.   [6] *Ibid.*
[7] *In.* IV, 20, 15.   [8] *CR* 40, 713.   [9] *CR* 53, 139.

recognize this and exercise their rule with arrogance and self-will must give heed: "Though to-day they do not admit that they are subject to the Word of God, they will one day appear before that tribunal where they will be forced to realize how perversely they have misused their power."[1] The hour when that happens is supremely the hour of God and lies solely within His power of determination. "As the life of an individual man has an absolute limit, and as God has determined what is to become of the kingdoms of the whole earth, so the course and the termination of every kingdom and people lies utterly in the hand and the counsel of God."[2]

But rulers are not only called to responsibility by the Word, but the comfort of the Word stands at their disposal. They need not let themselves be afraid at the difficulties which pile up against them; rather they can look upwards to God with the comfortable assurance that He will support them in their work. They are indeed invited to turn to Him and to pray to Him for His help.[3] "They must recognize that their duty is to meditate on the divine Word at all times and that they need the constant help of the Holy Spirit."[4] The bearers of civil authority who rightly understand their duties have their place in the hearkening and praying congregation of the church. The duty of punishment which they have to fulfil does not render them unworthy to belong to the congregation of Christ. On the contrary, the great responsibility which lies upon them has as a natural consequence that they should be eminent members of the church.[5] For a ruler, membership of the church is the highest honour which can come to him.[6]

4. OBEDIENCE TO THE SECULAR GOVERNMENT

The citizens are obliged to be obedient to those whom God has deemed worthy to be the delegates of His power on earth. Calvin never tired of sharply calling attention to this duty,

[1] CR 38, 322. [2] CR 38, 545. [3] CR 29, 660 ff.
[4] CR 29, 553; 27, 468 ff. [5] CR 53, 137 ff.
[6] CR 28, 511.

especially in his sermons. God wills that we should respect the dispositions He has made on this earth. But he demands not merely outward obedience. We are to recognize in the institution of the secular government His providence and fatherly care for us,[1] and must realize that authority is there for our good[2]; for without it there would be chaos and confusion in the world. Finally we should appreciate the fact that the persons invested with authority are the representatives of God Himself. This is the real ground of the demand that we should obey them.[3] "If we obey men who rule over us according to the will of God, we are obeying Him who has appointed and authorized them."[4] Hence Christians must gladly and without constraint yield obedience to civil authority whatever form it may take.[5] In fact Calvin goes a step further: "Even if we lived under Turks, tyrants or deadly enemies of the gospel it would still be incumbent upon us to be subject to them. Why? Because it is the good pleasure of God."[6] This does not mean that it should be a matter of indifference to Christians whether God-fearing or godless men exercise rule over them. On the contrary, every Christian should realize his responsibility for securing a God-fearing government, and, whenever opportunity offers, help to see that upright men obtain office.[7] But those who will not allow themselves to be governed according to the order which God has established in this world are resisting God Himself.[8] Whoever rebels against authority is attacking God and must be clear about the fact that in such a struggle he will in any event succumb.[9]

But the obedience towards authority required of us is no bondage. The subjection of the governed is "not of such a kind as would allow princes to exploit it as they please". Of course "subjects find themselves under the control and at the disposal of kings; but in return kings must be concerned about the common weal".[10] "God has created governments

---

[1] *CR* 26, 314.   [2] *CR* 34, 656.   [3] *CR* 26, 315.
[4] *CR* 54, 558.   [5] *CR* 30, 488.
[6] *CR* 54, 557; 27, 455; 30, 488; 45, 602.   [7] *CR* 27, 467.
[8] *Ibid.*   [9] *CR* 26, 317; 23, 107   [10] *CR* 29, 554.

and kingdoms and the order of this world, not with the purpose of giving pre-eminence to some, but because we cannot do without such means of help." Rulers "are therefore not appointed for their own pleasure but to promote the common good". "Since then God has appointed magistrates under this condition it is certain that they are subject to those whom they must serve by ruling."[1] The rule which authority exercises over the people is by its very nature nothing but a service.[2] The people are submitted to authority and authority is subject to the people it serves. This reciprocal relationship of mutual service is founded on the fact that the sovereign Lord Himself stands over rulers and ruled and has established civil government for the good of men.

Subjects owe obligation to the government only so long as it really holds office. They must serve it with body and soul. If it collapses through some chance and is replaced by another, then the subjects are released from their obedience, even from their oath of allegiance; "because it does not lie within the power of the people to determine who their ruler shall be; for it is the affair of God to change governments as it pleases Him".[3] Obedience to authority rests solely on the fact that God Himself sets up rulers. This again becomes clear from the limit which Calvin here sets to obedience.

5. THE LIMITS OF SECULAR GOVERNMENT

So far we have been speaking almost exclusively of secular authority which, in contradistinction to unlawful power, Calvin describes as legitimate. That authority is legitimate which keeps within the bounds divinely prescribed for it.[4] It recognizes the fact that it has received its office from God, and therefore may not attempt to rule over its subjects in any arbitrary manner but solely on the basis of the mandate it has received from God.[5] The legitimacy of a secular government is not a secure and permanent possession. It stems

[1] *CR* 51, 732. [2] *CR* 29, 555. [3] *CR* 39, 158.
[4] *CR* 29, 552. [5] *CR* 29, 554.

from the relationship in which the rulers stand to the Lord of all lords and depends on how far those rulers remain in obedience to God.[1]

Rulers are threatened by the temptation "of supposing that they can stand in their own strength and of evading the command of God, as though there were no Judge in heaven".[2] They no longer remain within that responsible position which devolves upon them as mediating between God and mankind, and they forget that they are mortal creatures and fondly imagine themselves to be demi-gods.[3] "Because they hold the reins of earthly power they think that they tower so far above the status of men as to have the right to require from them sheer divine honours."[4] "Although in their pride they despise God, yet they need the sanction of religion in order to buttress their authority, and to this end simulate an attitude of religious veneration in order to keep the people fettered to their duty."[5] They do not deny the existence of God; but "they shut God up in heaven and suppose that He is so content with His felicity as not to wish to interfere in the affairs of men".[6]

Rulers who in this way attempt to eliminate from the sphere of earthly affairs the living God who has called them to their office, and set themselves up in His place, are in Calvin's opinion no longer legitimate. But this certainly does not mean that they are no longer in possession of authority. In this respect there is a notable difference between secular and ecclesiastical authority. If the latter rebels against God, it not only loses its legitimacy but also every kind of claim to obedience. The position is different with regard to secular authority: "We must by no means consider whether persons in authority are fulfilling their duty or not, but must have regard to the order which God has instituted. The latter can never be so seriously harmed by the wickedness of men or rather so fully effaced that no traces of it any longer remain. Thus, even if those who stand in power and hold the sword

---

[1] *CR* 40, 622.   [2] *CR* 40, 715.   [3] *CR* 27, 479.
[4] *CR* 29, 555; 27, 479.   [5] *CR* 40, 626.   [6] *CR* 40, 682.

of justice in their hands perform their functions never so badly, even if they cause greater distress and confusion than would such as have no office or duty, even if they are the declared enemies of God, it must still be recognized that God has set up kingdoms, principalities, and the throne of justice in order that we may peaceably pass our day in His fear and lead an honourable life: and this"—so Calvin declares—"is something which the wickedness of men can never frustrate."[1] "The right to command as such has been instituted by God for the good of mankind."[2] For this reason the worst tyranny is "more bearable than no order at all".[3] It is better and more profitable than anarchy[4] for it still serves in some sense to hold human society together.[5] But this must not be understood to mean that secular government as such is endowed with an intrinsic quality which, even when corrupted by the greatest degeneracy, it could not lose. The fact is rather that God does not completely withdraw His grace even from those rulers who rebel against Him.[6] If the secular authority fulfils its function, if even what is degenerate to some extent performs a service, this is due utterly to the grace of God.

Hence subjects are obliged to yield obedience even to a bad government. In fact, even in such circumstances they must love what God has ordained.[7] Further, they should consider that it is their own fault if God withdraws from them the benefits of good government. "For it is the wrath of God which sends us evil rulers."[8] "Because we repel God from us He is obliged to withdraw His favour, and revoke His benefits, sending to rule over us people who subvert all that is right and good."[9] In such cases subjects have no occasion for complaint; rather they should look into their own hearts and confess their sins.[10] God has, of course, placed one means of help at their disposal; namely, prayer. "We must pray to God that He will bring good out of the evils of bad rulers." Finally the oppressed must by their prayers seek

---

[1] *CR* 53, 130.   [2] *CR* 49, 249.   [3] *CR* 53, 131; 54, 559.
[4] *CR* 55, 245.   [5] *CR* 49, 250.   [6] *CR* 29, 574.
[7] *CR* 52, 266.   [8] *CR* 52, 267.   [9] *CR* 54, 558; 53, 131.
[10] *CR* 53, 131; *In.* IV, 20, 29.

to turn away from themselves these scourges which have come upon them as a result of their sins.[1] We must "call upon God that it would please Him to give us such magistrates as would establish the reign of justice, so that we may serve God and that all may worship Him with one mind".[2]

But until such time as God intervenes we must give obedience to tyranny.[3] Authorities who do not exercise their office with a sense of responsibility towards the Lord of all lords will discover "that the kingdom of our Lord Jesus is as a stone of stumbling" which "will ruin the powers of this world when they rise against the majesty of our Lord Jesus Christ".[4] Calvin has also indicated how such intervention of God can take effect: "Sometimes He summons from among His servants public avengers and arms them with the command to bring to just retribution this odious rule and to free the unjustly oppressed people out of the misery of their bondage; at other times He uses for this purpose the fierce anger of men who have quite other thoughts and other intentions."[5] Because the former have received a special and rightful call of God, they do not violate by their action the dignity of the civil order and authority. The latter commit a crime because they lead a revolt against legitimate authority; but unwittingly they must do the work of God.[6] Yet in either case there is no question of an ethical possibility of self-help. Calvin is considering only those resources which God alone is able to bring into operation. He considers that only holders of subordinate office have the right to proceed against a government which has degenerated into tyranny.[7]

There is, however, one limit to the obedience of even the simplest subject: "If princes forbid us to serve and honour God, if they command us to sully our conscience with idolatry, and to concur and engage in abominations which are contrary to the service of God, then they are not worthy to be regarded as princes or to be recognized as having any

---

[1] *CR* 52, 267; *In.* IV, 20, 29.   [2] *CR* 53, 131.   [3] *CR* 53, 548.
[4] *CR* 41, 417.   [5] *In.* IV, 20, 30.   [6] *Ibid.*
[7] *In.* IV, 20, 31, *intercedere* (French: *de s'opposer et resister*); *CR* 29, 552.

sort of authority. And why so? Because there is only one foundation for the power which princes may legitimately enjoy. This is that God has placed them in their office. And if they would dethrone God, must we continue to pay heed to them?" [1] The fear of God must precede everything else. It is the foundation of obedience. Once it is destroyed there is no longer any ground for the connexion which binds subjects to their rulers.[2] "They have lost every vestige of authority." [3] "They are then nothing but ordinary men." [4] "Hence, if religious considerations compel us to withstand tyrannical decrees which forbid us to give to Christ and to God the honour and worship which we owe them, then it can rightfully be claimed that we are not violating the majesty of kings." "If they are not content with their lawful authority and wish to uproot in us the fear and worship of God, then there is no reason for anyone to say that we are despising them because the kingdom and the glory of God are of more worth to us." [5] "The Lord is the King of kings; when He speaks His Word He must be heard before all and above all. According to this Word we are subject to the rulers set over us, but only in Him." [6]

Calvin realized how difficult it is for a man to prove himself a Christian when involved in a conflict between the divine command and human authority. He warned his countrymen, who had to suffer severe persecutions for their faith, time and again, to stand fast. He wrote in reproof of those followers of Nicodemus who dared only in secret to confess their allegiance to Christ.[7] But he also advised Christians who found themselves in isolation and thus in very special danger to take the decision which he himself had taken with a very heavy heart. He wrote to such oppressed and persecuted Christians to the effect that "there was nothing better than to dwell within His congregation, where He abides and has made His seat", and that thus "we should

---

[1] *CR* 41, 415 ff.; 11, 707.   [2] *CR* 26, 315.
[3] *CR* 26, 318.   [4] *CR* 48, 109.
[5] *CR* 48, 398; *In.* IV, 20, 32.   [6] *Ibid.*   [7] *CR* 6, 537 ff.

prefer to our own country any place where the sincere worship of God is practised".[1] "If it is possible for us to live in a place where God is truly honoured and worshipped, then it is by far better to live in exile than to remain in the fatherland from which Christ the King of heaven and earth has been banished."[2]

In this sentence there resounds once again the theme of Calvin's whole life and work. It is the name of Jesus Christ.

[1] *CR* 12, 453.   [2] *CR* 14, 742.

Chapter 16

THE THEOLOGY OF CALVIN
AND ITS STRUCTURAL ORGANIZATION

IT is not strictly necessary that we should now summarize the progress of our enquiry and set out the conclusions reached. We think we have showed plainly enough that in every aspect of doctrine Calvin is concerned only about one thing: namely, the God revealed in flesh. But in conclusion we wish to draw attention to two sets of considerations:

1. We are now in a position to understand to some extent the many attempts of Calvin researchers to interpret the theology of the Reformer from the point of view of some one predominant element in the content of his doctrine.

If Calvin is concerned about Jesus Christ, then the idea of the honour of God will inevitably play a part in his thinking. If only people had heeded the fact that it is a question of the honour of the God who in Jesus Christ has disclosed to us the depths of His mercy! It is this God whom according to Calvin we should honour and praise.

It has been rightly noticed that the law occupies an important place in the doctrine of Calvin. How could it be otherwise, when he wishes to glorify the Son of God and His saving work? Only it ought to have been appreciated that Calvin understands the law from the point of view of its fulfilment in Jesus Christ.

It has been emphasized that the thought of sanctification controls both the teaching and the life of Calvin. Again we must say: with reason, provided that we belong to Christ and He, the living Lord, claims our life for Himself.

STRUCTURAL ORGANIZATION

It was completely correct to refer to the emphasis on the transcendent in the preaching of Calvin. Because he proclaims the Lord who will come again, his theology must of necessity be eschatological in bearing.

A very important contribution was made when it was noted that the sacraments were central to the doctrine of Calvin and to the parochial life which he organized. How could it be otherwise, since the sacraments promise us and bestow upon us communion with Jesus Christ?

And so we could go on with this enumeration. There is hardly an aspect of theology which someone or other has not considered as quite specially typical for Calvin's doctrine. The variety of these proposals need no longer astonish us; for we have seen that Calvin was concerned to expound in all its fullness and depth the self-revelation of God to which Holy Scripture bears witness.

2. Just as each individual facet of the theology of Calvin is determined by the central theme which he wishes to bring home to his readers, so is its structural organization. We do not wish to deny that Calvin has moulded his doctrine by the help of those resources which history and his own disposition suggested. How could it have been otherwise? But the observation of what is after all a matter of course does not take us far in the understanding of Calvin. More decisive is the appreciation of the fact that the form of Calvin's theology was shaped by the axis on which it revolves. Jesus Christ controls not only the content but also the form of Calvinistic thought. In proof of this assertion we refer to two important characteristics which constantly recur in Calvin's sequences of thought:

(a) We have seen that Calvin understood the conjunction of the two natures in the Person of the Mediator in harmony with the Chalcedonian dogmatic definition: union but not fusion: distinction but not separation.[1] The thought of Calvin in many other doctrinal matters is guided by this attempt to apprehend and describe the Person of Jesus Christ.

[1] See above, pp. 115 ff.

247

Thus in the light of it he seeks to understand the essential character of Holy Scripture. The relation between the words of Scripture and the incarnate Word is analogous to that between the human nature of Christ and the Logos. The written word is not interchangeable with the one Word but neither is it separable from the latter.[1] Exactly in the same way Calvin solves the question of the relation between the divine word and the human word in preaching[2] and the problem which was then so much discussed: the relation between sign and thing signified in the Eucharist.[3]

Calvin similarly defined the nature of our relation to Christ: a real communion of persons but not a fusion of being.[4] He insisted upon this, especially in his interpretation of the sacrament.[5] The sacramental gift is imparted to the communicant on the ground of the divine promise and in virtue of the action of the Holy Ghost; but this does not result in any fusion of the being of Christ with that of man. Even the communion which man originally had with God, Calvin thinks, is to be understood in the same way.[6]

As regards the gracious gifts of justification and sanctification, Calvin teaches that while they are inseparably contained in Christ they must nevertheless be distinguished.[7] Again, in the same way, in spite of all the divergences which are to be noted, he sees the unity of the Old and the New Testament implied in the living fact of Christ,[8] and by the same direction of his thought he seeks to solve the complementary problem of the law and gospel.[9] In a similar way he defines the relation between the spiritual and the secular power.[10]

From the same point of view he characterizes the effects wrought by the graces of justification and sanctification within us: "Here Paul reckons penitence and faith as two different things. How so? Can then penitence subsist without

---

[1] See above, pp. 33 ff.   [2] *In.* IV, 1, 5.   [3] See above, p. 224.
[4] See above, p. 124.   [5] See above, pp. 225 f.
[6] See above, pp. 68 f.   [7] See above, pp. 137 f.
[8] See above, pp. 105 ff.
[9] *CR* 50, 39 ff., 354; 24, 727 f.; 28, 539; 53, 33.
[10] *OS* 2, 362, 14; *CR* 10b, 263.

faith? By no means. But although they cannot be separated from each other, yet they must be distinguished. Just as faith cannot live without hope, and yet faith and hope are two different things, so it is with penitence and faith: although they are inseparably bound up with each other yet they must be united rather than fused." [1]

Finally, it is especially worthy of note that even in regard to the doctrine of the Trinity Calvin works with the same apparatus of ideas. He teaches us to distinguish but not to separate both person and being and person and person. [2] Even his formulation of this doctrine is moulded by the data of revelation.

(b) Calvin goes yet a step further in this direction. In thinking of the outcome of the actions of God, he suggests that their effects are both distinguishable and interrelated. Thus as regards justification and sanctification he explains as follows: "Just as Christ cannot be torn asunder, so these two benefits which we receive in Him both simultaneously and in conjunction (*simul et coniunctim in ipso*) are not to be separated from each other." [3] Since it is here a question of the saving action of God, the characteristic ideas—*simul et coniunctim*—serve to express the sense of juxtaposition and interrelatedness. But in the sentence just quoted what is above all essential is the reference to Christ as the ground of this indissoluble nexus.

As we have shown, the *simul* plays a great part in the sacramental doctrine of Calvin. The outward completion of the rite ordained by God, and the action of the Holy Ghost by which Christ is imparted to us, take place at the same time. [4] In considering this point we drew attention to the fact that this simultaneity refers to a divine and not a human moment. Hence we need here do no more than recall the fact that the simultaneity in Calvinistic doctrine cannot be understood from the standpoint of our human sense of time.

---

[1] *In.* III, 3, 5.
[2] See above, p. 59, note 3 and p. 60, note 6.
[3] See above, p. 137, note 4.   [4] See above, pp. 218 ff., 223 ff.

Calvin used similar expressions with regard to the effect wrought upon us by the Word of God. The Holy Spirit must at one and the same time be present in the Word and move within us as we hear it, if that Word is to find an entrance into our hearts.[1] But the Spirit is in no sense bound to the word as proclaimed by man.[2]

All this applies equally to the special case of man's call to hold an office in the church. To the outward call by the church corresponds the inner call by the power of the Holy Spirit. Since no one can read in the heart of another, that person is considered to be truly called who has been commissioned by the church; but if the inner vocation is lacking, he is nothing but a hireling.[3]

These references may suffice. They show plainly enough how closely the structure of Calvin's thoughts is dependent on the Chalcedonian definition and so on the living fact of divine self-revelation.

---

[1] See above, pp. 37 ff. 　　[2] *CR* 50, 40.

[3] See above, pp. 203 ff. and *OS* 5, 52, 21 f. Cf. H. Obendiek: "Vocatio legitima" (*Ev. Theologie*, 5, 1938, pp. 89 ff.).

Supplement

SURVEY OF RECENT STUDIES
OF CALVIN'S THEOLOGY

First of all Wilhelm Kolfhaus must be mentioned here. During his life he occupied himself with Calvin and strove to get a grasp on the innermost intent of the Reformer's teaching. The work he completed at a very advanced age, *Die Christusgemeinschaft bei Johannes Calvin*, is the mature fruit of extensive research and, on the whole, one of the best books on Calvin.[1] The title does not designate any particular segment of Calvin's teaching, but his whole program: it is concerned with Christ and the Christ-community. To Christology as such E. Emmen and Max Dominicé have made important contributions.[2] John Frederick Jansen has produced a study of the long-neglected doctrine of the work of Christ on the grounds that it is high time to give more attention to this subject, "for Christology is the measure of every theology."[3] These few words mark the great revolution which has occurred in the understanding of Calvin's theology.

Paul Jacobs has shown that the doctrine of predestination, which has for so long a time been viewed as the determinative foundation of the Calvinistic system, is Christocentric: "Christ is election itself."[4] At the same time he has pointed to the

[1] Wilhelm Kolfhaus: *Christusgemeinschaft bei Johannes Calvin*, Neukirchen, 1939; see also: *Die Seelsorge Johannes Calvins*, Neukirchen, 1941.

[2] E. Emmen: *De Christologie van Calvijn*, Amsterdam, 1935. Max Dominicé: *L'Humanité de Jésus d'après Calvin*, Paris, Ed. Je Sers, 1933.

[3] John Frederick Jansen: *Calvin's Doctrine of the Work of Christ*, London, James Clarke, 1956, p. 11.

[4] Paul Jacobs: *Prädestination und Verantwortlichkeit bei Calvin*, Neukirchen, 1937, p. 77.

THE THEOLOGY OF CALVIN

"Christ content" in Calvin's ethics. On the same subject we received at almost the same time a very meticulous work by Heinz Otten.[5] It likewise demonstrates that God's eternal decree of redemption is embodied in and through Christ; but it must not go unmentioned that Calvin—especially in conflict with opponents—did not always insist on carrying this viewpoint to all its logical conclusions.

In the list of these works belong the excellent dissertations (University of Halle) of Heinrich Quistorp[6] and Hans-Heinrich Wolf.[7] The former comes to the conclusion that "Calvin's eschatology is essentially Christology," and the latter shows that Calvin's perception of both Testaments is determined by Christ. The importance of Calvin's teaching about Christ and the Christ-community for his view of Word and sacrament has been very ably worked out in the book by Ronald S. Wallace.[8] At this point we should also mention the 1937 dissertation (University of Heidelberg) of Wilhelm Albert Hauck, which he later expanded—in length and depth—in several publications.[9] These publications reached their culmination in *Christusglaube und Gottesoffenbarung*, especially in the statement that, according to Calvin, every revelation of God is strictly Christocentric. Thomas F. Torrance's fine study of Calvin's doctrine of man gets into the question of the knowledge of God and the role of natural theology, and ends with the assertion that knowledge of God is possible for man only if he bows before the cross of Christ

[5] Heinz Otten: *Calvins theologische Anschauung von der Prädestination*, Munich, Chr. Kaiser, 1938.

[6] Heinrich Quistorp: *Die letzten Dinge im Zeugnis Calvins. Calvins Eschatologie*, Gütersloh, Bertelsmann, 1941.

[7] Hans-Heinrich Wolf: *Die Einheit des Bundes. Das Verhältnis von Altem und Neuem Testament bei Calvin.* 1940 dissertation, Neukirchen, 1958

[8] Ronald S. Wallace: *Calvin's Doctrine of the Word and Sacrament*, Edinburgh, Oliver and Boyd, 1953.

[9] Wilhelm Albert Hauck: *Sünde und Erbsünde nach Calvin*, Heidelberg, Comtesse, 1938; *Calvin und die Rechtfertigung*, Gütersloh, Bertelsmann, 1938; *Christusglaube und Gottesoffenbarung nach Calvin*, Gütersloh, Bertelsmann, 1939; *Vorsehung und Freiheit nach Calvin*, Gütersloh, Bertelsmann, 1947; *Die Erwählten. Prädestination und Heilsgewissheit bei Calvin*, Gütersloh, Bertelsmann, 1950.

and is renewed by Christ.[10] T. H. L. Parker has proved this in detail in his book on Calvin's conception of the knowledge of God.[11]

On the other hand, Edward A. Dowey, in a very thorough book in connection with the theological position of Emil Brunner, has advocated the thesis that Calvin taught a natural knowledge of God.[12] We will have to concern ourselves with this assertion at another time.[13] Here we need stress only the fact that in the end Dowey recognizes the Christocentric character of Calvin's theology.[14] A frank evaluation of this book shows it to be an indisputable witness of the Reformer's theological intent.

The Strasbourg theologian François Wendel has offered in French a fine presentation of the most important teachings of the *Institutes*.[15] His prudent book accepts the new line of Calvin research. He rejects the notion that a central idea dominates the whole of Calvin's theology; rather, he emphasizes that in the Reformer we find, in general, no comprehensive closed system of thought, for Calvin simply strings biblical truths together. Wendel also makes reference to the crucial position of Christ in Calvin's thought and work. That Wendel does not ignore the limitations in Calvin's presentation only serves to increase the value of his excellent book.

We cannot conclude this survey of recent literature on Calvin without mentioning the lifework of Josef Bohatec. Already at the Reformed candidate-school in Elberfeld (later a theological seminary), he contributed a significant article on Providence to

[10] T. F. Torrance, *Calvin's Doctrine of Man*, London, Lutterworth Press, 1949, pp. 169, 182f.

[11] T. H.L. Parker: *The Doctrine of the Knowledge of God. A Study in the Theology of John Calvin*, Edinburgh, Oliver and Boyd, 1952.

[12] E. A. Dowey: *The Knowledge of God in Calvin's Theology*, New York, Columbia University Press, 1952.

[13] Already defended by Günter Gloede: *Theologia naturalis bei Calvin*, Stuttgart, 1935. Today the author realizes that this his first work cannot be so considered. See instead his fine book *Calvin, Weg und Werk*, Leipzig, Koehler und Amelang, 1953.

[14] P. 241.

[15] François Wendel: *Calvin. Sources et Evolution de sa Pensée religieuse*, Paris, Presses Universitaires, 1950.

the volume of Calvin studies published for the anniversary year of that institution (1909). As a professor in Vienna he wrote his great volumes on Calvin.[16] His works aim at being "strictly historical," conveying his belief that "the personalities who form history disappear from the stage of history; their writings speak to us and turn the past into the present."[17] Thus he understands Calvin's theological accomplishment (as had earlier been attempted) from the Reformer's great personality: "Calvin's organic world-and-life view is the result of this unified organic nature which, through a master will, governed all antitheses (and there were many of them), binding them dialectically in the thought system."[18] It is in connection with this that Bohatec, in surpassing mastery of the material, undertook to classify the position of Calvin's thought-world within the intellectual history of the West. As a result Bohatec occupies a special place in recent Calvin research. Nevertheless, the theologian can learn much from the abundance of material in the books to which we have referred.[19] In a book which appeared at the same time, Marc-Edouard Chenevière, a lawyer, has remarkably pointed out how the problems discussed by Bohatec can be seen and handled differently: "Calvin is not a master teacher like the others, whose instruction can be easily grasped and followed. To put it exactly: Calvin is no master teacher; he is only a witness."[20] That is a different understanding. It is the viewpoint of the new Calvin research.

[16] Josef Bohatec: *Calvin und das Recht*, Feudingen, Verlagsanstalt, 1934; *Calvins Lehre von Staat und Kirche mit besonderer Berücksichtigung des Organismusgedankens*, Breslau, Marcus, 1937; *Budé und Calvin*, Graz, Böhlau, 1950.

[17] *Calvins Lehre*, p. VII.

[18] *Ibid.*, p. 749.

[19] Bohatec succeeded in proving, for example, that Calvin came to an understanding with Budé in the letter to Francis I at the beginning of the *Institutes*.

[20] Marc-Edouard Chenevière: *La Pensée politique de Calvin*, Geneva, Labor, 1937, p. 14.

INDEX

Adam, 43 f., 81, 83 ff., 115, 127

Assurance of salvation, 111, 117, 138, 166, 168 ff., 190, 213

Augustine, 81, 191, 215

Authority, right, 146, 148, 235

Backsliding, 149

Baptism, 40, 60, 197, 212, 220
Its essence, 211

Baron, H., 229

Barth, Karl, 17, 39 ff., 159

Barth, Peter, 18, 20 f., 39 f., 51 f., 140, 159, 182, 229

Bauke, Hermann, 10 ff., 38

Bearing the cross, 143, 145 ff., 152, 209

Bohatec, J., 182, 229

Brunner, Emil, 39

Brunner, Peter, 17, 30 ff., 38 f., 111 ff., 116, 140

Bullinger, 216

Caroli, 55

Castellio, 44

Ceremonies, 95, 100, 106, 206 ff.

Christ:
Communion with, 85, 114, 126 ff., 144 ff., 152, 163, 179, 182, 187, 190, 217 ff., 230, 247, 248
Cross of, 50, 76 f., 144 f., 147, 179
End of the law, 27, 32, 95 ff., 100, 106 f.
Extra Calvinisticum, 118 f.
Head of the Church, 188 f., 200, 202, 207 f., 230
Image of God, 69

Christ—*continued*
Intercessor, 154 f.
Lordship of, 183, 230 ff., 234, 236 f., 243
Mediator, 27, 36, 106, 110 ff., 219, 221
Obedience of, 115, 131, 141, 145
Revealer of God, 33 ff., 43, 49 ff., 57 ff., 62, 118 f., 120, 163 f., 221, 247
Righteousness of, 131 ff.
Saving work of, 96, 97, 106, 113, 115, 120, 126 f., 133, 142, 145, 153 f., 169, 188
"Scopus" ("end") of the Scriptures, 26, 30, 32, 107 f.
Second coming of, 150
Substance of the Gospel, 27, 107 f., 248
True God, 57 f., 109, 111 ff., 133 f., 163 f.
True Man, 113 ff., 133 f., 224
Unio Personalis, 115 ff.

Church, 64, 66, 73 f., 78, 93, 97, 99 f., 105, 156 f., 165, 179, 182 ff., 212, 230, 232 ff.
Confession, 55
Congregation, 194, 197, 209
Form, 206 ff.
Guidance, 236
Order, 99 f., 185, 199 ff.
Unity, 195 ff., 206

Church discipline, 197 ff.

Condescension, 35, 93, 113, 187, 214

255